MW00584173

BAPTIST
HISTORY
NOTEBOOK

Copyright © 2017 by Donnie Burford

All rights reserved. This book or any portion thereof may not be reproduced, distributed, or transmitted in any form or by any means, including photocopying, recording, or other electronic or mechanical methods, without the express written permission of the publisher except for the use of brief quotations in a book review or scholarly journal.

Third Edition, 2017

Printed in the United States of America

Baptist Training Center Publications
A Ministry of:
Westwood Missionary Baptist Church
Winter Haven, FL
www.baptisttrainingcenter.org

Library of Congress Control Number: 2017950775
Hisel, Berlin
Baptist History Notebook / Berlin Hisel
ISBN: 978-1-947598-01-0 (paperback)
ISBN: 978-1-947598-02-7 (ebook)

All Scripture quotations are taken from the King James Version

Cover Art: *The Christian Martyrs' Last Prayer* by Jean-Léon Gérôme 1883. This work has been released into the public domain by the Walters Art Museum according to a CC0 license for unrestricted use.

BAPTIST HISTORY NOTEBOOK

Berlin Hisel

Donnie Burford, editor

BAPTIST TRAINING CENTER PUBLICATIONS
WINTER HAVEN, FLORIDA

TABLE OF CONTENTS

NOTE FROM THE EDITOR...13

FORWARD...15

INTRODUCTION TO THE THIRD EDITION 17

ABOUT THE AUTHOR..19

SPECIAL THANKS 21

1   THE TRACING OF BAPTIST HISTORY.......................23
    Invisible Warfare.. 24
    What is Meant by Kingdom? 25
    Israel in the Old Testament................................... 25
    The New Testament Trail of Blood............................ 26
    Victims of This Warfare 27

2   JESUS ESTABLISHES HIS CHURCH............................29
    Christ's Church Built.. 30
    Identifying Doctrine 31
    1. Church Government Changed............................. 32
    2. Plan of Salvation Changed................................. 38
    3. Infant Baptism 40

3   PERSECUTION BY THE ROMAN EMPIRE 43
    Reasons for the Persecutions.................................. 44
    Different Emperors 46
    Terrible Days.. 57
    Days of Strength 57

4   THE MONTANISTS...59
    A Word of Caution 59
    False Charges.. 60
    Eusebius.. 60
    Montanists: Origin and Beliefs 63
    David Benedict... 64
    John T. Christian.. 65
    Henry C. Vedder 66
    Thomas Armitage 67
    W. A. Jarrel.. 67
    Final Notes on the Montanists..................................... 68

5   THE NOVATIANISTS..71
    The Novatian Rupture.. 72
    Gieseler... 73
    Origin of Novatianism.. 74
    J. M. Cramp... 76
    Their Doctrines 77
    Persecuted 79

6   CONSTANTINE THE GREAT 83

    Leo I and Boniface III... 84
    Flavius Valerius Constantinus A. D. 306-337............... 84
    His Early Life 85
    Constantine's Supposed Conversion 85
    Religion United to the State... 87
    The Edict of Milan 313 A. D. 89
    Changes in the False Churches 91
    The Privileges and Immunities of the Clergy............... 93
    Unity Among All Churches 94
    Constantine's Life.. 96
    Constantine's Baptism 96
    Conclusion 97

7   THE DONATISTS 99
    J. M. Cramp... 100
    Identified with The Novatians...................................... 101

The Church.. 102
Separation of Church and State............... 103
Baptism... 104
Donatist Persecution................................ 105
The Donatists on Persecution 107
Conclusion 108

8 PATERINS, PURITANS, CATHARI 111
Paterins (Patarenes) 111
Etymology.. 114
Paterines Were Baptists............................ 116
Puritans 116
Cathari... 117
Widely Applied... 118
The Catharist Doctrine............................... 118
The Cathari Were Baptists 120

9 THE PAULICIANS 121
Photius... 121
Siculus.. 122
Origin, Doctrine, Persecution..................... 123
Paulicians Were Baptists............................ 128
Persecuted 129

10 DEVELOPMENTS IN THE HIERARCHY 131
The Sign of the Cross 132
Wax Candles 132
Mother of God 133
Purgatory.. 134
Origin of Purgatory 135

11 MORE DEVELOPMENTS IN THE HIERARCHY 137
List of Heresies.. 137
Extreme Unction 140
Baptism of Bells 141
Transubstantiation...................................... 141
A Roman Miracle (?).................................... 141

Catholic Church Councils.. 143
Roman Catholic and Greek Orthodox 145

12 THE PETROBRUSIANS 147
Peter de Bruys.. 147
Their Doctrine 148
Augustus Neander 149
Peter de Bruys Was a Baptist.................................. 150
Information Source 151
Persecution 151

13 THE HENRICIANS... 153
Description of Henry.. 153
Henry in Mans 154
St. Bernard's Account of Henry's Influence 156
Henry Was a Baptist 156
Historians Say the Henricians Were Baptists 158
Persecution 159

14 THE ARNOLDISTS 161
Orchard's Sketch of Arnold of Brescia..................... 161
Was Arnold a Baptist? 164
Persecuted 165

15 THE WALDENSES 167
Their Name 167
Their Antiquity 168
Historical Testimony.. 169
Waldenses by Various Names................................... 170
Another Word on Origin 172
Concluding Remarks 173

16 THE WALDENSES CONTINUED.............................. 175
Waldenses Not Protestants 175
The Antichrist.. 176
Confession of Faith 178
What Say the Historians 181

17 THE WALDENSES CONCLUDED ... 183
    Milton's Poem ... 183
    Loss of Houses and Goods ... 184
    Everywhere Persecuted ... 185
    Persecution by Crusades ... 185

18 THE ALBIGENSES ... 191
    Origin ... 191
    Their Doctrine ... 192
    Their Persecution ... 195
    Bright Lights in Dark Times ... 197

19 THE ANABAPTISTS ... 201
    Mosheim ... 201
    Depths of Antiquity ... 203
    Anabaptists Ancestors ... 205
    Waldenses Were Anabaptists ... 205
    Anabaptist Beliefs ... 206

20 THE BOGOMILS ... 209
    Location ... 209
    Agreed with the Cathari ... 210
    Antiquity of the Bogomils ... 212
    Charges Against Them ... 212
    John T. Christian ... 214
    Their Persecution ... 214

21 THE LOLLARDS ... 217
    Origin of the Lollards ... 218
    Walter Lollard ... 218
    Spurgeon in Connection with the Lollards ... 220
    Their Doctrines ... 221
    Their Persecutions ... 222

22 THE BOHEMIAN AND MORAVIAN BRETHREN .. 227
    Description of the Land ... 227
    The Gospel in Bohemia ... 228
    Peter Waldo ... 229
    Called Waldensians ... 229

John Huss.. 230
Robert Robinson Again 231
Two Classes.. 231
Their Persecution 232

23 THE PICARDS AND BEGHARDS 235
Picards or Pickards..................................... 235
Bohemia 236
Maximilian II.. 236
Doctrine of the Picards 237
The Beghards... 238
The Name "Beghards" 239
Conclusion 240

24 ANABAPTISTS AND THE REFORMATION 243
God's Overruling Providence...................... 244
The Good Doesn't Last................................ 245
An Illustration 245
The Anabaptist Doctrine Very Old 246
Church Truth 248
Conclusion 249

25 ANABAPTISTS AND THE REFORMATION
CONTINUED... 253
Christianity Not a Culture 254
Constantine.. 254
The Reformation.. 254
The Same Problem....................................... 255
Religious Force... 255
Luther's Choice 256
Church Requirements 257
Salvation by Faith Alone 258
Non-Public Worship.................................... 259

26 ANABAPTISTS AND THE REFORMATION
CONCLUDED.. 261
Peace Between Catholics and Reformers................. 261
The Peace of Augsburg 1555 A. D............................. 262
The Peace of Westphalia 1648 A. D. 262

Lutheran Persecution.................................... 262
Luther: A Persecutor 264
Death Warrants...................................... 265
John Calvin... 265
The Reformers All Alike............................. 267
Conclusion 267

27 THE ANABAPTISTS OF MUNSTER............................ 269
W. A. Jarrel.................................... 269
The Munster Disorders 271
Common Sense 273
Anabaptists Denial.................................. 273
Martyr's Testimony.................................. 274
Non-Baptist Vindication............................. 275
Conclusion 276

28 THE WELSH BAPTISTS.................................... 277
The Gospel in Wales 277
Concerning Paul..................................... 278
Claudia.. 278
Baptists Alone...................................... 279
Were Ancient World Christians Baptists? 281
David Benedict...................................... 282
Conclusion 284

29 WALDENSIAN CONFESSIONS OF FAITH 285

30 BIBLIOGRAPHY... 289

NOTE FROM THE EDITOR

This work is presented as composed from the lecture notes of Bro. Berlin Hisel. They are, for the most part, presented just as they were constructed by the author. The only additions are the index to the chapters and spelling and grammatical changes for which the editor takes responsibility and, in advance, asks for forgiveness for any discrepancies and errors that may appear.
Donnie Burford

FORWARD

Unfortunately, to many this work will only be an intellectual exercise in Biblical and historical facts. Sadly, the one thing that cannot be communicated in this work is the passion of heart the author had for these truths concerning the Lord's church.

Although Bro. Hisel's insight into this most blessed of subjects had been heard for many years both in lecture and through preaching, it was not until this editor was privileged to sit under his personal instruction in the class room of Lexington Baptist College that his heart-felt conviction and love was witnessed.

It is remembered on one special occasion. It was as though in the midst of his great technical and intellectual renderings of these truths that his heart was revealed as he began to weep over the fact that, by the grace of God, he had been privileged not only to be placed in one of his Lord's churches but, wonder of wonders, had been counted worthy to be a pastor over that which Christ Himself loved and loves so dearly. Bro. Hisel's great concern, even knowing the sovereign purpose of God in the perpetuity of His kind of churches, was that many were letting these truths of the Lord's churches fall in the streets.

It is with this reality in mind, knowing that those who let the truth fall are those who once were in possession of it, and seeing many today who once professed these truths deny them either in part or in whole, that this work is set to print by the editor.

It is a shared hope of the editor, with the author, that men will see the truth, hold to the truth, and propagate the truth of that which their Lord built and purposed to continue until the end of the age; that being His ecclesia; the local, visible, called out assembly of baptized believers, each being recognized as His church. For this is the only revealed truth of God concerning His kind of ecclesia in His Holy Word.

May God bless this humble effort, and may He use it to bring glory unto Himself. Ephesians 3:21; 5:25-27

Donnie Burford, Editor
Pastor, Purity Baptist Church
Maysville, KY

INTRODUCTION TO THE THIRD EDITION

When our hopes and expectations are seen to be exceeded by the revealed purpose of God as He providentially works out His good pleasure and will in a matter, it still never ceases to amaze us!

Maybe only more than amazed, is how truly thankful I am that God has seen fit to use this work in which we have tried to set forth the truth, both historically and Biblically, concerning the people and churches that have existed from the time that Christ Himself walked upon the earth, even unto this day, and which are now known by the name, "Baptist!"

Our prayer continues to be that this book will be a help to those who seek the truth of the Lords kind of churches down through the ages and that the Lord may be glorified even in some small way by the efforts put forth in the publishing of this 3rd edition!

Ephesians 3:20-21; "Now unto him that is able to do exceeding abundantly above all that we ask or think, according to the power that worketh in us, Unto him be glory in the church by Christ Jesus throughout all ages, world without end. Amen."

Bro. Donnie Burford,
1Peter 4:7-11
August, 2017

ABOUT THE AUTHOR

Bro. Berlin Hisel was born August 25, 1936 in Jackson County, Kentucky. He moved to Dayton, Ohio in 1941 and served in the U.S. Navy from 1953-1957. In 1958, he married Dora B. Martin and they had 3 children.

He was born again into the kingdom of God in 1950. He served as deacon, teacher, and Supt. Of Missions at Bentley Memorial Baptist Church in Lexington, KY. In 1963, he received his A.B. degree from Lexington Baptist College, and in 1975 he received his Th. B. degree from Cincinnati Baptist College. He served as Bible Instructor at Cincinnati Baptist College from 1967-1975, and at Lexington Baptist College from 1975-1990. He pastored the South Irvine Baptist Church from 1964-1967. He then accepted the pastorate of the First Baptist Church of Harrison, Ohio where he ministered from 1967-1982. He returned to again pastor the South Irvine Baptist Church in 1982 until his death on July 13, 1990.

SPECIAL THANKS

To Sister Dora Hisel, who graciously gave permission for the publication of this work in memory of her late husband, and for her original efforts in the compiling of this work.

I would also like to thank Christina Thomas who helped greatly in re-typing and research in verifying some of the given quotes as foot-noted in this book.

And to my wife, Karen, for both her personal encouragement to complete this work, as well as her technical skills in grammar and proof-reading which made this present rendering a reality.

Chapter 1

THE TRACING OF
BAPTIST HISTORY

The people called Baptists have suffered much in their past history. The study of "Baptist Roots" is one mainly of persecution. Our history has been written in blood. Often Baptist history is studied under the heading of the Trail of Blood. We have not had a lot of historians to record our glorious past. Those who did write from among our ranks were martyred and their writings burned. Most of our history has been written by our enemies and written in blood. Therefore you may be sure that, whenever possible, the history has been changed by our enemies to seek to blacken our names. Dr. Clarence Walker, writing an introduction to *The Trail of Blood* says of J. M. Carroll: "He found much church history - most of it seemed to be about the Catholics and Protestants. The history of the Baptists, he discovered, was written in blood. They were the hated people of the Dark Ages. Their preachers and people were put into prison and untold numbers were put to death. The world has never seen anything to compare with the suffering, the persecutions, heaped upon Baptists by the Catholic Hierarchy during the Dark Ages. The Pope was the world's dictator. This is why the Ana-Baptists, before the Reformation, called the Pope the Anti-Christ."[1]

"This history of the ancient churches is very obscure. Much of the early recorded history was either lost or destroyed. A great part of the history that remains was changed to suit the interests of the Roman Catholic Church. All of church history has been involved in much controversy and was subject to the whims and fancies of each particular age."[2]

Baptists have a heritage for which they can be very thankful. One of the more discouraging features of the age in which we live is that preachers, young preachers, students do not have a love for the churches of the Lord Jesus Christ like they ought. Church members do not have a love for the Lord's church like they ought. The reason, or one of the reasons, is that they are unacquainted with the glorious history of the churches of the Lord Jesus Christ. Hopefully, the *Baptist History Notebook* will be used of the Lord to create interest in a study of Baptist history.

In order to study the history of the Baptists we need an introductory study of an underlying principle that has produced the outward malice toward the Baptists and the persecutions that caused the trail of blood. There is reason behind the twelve hundred years of the dark ages when millions of our Baptist ancestors sealed their testimonies by their blood. There is reason for the persecution, even unto death, of our Baptist brethren today in Communist countries.

Invisible Warfare

"And I will put enmity between thee and the woman, and between thy seed and her seed; it shall bruise thy head, and thou shall bruise his heel" (Genesis 3:15). From the beginning until the end of what we call time, a battle has been raging and will continue to rage. This has been, and is a battle between two kingdoms. These are the kingdom of God and the kingdom of Satan. They are known as the kingdom of light and the kingdom of darkness; the kingdom of truth and kingdom of lies; the kingdom of good and the kingdom of evil. Even though these kingdoms are invisible they are none the less real. "For we wrestle not against flesh and blood, but against principalities, against powers, against the rulers of the darkness of this world, against spiritual wickedness in high places" (Ephesians 6:12). "Who hath delivered us from the power of darkness, and hath translated us into the kingdom of His dear Son" (Colossians 1:13). Manifestations of this invisible warfare are seen and experienced by people in the visible realm or in history.

What is Meant by Kingdom?

To understand what we are saying we must understand what is meant by "kingdom." The word, in its Bible usage means "rule." Thus the kingdom of God is the rule of God. The kingdom of Satan is the rule of Satan. Thus, "For the kingdom of God is not meat and drink: but righteousness, and peace, and joy in the Holy Ghost" (Romans 10:17), means that these three things will result in the lives of those with whom Christ rules in the heart. In the lives of those who are ruled by Satan, we see different results.

There are but two of these kingdoms, God's and Satan's. There is enmity between them and always has been. The people where the "kingdom of God is within" where the rule of God is seen in their lives, will be the people who experience the most outward manifestations of the spiritual warfare. It will be here that the Trail of Blood will be manifested for us to see in our search of history.

Israel in the Old Testament

In the Old Testament times, the most outward manifestations of the rule of God is to be observed in the nation of Israel. Certainly, I do not mean to say that no one outside of Israel was saved, for many were. Nor do I mean to say that all in Israel were saved, for they were not. What I do mean to say is that if any group of people in the Old Testament days would exhibit God's rule in their lives it would be Israel. "What advantage then hath the Jew? Or what profit is there in circumcision? Much every way: chiefly, because that unto them were committed the oracles of God" (Romans 3:1-2). Having the truth would draw Satan's concentrated efforts toward them. Hence, persecution for truth's sake would give Israel a Trail of Blood.

Abel's blood (Genesis 4:8) is the beginning of the fulfillment of Genesis 3:15. The drowning of babies in Exodus 1:22 is actually Satan's hatred and persecution of truth. We see this manifestation in the contrast between Moses (who represents the rule of God) and Pharaoh (who represents the rule of Satan). The infamous act of Athaliah in II Chronicles 22:10-12, in the slaying of the royal seed (except Joash) was the attempt of Satan to prevent the coming of our Champion, the Seed of the woman, who would be Truth incarnate. This principle shows what was behind the persecution of Israel by other nations and the persecution of Israel's prophets by some in Israel itself. It is Satan moving, behind the scene, to have his rule in the lives of people as opposed to them being ruled by the Lord. Thank God, we know the final outcome of this age long battle. One day "the earth shall be full of His knowledge and glory as waters that cover the sea."

The New Testament Trail of Blood

The Lord Jesus Christ built His church during His earthly ministry. To that church He gave the truth. "But if I tarry long, that thou mayest know how to behave thyself in the house of God, which is the church of the living God, the pillar and ground of the truth" (I Timothy 3:15). Israel of the Old Testament was to be a priesthood to the nations. They failed and Jesus commissioned the church which He built to take His truth into all the world (Matthew 28:16-20). As they take the truth into the world they will be persecuted by Satan. That church will be the place where the rule of God will be manifested in outward life, which thing Satan hates.

This is not to say that only Baptists are saved for that is not true. All who trust the Lord Jesus Christ savingly are saved. Not all Baptists are saved. So we are not saying that all Baptist churches (by name or identification) will exhibit a Trail of Blood. We are saying we are most likely to find this manifestation of warfare between the two kingdoms in true churches of the Lord Jesus Christ. Our search in the *Baptist History Notebook* will bear out this truth.

Victims of This Warfare

We should naturally and logically expect that those closely involved with this church Jesus built, and laboring in connection with it, would come under Satan's attack. So we are not disappointed as we check the record, to find out if this is so. It is true!

The first martyr to fall was John the Baptist (Matthew 14:1-12). Why John? He was the prophesied forerunner of Christ and the one who gathered the material out of which Jesus built His church (Acts 1:20-22). The beheading of John was done by Herod because of Herodias. Yet all should be able to see Satan at work behind the scene. He hates the truth, so he hates the one who gathered material for the church which was to be the depository of truth.

Next to fall was Jesus, Himself. He was Founder of His church which He commissioned to preach the "truth" into all the world. It is still the battle of the two kingdoms manifesting itself where the truth is. Where there is no truth there will be no manifestation of a battle. It was in the crucifixion of Jesus that Jesus bruised the head of the serpent. It was there also that the serpent bruised His heel. This was the ultimate fulfilling of Genesis 3:15. Even though persecution of God's kingdom by Satan continues, Satan and his kingdom received the death blow when Christ died at Calvary. He arose from the dead and is in the process of overthrowing Satan's kingdom (governments and individuals who are ruled by Satan). This will be finalized at the second coming. Oh! What a happy day!

The next pool of blood came from Stephen (Acts 7:54-60). Why Stephen? He was a Baptist deacon affiliated with, and a member of, the Jerusalem Baptist Church where "truth" was (Acts 6:5). He told them, the Jews, that they did not propagate the message God gave them (Acts 7:53), so God is to use His church and, for this, he died.

Who cannot see behind this visible manifestation of persecution the invisible hatred and malice of Satan?

The next blood shed was that of James (Acts 12:1-2). Why James? He had been one of the three closest men to the first pastor - Jesus. He died in Satan's opposition to the truth.

The "Trail of Blood" left by the Lord's churches is seen all through the New Testament. It begins slowly (Acts 4:13-21). It speeds up and up (Acts 5:17-18; 33-40). It gets worse and worse (Acts 8:1,3; 9:1,2; 14:19; 16:23-24; 18:12-17).

And thus it has been and shall be throughout history. Our "notebook" will bring this to light in the chapters that follow. There is no rest in this warfare. God has chosen you to be soldiers and to stand in the gap, contending for the truth. If it should become necessary for us to seal our testimony with our blood, may God's grace strengthen us to our duty. As Baptists, we have a noble heritage and a rewarding future. Through we may be like sheep among the wolves let us be courageous, even into the end.

NOTES ON CHAPTER 1

1 J. M. Carroll, *The Trail of Blood*, page 2.
2 Norman H. Wells, *The Church That Jesus Loved*, page 90.

Chapter 2

JESUS ESTABLISHES HIS CHURCH

We have observed the persecution of truth, first of Israel and secondly of the church. Satan persecuted the churches of Jesus Christ first by the Jews. This persecution is recorded in the book of Acts. It is also mentioned in some of the Epistles of the New Testament.

Next, Satan used the Roman Empire to persecute the churches of the Lord Jesus Christ. There were at least ten severe persecutions beginning with Nero and ending with Diocletian. We will devote space to these in the next chapter. These persecutions resulted in the death of a very large number of Christians.

Satan used the Roman Empire to persecute the Lord's churches while he was establishing a church of his own with which to oppose and persecute the true churches of Jesus Christ. Much of this *Baptist History Notebook* will deal with the development of Satan's church (the synagogue of Satan) and its persecution of the churches of our Lord.

Christ's Church Built

Doing this, we must begin with the church which Jesus built and observe how Satan sought to corrupt it from within which resulted in a separation by the pure churches from the corrupt churches.

"And I say also unto thee, That thou art Peter, and upon this rock I will build My church: and the gates of hell shall not prevail against it" (Matthew 16:18). The word "church" means assembly. The Lord said He would build "His" (My) church. This was to distinguish it from all other kinds of assemblies. He built His "kind" of assembly. That which distinguishes His from all the rest are the doctrines He gave to it. Those doctrinal peculiarities make it His kind of church.

What are those marks or doctrinal peculiarities? Dr. J. R. Graves in his book Old Landmarkism lists seven. Dr. Clarence Walker, in his introduction to the Trail of Blood (page 5) lists seven. Dr. D. B. Ray, in his Baptist Succession lists seven. To these could be added or subtracted, depending on the historian and what his purpose might be. Where one would list two doctrines under one head the next may list them separately. I will list eight but treat primarily three in this Notebook.

(1) The church's Head and Founder is Jesus Christ
   (Matthew 16:18; Colossians 1:18).

(2) Its only rule of faith and practice is the Bible
   (II Timothy 3:15-17).

(3) Its members are to be only saved people *(Acts 2:41).*

(4) Its government is congregational *(Acts 1:23-26 - equality).*

(5) Its teaching on salvation is that it is by grace
   (Ephesians 2:8-9).

(6) It has but two ordinances; Baptism and the Lord's Supper, and these are symbolic *(Matthew 28:19-20; I Corinthians 11:24).*

(7) Its commission is inclusive *(Matthew 28:16-20).*

(8) It is independent *(Matthew 16:19; Matthew 22:21).*

Wherever, in history, in whatever age, you find churches teaching these doctrines, you have a Baptist church, no matter what name it may go by. It matters not if we cannot, from church to church, trace it back to the First Baptist Church of Jerusalem. The succession is there but records may hinder or stop our search. What it teaches is the important thing. Jesus said the gates of hell would not prevail against His church so He guaranteed perpetuity.

Identifying Doctrine

Maybe this illustration will help us. Suppose we have a covered bridge one mile long. As we look at this bridge we see a wagon drawn by a mule enter one end of the bridge. The mule is black, broken down, long-eared, and thin with ribs showing. The wagon is of wood and is red. It also has white stripes on it. The wheels are blue with spokes. After the wagon and mule enter the covered bridge we wait about thirty minutes. We see the wagon and mule come out at the other end of the bridge that fits exactly the description of the ones we saw enter the bridge. One who has a sound mind realizes that this is the same mule and wagon we observed earlier. This is like the church that Jesus built. In the Bible we have an accurate description of what the church looked like. As that church entered the covered bridge of time we wait and watch. If we look and see a church fitting the description of the one we saw earlier in the Bible we are forced to conclude that it must be the same church. As we watched the covered bridge earlier we may have seen several wagons drawn by mules come out of it. We looked and saw they did not fit the description of the one we saw earlier. They may have looked alike in many ways but if they are not exactly alike, we know they are different wagons and mules. So today, when we look at so called churches and see that they look a lot like the first one, let us look closely. If they do not meet the Bible description, conclude that they are not of the first church.

Thus we believe that Baptist churches are identified in history by their doctrines. It is where these "truths" or doctrines are stood for and taught that we will be able to observe the "Trail of Blood." The history of these "kind" of churches is written in blood. Here you will find outward manifestations of the battle between the Kingdom of God and the Kingdom of Satan.

1. Church Government Changed

In developing his church Satan began by corrupting the doctrinal teachings of the Lord's church from within. He has his servants in all churches. The first corruption came in his seeking to change the form of church government that Christ gave. His subtlety is seen in this.

There was a plurality of elders (preachers) in the early churches. "And from Miletus he sent to Ephesus, and called the elders of the church" (Acts 20:17). It seems that today we have a scarcity of preachers but not then. These elders were to be equal, one was not to lord it over another. "The elders which are among you I exhort, who am also an elder... Feed the flock of God which is among you, taking the oversight thereof, not by constraint, but willingly; not for filthy lucre, but of a ready mind; Neither as being lords over God's heritage (clergy), but being ensamples to the flock" (I Peter 5:1-3). See our Lord's instruction on equality (Matthew 23:1-12).

Early in history Satan led some away from that truth. Diotrephes is an example given in III John 9. We read in Revelation 2:15, "So hast thou also them that hold the doctrine of the Nicolatians, which thing I hate." Without being positive what this doctrine was, I think the meaning lies in the name. It comes from two Greek words. The first is *nikaw* which means "to conquer." The second is *laos* which means "people." So then it means to conquer the people or laity. Thus we have a ruling clergy. Thus developed an episcopal church government in place of a congregational one. What kind of government is this? "Episcopacy, Episcopal." These terms are derived from the Greek *episcopos*, meaning 'bishop.' They refer accordingly to that system of church government in which the principal officer is the bishop."[1]

BIG PREACHERS - BIG CHURCHES

Thus, some bishops with big egos began to feel more importance attached to them than to others. Their strong personalities helped them "climb the ladder." Bishops of the larger city churches became known as Metropolitans. They began to preside over the smaller country churches. The development of this kind of church government was gradual. The result is what we see in Roman Catholicism in the past and today.

I will quote from the Lutheran historian, Mosheim, who is known as the father of modern church history:

"Let none, however, confound the bishops of this primitive and golden period of the church with those of whom we read in the following ages; for though they were both distinguished by the same name, yet they differed in many respects. A bishop during the first and second century was a person who had the care of one Christian assembly, which, at that time was, generally speaking, small enough to be contained in a private house. In this assembly he acted, not so much with the authority of a master, as with the zeal and diligence of a faithful servant. He instructed the people, performed the several parts of divine worship, attended the sick, and inspected the circumstances and supplies of the poor. He charged, indeed, the presbyters with the performance of those duties and services, which the multiplicity of his engagements rendered it impossible for him to fulfill; but he had not the power to decide or enact any thing without the consent of the presbyters and people; and though the episcopal office was both laborious and singularly dangerous, yet its revenues were extremely small, since the church had no certain income, but depended on the gifts or oblations of the multitude, which were, no doubt, inconsiderable, and were moreover to be divided among the bishops, presbyters, deacons and poor.

"The power and jurisdiction of the bishops were not long confined to these narrow limits, but were soon extended by the following means. The bishops, who lived in the cities, had, either by their own ministry, or that of their presbyters, erected new churches in the neighboring towns and villages. These churches, continuing under the inspection and ministry of the bishops, by whose labors and counsels they had been engaged to embrace the Gospel, grew imperceptibly into ecclesiastical provinces, which the Greeks afterwards called dioceses. But as the bishop of the city could not extend his labors and inspection to all those churches in the country and in the villages, he appointed certain *suffragans* or deputies to govern and to instruct these new societies; and they were distinguished by the title *chorepiscopi*, i.e. country bishops. This order held the middle rank between bishops and presbyters.

"The churches, in those early times, were entirely independent, none of them being subject to any foreign jurisdiction, but each governed by its own rulers and its own laws; for, though the churches founded by the apostles had this particular deference shown to them, that they were consulted in different and doubtful cases, yet they had no juridical authority, no sort of supremacy over the others, nor the least right to enact laws for them. Nothing, on the contrary, is more evident than the perfect equality that reigned among the primitive churches; nor does there even appear, in the first century, the smallest trace of that association of provincial churches, from which councils and metropolitans derive their origin. It was only in the second century that the custom of holding councils commenced in Greece, whence it soon spread through the other provinces."[2]

AGAIN: CONCERNING THE DOCTRINES AND MINISTERS OF THE CHURCH, AND THE FORM OF ITS GOVERNMENT.

"The form of ecclesiastical government, whose commencement we have seen in the last century, was brought in this to a greater degree of stability and consistence. One inspector, or bishop, presided over each Christian assembly, to which office he was elected by the voices of the whole people. In this post he was to be watchful and provident, attentive to the wants of the church, and careful to supply them. To assist him in his laborious province, he formed a council of presbyters, which was not confined to any fixed number; and to each of these he distributed his task, and appointed a station, in which he was to promote the interests of the church. To the bishops and presbyters, the ministers or deacons were subject; and the latter were divided into a variety of classes, as the state of the church required.

"During a great part of this century, the Christian churches were independent with respect to each other; nor were they joined by association, confederacy, or any other bonds than those of charity. Each Christian assembly was a little state, governed by its own laws, which were either enacted, or at least, approved by the society. But, in the process of time, all the Christian churches of a province were formed into one large ecclesiastical body, which, like confederate states, assembled at certain times in order to deliberate about the common interests of the whole. This institution had its origin among the Greeks, with whom nothing was more common than this confederacy of independent states, and in the regular assemblies which met, in consequence thereof, at fixed times, and were composed of the deputies of each respective state. But those ecclesiastical associations were not long confined to the Greeks; their great utility was no sooner perceived, then they became universal, and were formed in all places where the gospel had been planted. To these assemblies, in which the deputies or commissioners of several churches consulted together, the names of synods was appropriated by the Greeks, and that of councils by the Latins; and the laws that were enacted in these general meetings, were called canons i.e. rules.

"These councils of which we find not the smallest trace before the middle of this century, changed the whole face of the church, and gave it a new form: for by them the ancient privileges of the people were considerably diminished, and the power and authority of the bishops greatly augmented. The humility, indeed, and prudence of these pious prelates, prevented their assuming all at once the power with which they were afterward invested. At their first appearance in these general councils, they acknowledged that they were no more than the delegates of their respective churches, and that they acted in the name, and by the appointment of their people. But they soon changed this humble tone, imperceptibly extended the limits of their authority, turned their influence into dominion, and their counsels into laws; and openly asserted, at length, that Christ had empowered them to prescribe to his people authoritative rules of faith and manners. Another effect of these councils was the gradual abolition of that perfect equality which reigned among all bishops in the primitive times. For the order and decency of these assemblies required, that some one of the provincial bishops, meeting in council, should be invested with a superior degree of power and authority; and hence the rights of Metropolitans derive their origin. In the mean time the bounds of the church were enlarged; the custom of holding councils was fallowed wherever the sound of the gospel had reached; and the universal church had now the appearance of one vast republic, formed by a combination of a great number of little states. This occasioned the creation of a new order of ecclesiastics, who were appointed, in different parts of the worlds as heads of the church, and whose office it was to preserve the consistence and union of that immense body, whose members were so widely dispersed throughout the nations. Such were the nature and office of the patriarchs, among whom, at length, ambition, having reached its most insolent period, formed a new dignity, investing the bishop of Rome, and his successors, with the title and authority of prince of the patriarchs."[3]

AGAIN

"The face of things began now to change in the Christian church. The ancient method of ecclesiastical government seemed, in general, still to subsist, while, at the same time, by imperceptible steps, it varied from the primitive rule, and degenerated toward the form of a religious monarchy; for the bishops aspired to higher degrees of power and authority than they had formerly possessed, and not only violated the rights of the people, but also made general encroachments upon the privileges of the presbyters; and that they might cover these usurpations with an air of justice, and an appearance of reason, they published new doctrines concerning the nature of the church, and of the episcopal dignity, which, however, were in general so obscure, that they themselves seemed to have understood them as little as those to whom they were delivered. One of the principal authors of this change, in the government of the church, was Cyprian, who pleaded for the power of the bishops with more zeal and vehemence than had ever been hitherto employed in that cause, though not with an unshaken constancy and perseverance; for in difficult and perilous times, necessity sometimes obliged him to yield, and to submit several things to the judgment and authority of the church.

"This change in the form of ecclesiastical government, was soon followed by a train of vices, which dishonored the character and authority to those to whom the administration of the church was committed; for, though several yet continued to exhibit to the world illustrious examples of primitive piety and Christian virtues, yet many were sunk in luxury and voluptuousness, puffed up with vanity, arrogance, and ambition, possessed with a spirit of contention and discord, and addicted to many other vices that cast an undeserved reproach upon the holy religion, of which they were the unworthy professors and ministers. This is testified in such an ample manner, by the repeated complaints of many of the most respectable writers of this age that truth will not permit us to spread the veil, which we should otherwise be desirous to cast over such enormities among an order so sacred. The bishops assumed, in many places, a princely authority, particularly those who had the greatest number of churches under their inspection, and who presided over the most opulent assemblies. They appropriated to their evangelical function the splendid ensigns of temporal majesty; a throne, surrounded with ministers, exalted above his equals the servant of the meek and humble Jesus; and sumptuous garments dazzled the eyes and minds of the multitude into an ignorant veneration for this usurped authority. An example which ought not to have been followed was ambitiously imitated by the presbyters, who, neglecting the sacred duties of their station, abandoned themselves to the indolence and delicacy of an effeminate and luxurious life. The deacons, beholding the presbyters thus deserting their functions, boldly invaded their rights and privileges; and the effects of a corrupt ambition were spread through every rank of the sacred order."[4]

I realize this is a long quote but one that is necessary. This will be one area where the history of the Baptists and the history of the synagogue of Satan separates. For those who would like to further study this changing of church government by Satan, please read *Augustus Neander*. Volume 1, pages 179-201. For a most interesting statement of the development of the Roman Catholic Hierarchy, read Dowling's *History or Romanism*, pages 36-64.

NOTE: It is to be remembered that hundreds of churches kept to the original plan of church government given by our Lord. They did not follow the ungodly form of Episcopal Church Government devised by Satan. These churches, keeping to the original form were the true Baptist churches.

2. Plan of Salvation Changed

Those of Jewish background had always emphasized rites and ceremonies. Whole of Jewish religion laid stress on ceremony. The same can be said of the pagan world. Both Jews and Gentiles (apart from Christianity) upheld the shadows more than the substances. It is easy to understand why they might be tempted to place too much or give over importance to baptism which is a rite or ceremony. Their reasoning (because of their background) ran something like this: Much is said about baptism; hence it must have some saving ability. So many in our own day place their reasoning above the revelation God has given (the Bible).

D. B. Ray, in his great book on Baptist Succession tells us:

"The second leading error which originated in this period is the doctrine of baptismal salvation. This doctrine was based upon the false interpretation of those Scriptures which speak of baptism for remission of sins; and especially John, where they made born of water, mean baptism. It is admitted that baptism represents the washing away of sins. The same principles of Scripture interpretation which gave birth to baptismal salvation also gave birth to transubstantiation. Of this defection from the truth on the part of some, Miall remarks: "In the ante-Nicene period, sin was regarded much more in its overt demonstrations than in its spiritual destructiveness; repentance had degenerated into penance; regeneration into baptism; justification by faith, into just what the ninetieth number of 'The Tracts for the Times' declare it to be; and sanctification was lost in the names of sacred persons, sacred things, and sacred places. All this was before the Papacy had begun to blazon its triple crown, or to set its feet upon the necks of kings." It is difficult to ascertain at what precise point of time the error of baptismal salvation was first advocated; it is certain, however, that it was advocated by a large number as early as the middle of the third century; and it is likely that some embraced this view as early as the close of the second century. Baptismal salvation was an innovation brought in, in some places, along with the change of the form of church government to a hierarchy. Neander and Waddington both testify that baptismal salvation was a departure from the original doctrine of the design of baptism. And when this superstitious error concerning baptism was established, it opened the way for other superstitions, which tended to clothe the baptismal ceremony with a mysterious grandeur and importance which excited the admiration of the people. Among the attending superstitions added to baptismal salvation, may be mentioned the sign of the cross, blowing in the mouth of the candidate, the use of crism, and the giving of the new baptized persons milk and honey, as a symbol of the new life."[5]

Almost all the historians agree that baptism, at first, was for adults who expressed faith in Jesus Christ. This is believer's baptism. Hence, to baptize someone in order to get them saved is a departure from truth. All of this was, and still is, a clever invention of Satan to build for himself a false church with which to persecute the true churches of our Lord.

NOTE: It is to be remembered that hundreds of churches did not go off after the "baptismal regeneration" heresy. They continued preaching that baptism is a symbol - not substance. Thus they were the true Baptist churches keeping pure the doctrine as our Lord had given it to them.

Before passing from this point, let us hear from a couple of church historians. J. M. Cramp says, "The figment of baptismal regeneration, one of the earliest corruptions of Christianity, was an outrage on morals and religion. It encouraged men in sin, and bolstered them up with a false hope, substituting the outward form for repentance, faith and a changed heart and life."[6]

Dr. John T. Christian writes, "One of the earliest and most hurtful errors was the dogma of baptismal regeneration. This error, in one form or another, has marred the life and colored the history of all the Christian ages. It began early and the virus may be traced to this day, not only among ritualists, but likewise in the standards of evangelical Christians. Tertullian was influenced by it to oppose infant baptism, and under other conditions it became the frightful origin of that heresy."[7]

3. Infant Baptism

The third great error, introduced by Satan in the primitive churches was that of infant baptism. It is very easy to see how this would rapidly follow the doctrine of baptismal regeneration. If baptism washes away sin and regenerates, should it not be applied as early as possible was the reasoning. People die because of sin. Babies die. Babies must have sin. Baptize them quick to wash that sin away so they will go to heaven if they die. This is the reasoning Satan placed in the heads of many, then and now.

This error began, probably at the start of the third century, to be taught by some. In this area of church history we are blessed with several worthy histories of infant baptism. Check the bibliography at the end of this notebook for a partial listing. The historians (most of them) are in agreement that this practice originated about the third century.

G. H. Orchard writes, "We conclude this chapter with the words of Curcellus, 'Paedobaptism was not known in the world the two first ages after Christ; in the third and fourth it was approved by few; at length, in the fifth and following ages, it began to obtain in divers places; and therefore, we (paedobaptists) observe this rite indeed, as an ancient custom, but not as an apostolic tradition. The custom of baptizing infants did not begin before the third age after Christ, and that there appears not the least footstep of it for the first two centuries.'"[8]

This doctrine is of the devil and its evil is beyond description. D. B. Ray quotes J. Newton Brown (from *Baptist Martyrs*). "Infant baptism is an error from beginning to end; corrupt in theory, and corrupting in practice; born in superstition, cradled in fear, nursed in ignorance, supported in fraud, and spread by force: doomed to die in the light of historical investigation, and its very memory to be bathed in all future ages by a disabused church. In the realms of despotism it has shed the blood of martyrs in torrents: that blood cries against it to heaven: and a long suffering God will yet be the terrible avenger. The book before us is a swift witness against it."[9]

NOTE: Many, many churches opposed this error from the start. Not all churches were carried away by the satanic invention of infant baptism. These who stood firm were the true churches of our Lord. In the history we are to study we will see that these three errors which the true churches stood against brought them much persecution and death. It is my opinion that the Roman Catholic Church is built upon this unholy trinity of doctrine: episcopal government, baptismal regeneration, and infant baptism. These errors have led to hundreds more. We detest and protest these doctrines. We cry out against them as the arsenal of antichrist. Our Baptist ancestors died crying out against them! Can we do less?

NOTES ON CHAPTER 2

1 *Baker's Dictionary of Theology, page 184 - Article by Leon Morris.*
2 *Mosheim's Church History, pages 22-23.*
3 *Mosheim's Church History, page 41.*
4 *Mosheim's Church History, pages 63-64.*
5 *Baptist Succession, pages 306-307.*
6 *Baptist History, page 47.*
7 *A History of the Baptists, volume 1, page 28.*
8 *A Concise History of the Baptists, page 50.*
9 *Baptist Succession, page 311.*

Chapter 3

PERSECUTION BY THE ROMAN EMPIRE

Governments, in the Bible, are represented under the emblems of beasts. "And I stood upon the sand of the sea, and saw a beast rise up out of the sea, having seven heads and ten horns, and upon his ten horns ten crowns, and upon his heads the name of blasphemy. And the beast which I saw was like unto a leopard, and his feet were as the feet of a bear, and his mouth as the mouth of a lion: and the dragon gave him his power, and his seat (throne) and great authority" (Revelation 13:1-2). John here sees a composite of the beasts Daniel saw (Daniel 7:1-8). Daniel was told that these four beasts he saw represented four kings and kingdoms (Daniel 7:17-23). The point that I wish to make is that the kingdoms of this earth get their power, thrones and authority from Satan.

"Again, the devil taketh Him up into an exceeding high mountain, and showeth Him all the kingdoms of the world, and the glory of them; and saith unto Him, All these things will I give Thee, if Thou wilt fall down and worship me" (Matthew 4:8-9). Earthly kingdoms or governments belong to Satan. He is the prince of this world (John 12:31). He is the god of this world (II Corinthians 4:4). These kingdoms and the glory of them were his to give to Christ in exchange for the worship of Christ.

The Roman Empire was one of the beasts Daniel saw and John wrote about (Revelation 13:3; 17:9-11). So when the Roman Empire persecuted the children of God and the churches of our Lord Jesus Christ, it was really Satan behind it all. It is the spiritual warfare breaking out in the physical realm where God's rule was being exhibited in life. As we look at the reasons for those persecutions and examples of the suffering, please remember, that whatever the earthly reasons for it, Satan is behind it all.

Reasons for the Persecutions

Since the Christians denied the gods of the Romans and other nations the Christians were called and considered "atheists". They were the first people to be so-called. Since they observed the Lord's Supper they were called "cannibals" because it was said they ate the body and blood of Christ. They were considered guilty of treason because they had no king but Christ. There were many other reasons which we will list in the quotes of the historians. The Romans, since they believed these charges, found it very easy to blame the Christians for every evil which befell them and so sought to kill them all.

For those who would like to read the charges made against the Christians by the Empire and how the Christians responded, please read the *Apologies of Justin Martyr*:[1] Please also read *A Plea for the Christians by Athenagoras*;[2] See also *Tertullian's Apology*:[3] All these apologies were written during the times of the persecutions and therefore are very valuable to the student of Baptist history.

Neander gives several reasons for the persecution during this age (I value Neander most of the non-Baptist historians - bh). Following are two of his reasons:

"The Christians were often victims of the popular rage. The populace saw in them the enemies of their gods; and this was the same thing as to have no religion at all. The deniers of the gods, the atheists, was the common name by which the Christians were designated among the people: and of such men the vilest and most improbable stories could easily gain belief: - that in their conclaves they were accustomed to abandon themselves to unnatural lust; that they killed and devoured children; - accusations which we find circulated, in the most diverse periods, against religious sects that have once become objects of the fanatic hatred of the populace. The reports of disaffected slaves, or of those from whom torture had wrung the confession desired, were next employed to support these absurd charges, and to justify the rage of the populace. If in hot climates the long absence of rain brought on a drought; if in Egypt the Nile failed to irrigate the fields; if in Rome the Tiber overflowed its banks; if a contagious disease was raging; if an earthquake, a famine, or any other public calamity occurred, the populace rage was easily turned against the Christians. "We may ascribe this," was the cry, "to the anger of the gods on account of the spread of Christianity." Thus it had become a proverb in North Africa, according to Augustine, "If there is no rain, tax it on the Christians." And what wonder is it that the people so judged, when one who claimed to be a philosopher, when a Porphyry assigned as the cause why no stop could be put to a contagious and desolating sickness, that by reason of the spread of Christianity, Esculapius' influence on the earth was over.

There was, besides, no want of individuals who were ready to excite the popular rage against the Christians; priests, artisans and others, who, like Demetrius in the Acts, drew their gains from idolatry; magicians, who beheld their juggling tricks exposed; sanctimonious Cynics, who found their hypocrisy unmasked by the Christians. When, in the time of the emperor Marcus Aurelius, the magician whose life had been written by Lucian, Alexander of Abonateichus, observed that his tricks had ceased to create any sensation in the cities, he exclaimed, "The Pontus is filled with atheists and Christians;" and called on the people to stone them, if they did not wish to draw down on themselves the anger of the gods. He would never exhibit his arts before the people, until he had first proclaimed, "If any Atheist, Christian or Epicurean has slipped in here as a spy, let him begone!" An appeal to popular violence seems, at this time, to have been considered the most convenient course, by the advocates of religion among the pagans. Justin Martyr knew that Crescens, -one of the common Pseudo-cynics of the period, who were sanctimonious demagogues, - attempted to stir up the people against the Christians; and that he had threatened Justin's own life, because he had stripped him of his disguise."[4]

Different Emperors

In the next few pages we will look at how God's people and the churches of Jesus Christ fared under the different Emperors. You must remember that, at this time; all churches were, for the most part, alike. The Catholic church existed only in the plan of Satan. It seems reasonable, therefore, to think that the Christians all belonged to true churches even though a few errors had begun to creep in among some of the churches.

NERO 54-68 A. D.

It is hard to believe that Nero wasn't demon possessed. He surely made Adolf Hitler look like a kitten. It is no wonder that many, in those days, felt he was the man of sin, the son of perdition, the antichrist. Some even looked for his resurrection after his death.

Dr. John Henry Kurtz, the German Lutheran Historian, says of Nero:

"There may have been some historical foundation for the legend (however absurd at first sight it may appear), that TIBERIUS (14-37 A. D.), moved by the report of Pilate, had made a proposal to the senate to elevate Christ among the Roman deities, and when baffled in this, had threatened with punishment those who accused the Christians. At least, there is nothing in the character of Tiberius to render such a circumstance incredible. - At first the Christians were simply regarded as Jews; and therefore a number of them (Acts xviii. 2) were expelled from Rome when, in consequence of a tumult, the Emperor CLAUDIUS (41-54) banished the Jews from the capital. Much more serious were the persecutions of Christians (A. D. 64) which took place under NERO (54-68), on the occasion of a great fire which lasted nine days, and which was commonly imputed to incendiarism on the part of the Emperor himself. Nero threw the whole blame on the hated Christians, and visited them with exquisite tortures. They were sewn into skins of wild beasts, and thrown to the dogs to be torn to pieces; they were covered with wax and pitch, nailed to sharp poles, and set on fire to illuminate the imperial gardens at night. The persecution was not confined to Rome, and lasted to the end of Nero's reign. Peter and Paul obtained at that time the martyr's crown. Among the Christians the legend spread that Nero had retired to the banks of the Euphrates, whence he would return as Antichrist."[5]

The next quote is from Tieleman J. van Braght. His book is a must for every Baptist history student. On pages 78-86, he tells of Nero and his persecutions. He lists individuals who fell under Nero. The following quote deals with Nero's persecutions in general:

"Touching the manner in which the Christians were tortured and killed at the time of Nero. A. Mellinus gives the following account from Tacitus and other Roman writers: namely, that four extremely cruel and unnatural kinds of torture were employed against the Christians:

Firstly, that they dressed them in the skins of tame and wild beasts, that they might be torn to pieces by dogs or other wild animals.

Secondly, that they, according to the example of their Saviour, were fastened alive on crosses, and that in many different ways.

Thirdly, that the innocent Christians were burned and smoked by the Romans, with torches and lamps, under the shoulders and on other tender parts of their naked bodies, after these had been cruelly lacerated with scourges or rods. This burning was done also with shavings and fagots, they (the Christians) being tied to stakes worth half a stiver. Therefore they called the Christians sarmentieii, that is, fagot people, and semissii, that is, half stiver people; because they stood fastened to half stivers stakes, and were thus burned with the slow fire of fagots.

Fourthly, that these miserable, accused Christian martyrs were used as candles, torches, or lanterns, to see by them at night.

Of those who were burned, some were tied or nailed to stakes, and held still by a hook driven through the throat, so that they could not move the head when the pitch, wax, tallow, and other inflammable substances were poured boiling over their heads, and set on fire, so that all the unctuous matter of the human body flowing down made long, wide furrows in the sand of the theatre. And thus human beings were lighted as torches, and burned as lights for the wicked Romans at night.

Juvenal and Martial, both Roman poets, and Tertullian, state this in different manner, namely, that the Romans wrapped them in a painful or burning mantle, which they wound around their hands and feet, in order to melt the very marrow in their bones.

Futhermore, it is stated by A. Mellinus (from the aforementioned authors), concerning those mantles, that they were made of paper or linen, and, having been thickly coated with oil, pitch, wax, rosin, tallow, and sulphur, were wrapped around their whole body, and then set on fire. For this spectacle Nero gave the use of his gardens, and appeared himself among the people in the garb of a charioteer, taking an active part in the Circusian games; himself standing in the circus, and, as charioteer, guiding a chariot.

These proceedings, according to the testimony of Tacitus, although it had the appearance that the Christians were punished as malefactors who had deserved the extremest penalty, nevertheless moved the people to compassion; for they understood well enough that the Christians were not exterminated for the good of the common weal, but simply to gratify the cruelty of one man, Nero."[6]

TRAJAN 98-117

Remember, while these quotes come mainly from Kurtz and van Braght, all the historians, almost, have something to say about them.

Let us hear Kurtz:

"Under the reign of TRAJAN (98-117) commenced a new stage in the persecution of Christians. He renewed the former interdict against secret associations (the "Heteriae"), which was soon applied to those of Christians. In accordance with this law, Pliny the Younger, when Governor of Bithynia, punished with death those who were accused as Christians and persisted in their profession. But, partly staggered by the great number of persons accused, who belonged to every rank and age, and to both sexes - partly convinced by strict judicial investigation that the tendency of Christianity was morally pure and politically harmless, and that, as it appeared to him, Christians could only be charged with unyielding superstitiousness, the Governor applied for fresh instructions to the Emperor. Trajan approved both of his conduct and his proposals; and accordingly commanded that Christians should not be sought out, that no notice should be taken of anonymous accusations, but that if parties were formerly accused and found guilty, they should be put to death if they obstinately refused to sacrifice to the gods. This persecution extended as far as Syria and Palestine. There Symeon, Bishop of Jerusalem, the successor of James and a relative of the Lord, after cruel scourging, died a martyr's death on the cross, at the advanced aged of 120 years (107). Ignatius also, the excellent Bishop of Antioch, after an audience with the Emperor was, by his command, sent in chains to Rome, and there torn by wild beasts (115)."[7]

One of many illustrations that comes to us from van Braght:

"Phocus, a some of Pamphilius, the first bishop of the church in Pontus in the city of Sinope, on being brought, in the time of Trajan, before Africanus, the Governor of Pontus, who urged him to sacrifice upon the alter of Neptune, steadfastly refused to do this; on account of which he was sentenced by the Governor to die for the name of Christ; which death he suffered after many pains and torments, and was thus numbered with his slain fellow brethren. Regarding the death of this man, see A. Mell., *1st Book of the Hist, der vervolg. in Marti*, fol. 27, col. 1, ex Adone, in comment At. 6 Aster. Oral, de Phoca. Also, concerning the time of his death, for the year 118, see Joh. Gysii Hist. Mart., fol. 15, col. 4. Touching the manner of his death, P.J. Twisck gives the following account: "Phocus, in Pontus, refusing to sacrifice to the gods, was thrust, according to the command of Emperor Trajan, and for the name of Christ, into a lime-kiln full of glowing coals, then cast into boiling water and thus killed. P.J. Twisck. *Chronicles*. 2nd book, for the year 118; p. 37, col. 2 from Adon. Vinnens, lib. 6, fol. 166, Vinefol 159."[8]

SEPTIMUS SEVERUS 193-211

Let us hear Kurtz again:

"Septimus Severus (193-211), whom Proculus, a Christian slave, had healed from dangerous illness by anointing him with oil (James v. 14), was at first friendly to Christians. But political suspicions or the extravagances of Montanism changed this disposition. He forbade conversion to Christianity (203); and in Egypt and North Africa, persecution again raged. In Alexandria, Leonidas, the father of Origen, was beheaded. Potamiaena, a virgin equally distinguished for moral purity and beauty, suffered the most exquisite tortures, and was then to be given up to the gladiators for the vilest purposes. The latter indignity she knew to avert; but she and mother Marcella were slowly immersed in boiling pitch. Basilides, the soldier who had been commissioned to lead her to martyrdom, himself became a Christian and was beheaded on the day following. Not less searching and cruel was the persecution of Carthage. Perpetua, a lady of noble descent, and only twenty-two years old, with a babe in her arms, remained stedfast, despite the entreaties of her father, imprisonment, and tortures. She was gored by a wild cow, and finally dispatched by the dagger of a gladiator.

Felicitas, a slave, who in prison became a mother, dispatched equal constancy in suffering."[9]

Note to Albert Henry Newman in his excellent work:

"Septimus Severus (193-211) was not intensely hostile toward Christianity. In fact, it has been commonly supposed that up to 202 he was somewhat favorably disposed, it is related by Spartianus that on his return from a victorious campaign against the Armenians and the Parthians (202), while sojourning in Palestine, he enacted a law forbidding conversions to Judaism or Christianity. It does not appear to have been his purpose to attempt the extermination of Christianity, but simply to put a check upon proselytizing. But the enforcement of the Trajanic law against Christianity as an unauthorized religion involved many Christians in severe suffering. It does not appear that the emperor issued an edict of persecution; but he no doubt encouraged the local officials diligently to enforce the old laws.

Clement of Alexandria, who was at the head of the Catechetical school, wrote some time before the close of the second century: "Many martyrs are daily burned, crucified, and beheaded before our eyes." About 202 or 203 he was obliged to abandon his work and retire from the city. The father of Origen suffered martyrdom at this time. Origen himself, then a zealous and brilliant youth, was saved from a like fate by the tact of his mother, who hid his clothes and thus prevented him from publicly proclaiming himself a Christian and gaining the martyr's crown. About 200, a number of Christians, including three women, suffered joyfully in Scillte, in Numidia, falling on their knees and praising God. At Carthage two young women, Perpetua and Felicitas, won the highest admiration of their contemporaries and of posterity by resolutely refusing to yield to the entreaties of parents and friends or to the promptings of material affection, to save their lives by denying the faith, and by cheerfully confronting the maddened beasts. These last and their companions in suffering are supposed to have been Montanists. Tertullian refers to the persecutions in Numidia and Mauritania about 211."[10]

DECIUS TRAJAN 249-251

Of this Emperor, Kurtz has the following: "But with the accession of DECIUS (249-251) commenced a fresh, and indeed the first general persecution, surpassing in extent, combination, continuance, and severity, all that had preceded it. In other respects, Decius was an able monarch, who combined the ancient Roman earnestness with firmness and energy of purpose. But this very circumstance induced him to resolve on wholly exterminating Christianity as a religion equally hostile to the commonwealth and to the gods. Every conceivable means - confiscation, banishment, exquisite tortures, and death - were employed to induce Christians to apostatize. In too many cases these measures proved successful, the more so as the long period of peace had led to false security. On the other hand, a longing after the martyr's crown led many of their own accord to rush into prison or to the scaffold. Those who recanted (lapsi) were either:

1. *thurificati* or *sacnficati,* who, in order to preserve their lives, had sacrificed to the gods;

2. *libellatici.* who without having actually sacrificed, had bribed the magistrates to give them a certificate of having done so; or

3. *acta facientes.* who made false depositions in reference to their Christianity.

Again, those who openly confessed Christ even amid tortures, but escaped with their lives, were called confessors (*confessores*); while the name of martyrs was given to those who, for their profession, had suffered death."[11]

Dr. Newman gives us a concise statement concerning Decius:

"Decius Trajan (249-251), an Italian soldier, was raised to the throne by the Danubian army after the battle with the Goths at Verona, in which Philip lost his life. He seems to have had an earnest desire to restore the empire to its pristine order and vigor. The millennium of the city was being celebrated with great splendor when Decius returned from the Gothic war. Special occasion was doubtless afforded thereby for remaking the decay of the State religion. The fact that Christians had been especially favored by the predecessor probably led Decius to suspect them of disloyalty to himself. It may be assumed from what we know of this ruler that his exterminating measures against Christianity did not proceed from sheer wantonness, but were, from his point of view, a political necessity. Only by the extermination of the State religion could the unity and the stability of the empire be secured. In 250 was issued the first imperial edict aiming at the universal suppression of Christianity. Christians everywhere were required to conform to the State religion by participating in its ceremonies, and officials were commanded, under heavy penalties, rigorously to enforce the requirement. In each official district all Christians were required within a definite time to appear before the magistrates and to offer sacrifices to the gods. The flight of Christians before the expiration of the time allowed was not hindered, but the property of fugitives was confiscated and death was the penalty of returning. Those who were not in a position to prove that they had fulfilled the requirement were brought before a commission composed of officials and citizens. First they were threatened with the direst punishments in case of obstinacy. Threats were followed by torture. This failing, imprisonment and repeated tortures, including hunger and thirst, were resorted to as a means of breaking down the wills of the victims. All the influence and machinery of the imperial government were employed to prevent laxity on the part of the officials. The magistrates were enjoined to use special severity toward bishops and other influential leaders.

Immunity from persecution had brought into the churches multitudes of people who had no proper idea of the obligations of the Christian life and many who cannot be regarded as possessing a saving knowledge of the truth. Lamentable worldliness characterized many of the clergy, who were spending their energies in secular pursuits rather than in the ministry of the word. The imperial edict struck terror to the hearts of all whose faith was weak. "Before the battle," writes Cyprian, "many were conquered, and without having met the enemy, were cut down; they did not even seek to gain the reputation of having sacrificed against their will. They indeed did not wait to be apprehended ere they ascended, or to be interrogated ere they denied. Many were conquered before the battle, prostrated before the attack. Nor did they even leave it to be said for them that they seemed to sacrifice to idols unwillingly. They ran to the market place of their own accord." Many were so impatient to deny their faith that they could hardly wait their turn. Cyprian himself retired before the fury of the persecution and thereby greatly injured his reputation among the stricter sort. Many who would neither flee nor sacrifice suffered the most terrible tortures and died in prison or were at last cruelly executed. Some, by bribing the officials, procured certificates of having sacrificed without committing the overt act. Some allowed others to say that they had sacrificed or to procure certificates for them. Holders of these fraudulent certificates were called libellatici and were regarded as scarcely less culpable than the Lapsi, or those who actually denied their faith. Decius was, after a few months, called away by a fresh Gothic invasion and was slain in 251, but not until he had spread desolation throughout the churches. There was a slight lull in the storm of persecution from Callus, but a year of public disasters (plague, drought, famine, barbarian invasions) drew the attention of the populace afresh to the Christians, whose hostility to the gods was supposed to be responsible for the calamities. Many were sent to the mines, which involved the direst hardship and often death."[12]

DIOCLETIAN 284-316

There were other emperors who persecuted Christians. Most of them did in one manner or another. The last one we will consider in this Notebook is Diocletian. We will let Kurtz speak again:

"In 284 DIOCLETIAN and Maximianus Herculius became joint Emperors. In 292 the two caesars, Galerius and Constantius Chlorus (in the West), were associated with them. Diocletian was an excellent monarch; but being zealously attached to the old faith, he hated Christianity as introducing an element of disturbance. Still the edict of toleration issued by Gallienus, political considerations in regard to the large number of Christians throughout the empire, and a certain amount of natural kindness, for some time retarded decisive measures. At last the continued urgency of his son-in-law and colleague, Galerius, led to the most terrible of all persecutions. As early as the year 298, Galerius commanded that all soldiers in his army should take part in the sacrifices, - a measure by which he obliged all Christians to leave the ranks. At a meeting between the two monarchs, at Nicomedia in Bithynia (303), he prevailed on the Emperor to disregard what had formerly been the causes of his toleration. An imperial ordinance to pull down the splendid church at Nicomedia was the signal for the persecution. Soon afterwards an edict was affixed which forbade all Christian meetings, and ordered that the churches should be pulled down, the sacred writings destroyed, and all Christians deprived of their offices and civil rights. A Christian who tore down this edict was executed. A fire broke out in the imperial palace, when Galerius immediately accused the Christians of incendiarism. The persecution which now commenced extended over the whole empire, with the exception of Gaul, Spain, and Britain, where the protection of Constantius Chlorus shielded the Church. Whatever tortures or modes of death ingenuity could devise were put in requisition. When, in 305, Diocletian and Maximianus abdicated, Maximinus, the colleague of Galerius, proved quite as bitter an enemy as his predecessors, and raised anew the storm of persecution. In the year 308 Galerius even caused all articles of food or drink, sold in the market, to be moistened or mixed with sacrificial water or wine. At last, when a fearful disease brought Galerius to a different state of mind, he ordered in 311 a cessation of this persecution, and in return demanded the prayers of the Church for the Emperor and the empire. During those eight years of unceasing and unprecedented persecution, Christians had given the brightest proofs of moral heroism and of enthusiastic readiness to suffer as martyrs. In proportion, the number of lapsi was much smaller than it had been during the Decian persecution. But the command to give up sacred writings had originated a new kind of recantation. Those who had complied with this demand were called traditiores. Some, instead of delivering the sacred, handed in heretical writings, on pretence that they were the sacred books. But the spiritual earnestness of that period was such that these parties were ranked with the ordinary traditores, and, like them, were excommunicated."[13]

Let us look at one example from the pen of Thieleman J. van Braght:

"Not long afterwards, under the same Emperor and Proconsul, and in the same year, Zenobius, Bishop of the church of Aegaea in Cilicia, and his sister, were apprehended; and when there were held out to him on the one hand, great wealth, honor, and position, if, in accordance with the command of the Emperor, he would serve the gods, but on the other hand, manifold torments, Zenobius answered: "I love Jesus Christ more than all the riches and honor of this world. Death and torments with which you threaten me, I do not consider a disadvantage, but my greatest gain."

Having received this answer from the martyr, Lysias caused him to be suspended on the rack, and inhumanly tormented his whole body.

While the executioners were busy with Zenobius, his sister Zenobia, having learned of it, came running, crying with a loud voice: "Thou tyrant, what villainy has my brother committed, that thou dost thus cruelly torment him?"

Having thus addressed Lysjas, and set at naught his entreating as well as his threatening words, she, too, was seized by the servents, stripped naked, and stretched out, and roasted beside her brother on a red-hot iron bed, or roasting pan. The tyrant, deriding the martyrs said: "Now let Christ come and help you, seeing you suffer these torments for Him."

Zenobius replied: "See, He is already with us, and cools, with His heavenly dew the flames of fire on our bodies; though thou, surrounded as thou art with the thick darkness of wickedness, canst not perceives it on us."

Lysias, almost beside himself, commanded that they should be put naked into boiling caldrons. But seeing that the boiling water did not injure them, or at least, that they could not thereby be made to apostatize, he had them taken out of the city and beheaded. Their dead bodies were buried by Cauis and Hermogenes in the nearest cave. This happened in A.D. 285, on the 30lh day of October, in the city of Aegaea in Cilicia."[14]

Terrible Days

These were terrible days for the churches of God. Many a saint gained a martyr's crown. Of this period Dowling says, "For three centuries after the ascension of Christ, His disciples were exposed, with but few and brief intermissions, to a succession of cruel and bitter persecutions and sufferings. The pampered wild beasts, kept for the amusement of the Roman populace, fattened upon the bodies of the martyrs of Jesus in the amphitheaters of Rome or of other cities of the empire, and hundreds of fires were fed by the living frames of those who loved not their lives unto death."[15]

Days of Strength

Those bitter persecutions of Satan upon Christians by the use of the Roman Empire served to strengthen the churches in the faith. No one dared unite with one of the churches unless he or she really meant business for God. The result was that churches were stronger. Persecution would surely thin our ranks today but would be a spiritual medicine for our churches. Most church members of today are settled on their lees. Our ancestors brought the truth down to us at a great personal cost. We shouldn't take that lightly or for granted.

NOTES ON CHAPTER 3

1 *The Anti-Nicene Fathers: Volume 1, pages 163-193.*
2 *The Anti-Nicene Fathers: Volume 2, pages 129-148.*
3 *The Anti-Nicene Fathers: Volume 3, pages 17-55.*
4 *History of the Christian Religion and Church, Volume 1, pages 92-93.*
5 *Church History, page 86.*
6 *Martyrs Mirror, page 79.*
7 *Church History, pages 86-87.*
8 *Martyrs Mirror, pages 108-109.*
9 *Church History, page 88.*
10 *A Manual of Church History, pages 160-161.*
11 *Church History, page 89.*
12 *A Manual of Church History, pages 164-166.*
13 *Church History, pages 90-91.*
14 *Martyrs Mirror, page 145.*
15 *History of Romanism, page 26.*

Chapter 4

THE MONTANISTS

Baptists have been known by many different names in the past. They have been called by the name of the place in which they lived. They have been called by the name of the powerful leader among them. In was not until the time of the Reformation that they were called "Baptists." If time stands, we may be called by another name. This first group of our ancestors which we shall study gets their name from a man.

A Word of Caution

Not everyone today who calls himself a "Baptist" would be a "Baptist" as we consider it. In "Baptist" seminars, there are so-called Baptists who teach that a man can "fall from grace." They teach that the Bible is not infallible. They teach that Baptists began with John Smyth. Some of them teach that Jesus Christ was only a man. They call themselves Baptists. They pastor churches which call themselves Baptist churches. Yet, they are not Baptists at all. They deny many (most) of the cardinal doctrines that make a "Baptist" church. They do not bear the marks or the doctrinal peculiarities that Christ gave to His church when He founded it. So, in reality, they are Baptists who are not Baptists.

We will find this in our study of the Montanists and all other groups that we shall study about. We will not try to maintain that every Montanist was a true Baptist any more than we would maintain and do maintain that "among" them were the churches holding the truth as Christ gave it to His church.

False Charges

Much of the history we have of the Montanists was written by their enemies. There are many charges against them in the various church histories that are absolutely false.

If we use common sense in our investigation, this will be evident. When one person is writing about another person who believes differently, false charges are often made, consciously or unconsciously. Example: A Baptist would say that everybody who is going to heaven will go like a Baptist goes. A Methodist, hearing this, says the man who said it believes only Baptists are going to heaven. This is a false charge. Our ancestors, who refused the baptisms of the apostate churches, are charged as not believing in baptism. Since we do not believe baptism saves, the Campbellites say we do not believe in baptism. Many false charges against the Montanists and others have crept into histories by this line of reasoning.

Eusebius

It is my opinion that Mosheim and others relate certain charges against the Montanists because they follow the *Ecclesiastical History* of Eusebius. Eusebius was born about 275 A.D. and died about 339 A.D. He was bishop of Caesarea in Palestine and is revered, by most, as the father of church history. He was a close friend to Constantine, the ruler of the Roman Empire who united false churches to the state power. It is believed by many that Constantine commissioned him to write this history and financed his travel and investigations. Knowing what Constantine did to our Baptist ancestors should make us leery of him. Knowing he was a friend of Eusebius should make us careful of Eusebius too.

Eusebius quotes authors whom we know nothing about, against the Montanists. "He had also transmitted to us what we know of Miltiades and his works, especially on the Montanists. Extracts from Apollonius of Rome, caused much zeal in refuting the pretended prophets. Serapion, bishop of Antioch, is cited on the same subject."[1]

Eusebius gives: "Their combination, therefore, and the recent heretical severance of theirs from the church, had for its origin the following cause: - There is said to be a certain village of Mysia in Phrygia, called Ardaba. There, they say, one of those who was but a recent convert, Montanus by name, when Cratus was proconsul in Asia, in the excessive desire of his soul to take the lead, gave the adversary occasion against himself. So that he was carried away in spirit, and wrought up into a certain kind of frenzy and irregular ecstasy, raving, and speaking, and uttering strange things, and proclaiming what was contrary to the institutions that had prevailed in the church, as handed down and preserved in succession from the earliest times. But of those that happened then to be present, and to hear these spurious oracles, and being indignant, rebuked him as one under the influence of demons and the spirit of delusion, and who was only exciting disturbances among the multitude. These bore in mind the distinction and the warning given by our Lord, when he cautioned them to be vigilantly on their guard against false prophets. Others again, as if elated by the Holy Spirit, and the gift of grace, and not a little puffed up, and forgetting the distinction made by our Lord, challenged this insidious, flattering, and seducing spirit being themselves captivated and seduced by him; so that they could no longer restrain him to keep silence. Thus, by an artifice, or rather by a certain crafty process, the devil having devised destruction against those that disobeyed the truth, and thus excessively honoured by them, secretly stimulated and fired their understandings, already wrapt in insensibility, and wandering away from the truth. For he excited two others, females, and filled them with the spirit of delusion, so that they also spake like the former, in a kind of extatic frenzy, out of all season, and in a manner strange and novel, whilst the spirit of evil congratulated them, thus rejoicing and inflated by him, and continued to puff them up the more, by promises of great things. Sometimes pointedly and deservedly, directly condemning them that he might appear also disposed to reprove them. Those few that were deceived were Phrygians; but the same inflated spirit taught them to revile the whole church under heaven, because it gave neither access nor honour to this false spirit of prophecy. For when the faithful held frequent .conversations in many places throughout Asia for this very purpose, and examined their novel doctrines, and pronounced them vain, and rejected them as heresy, then indeed they were expelled and prohibited from communion with the church."[2]

Eusebius, speaking so severely against them, makes me think they must have been Baptists. Guess we all have our bias.

One last reference of this sort: Mosheim, in speaking of what he calls sects of this time period, says, "These sects, which we have now been slightly surveying, may be justly regarded as the offspring of philosophy. But they were succeeded by one in which ignorance reigned, and which was the mortal enemy of philosophy and letters. It was formed by Montanus, an obscure man, without any captivity or strength of judgment, and who lived in a Phrygian village called Pepuza. This weak man was so foolish and extravagant as to imagine and pretend that he was the paraclete, or Comforter, whom the divine Saviour, at his departure from the earth, promised to send to his disciples to lead them to all truth."[3] Mosheim follows Eusebius and his unknown sources here.

I must give here a quote by Archibald Maclaine, the translator of Dr. Mosheim, given at the same place of the above quote in a footnote. "Those are undoubtedly in an error, who have asserted that Montanus gave himself out for the Holy Ghost. However weak he may have been in point of capacity, he was not fool enough to push his pretensions so far. Neither have they, who inform us that

Montanus pretended to have received from the same spirit or paraclete which formerly animated the apostles, interpreted with accuracy the meaning to observe here, that Montanus made a distinction between the paraclete promised by Christ to his apostles, and the Holy Spirit that was shed upon them on the day of Pentecost."[4]

I think most Baptists see the difference between the Holy Spirit dwelling in a believer and in the Holy Spirit empowering the church on the day of Pentecost. It seems to me that Montanus felt he was a teacher in the true church, empowered in a special way to teach the truth. Churches (true churches) have the Holy Spirit in a special way. True churches have the truth, so the best place to hear the truth is in a true church.

Montanists: Origin and Beliefs

Sylvester Hassell writes of these people: "The chief opposition to the Alexandrian School and to Gnosticism and to the substitution of philosophy for Christianity was, in the second century, made by those called the Montanists, of whom Tertullian became, in the third century, the ablest writer. They took their name from Montanus, a native of Phrygia in Asia Minor, and were hence also called Cataphrygians, and Pepuzians, from Pepuza in Phrygia. They sought to emphasize the great importance of the spirituality and purity of the church and especially the absolute indispensability of the work of the Holy Ghost and the dispensableness of human philosophy."[5]

Who cannot see herein, men of Baptist principles? A spiritual and pure church speaks of a regenerated church membership. This opposed to infant baptism and to baptismal regeneration. This is a Baptist distinctive. Baptists have always preached that the power of the Holy Spirit is needed in the salvation of sinners and the building of churches. Others believe that human wisdom can accomplish these things. It seems, to me, that these folks believed what true churches believe.

David Benedict

Benedict has the following to say about the Montanists:

"Montanists - According to the representations of most writers, this sect took its name from Montanus; others suppose they were so called from their dwelling in the mountains, to avoid the persecutions of their enemies.

The Montanists were in a flourishing condition towards the latter part of the second century. They began in Phrygia, and spread abroad throughout Asia, Africa, and a part of Europe. The severity of their doctrines, says Mosheim, gained them the esteem and confidence of many who were far from being the lowest order."

With this party the famous Tertullian united, about A.D. 200, and wrote many books in defense of their sentiments. It is proper here to remark that heresies in abundance were attributed to this people, relative both to their faith and practice; but when we consider that such a man as Tertullian, with many other eminent characters, became their associates and defenders, it seems to relieve in a measure the gloomy picture which many have drawn of their ignorance and fanaticism.

As the first church of this sect was formed at Pepuza, in Phrygia, as also Quintilla, a famous lady, was a prophetess among them, from all these circumstances these early dissenters went by the name of Cataphrygians, Quintillianists, and Pepuzians, as well as Montanists. These people will be referred to in the narratives which will follow. After the Donatists arose they were often called by that name."[6]

We have all of Tertullian's writings available in the Anti-Nicene Fathers, volume 3 and 4. When Benedict here identifies them with the Donatists, he states they were Baptists. We will see something of the Donatists in a future chapter in this Notebook.

John T. Christian

In his most excellent history, Dr. Christian writes: "The first protest in the way of separation from the growing corruptions of the times was the movement of the Montanist churches. This Montanus, the leader, was a Phrygian, who arose about the year A.D. 156. The most distinguished advocate of Montanism was Tertullian who espoused and defended their views. They held that science and art, all worldly education or gay form of life, should be avoided, because such things belonged to paganism. The crown of life was martyrdom. Religious life they held to be austere. Against a mortal sin the church should defend itself by rightly excluding him who committed it, for the holiness of the church was simply the holiness of the members. With such principles, they could not fail to come in conflict with the popular Christianity of the day. The substance of the contentions of these churches was for the life of the Spirit. It was not a new form of Christianity; it was a discovery of the old, the primitive church set over against the obvious corruptions of the current Christianity. The old church demanded purity; the new church had struck a bargain with the world, and had arranged itself comfortably with it, and they would, therefore, break with it." (Moeller, "Montanism" in *Schaff-Herzog Encyclopedia,* III, 1562)

Their contention was not so much one of doctrine as of discipline. They insisted that those who had "lapsed" from the true faith should be rebaptized, because they had denied Christ and ought to be baptized anew. On this account they were termed "Anabaptists," and some of their principles reappeared in Anabaptism (Schaff, *History of the Christian Church,* II, 427). Infant baptism was not yet a dogma, and we know that it was rejected by the Montanists. Tertullian thought only adults ought to be immersed. The Montanists were deeply rooted in the faith, and their opponents admitted that they received the entire Scriptures of the Old and the New Testaments, and they were sound in their views of the Father, and of the Son, and of the Holy Spirit (Epiphanius, Hoer, XLVIII, 1). They rejected episcopacy and the right of the bishop's claim to exercise the power of the keys.

The movement spread rapidly through Asia Minor and North Africa and, for a time, in Rome itself. It appealed very powerfully to the sterner moralists, stricter disciplinarians, and more deeply pious minds among all Christians. Montanism had the advantage of claiming divine revelation for stricter principles. Montanism had made so much stir in Asia Minor, before the close of the second century that several councils were called against it, and finally the whole movement was officially condemned. But Montanism continued for centuries, and finally became known under other names (*Eusebius, The Church History*, 229, note 1 by Dr. McGiffert). In Phrygia, the Montanists came in contact with the Paulicians. We know that they were still in existence in the year 722 (Theophanes, 617. Bonded).[7]

While many churches were becoming corrupt by the doctrines of church government and baptism regeneration, these churches stood firm for truth. They accepted the Scripture as their guide.

Henry C. Vedder

Dr. Vedder, though not too highly favorable to perpetuity, says the following things about their beliefs:

"First, they clearly apprehended the fundamental truth that a church of Christ should consist of the regenerate only. As a result of the doctrine of sacramental grace, large numbers were becoming members of the church who, in the judgment of the most charitable, could not be regarded as regenerate. This was true of the adults baptized on profession of faith, and the case became continually worse as the practice of infant baptism extended. Montanus advocated a return to the principle of the New Testament - a spiritual church. His immediate followers called themselves "spiritual" Christians, as distinguished from the "carnal" who were found in the Catholic Church in great numbers. The Spirit of God has not only regenerated every Christian, they taught, but dwells in an especial manner in every believer, even as Jesus promised the Paraclete (John 16:13)."[8]

Concerning the second coming of Christ, Vedder says, "The second of the chief features in Montanism was a belief in the speedy coming of Christ to reign with his saints a thousand years. The fragmentary says of their prophets that have come down to us, the writings of Tertullian, and the testimonies of the Catholic writers against Montanism combine to make this certain."[9]

You know, that sounds Baptistic to me. Vedder also writes: "Of course the Montanists immersed -no other baptism, so far as we know, was practiced by anybody in the second century. There is no evidence that they baptized infants, and their principle of a regenerate church would naturally require the baptism of believers only."[10]

Thomas Armitage

This historian, though against church perpetuity, says the following: "The one prime idea held by the Montanists in common with Baptists, and in distinction to the churches of the third century was, that membership in the churches should be confined to purely regenerate persons; and that a spiritual life and discipline should be maintained without any affiliation with the authority of the State."

Again: "They believed in the literal reign of Christ upon the earth, and longed for his coming, that he might hold his people separate by the final overthrow of sin and sinners, and then his saints would reign with him in his glory."[11]

W. A. Jarrel

Jarrel's chapter on the Montanists is very good. He quotes from various writers whose works we do not possess but would like to. He writes: "In historic times Phrygia comprised the greater part of Asia Minor. 'Montanism' appeared there about the middle of the second century. Montanism enrolled its hosts and was one of the greatest Christian influences throughout early Christian centuries. As there was at the time, when Montanism arose, no essential departure from the faith in the action, the subjects of Baptism, church government or doctrine, the Montanists, on these points, were Baptists."[12]

He quotes Moller as saying of Tertullian, "To him the very substance of the church was the Holy Spirit and by no means the Episcopacy whose right to wield the power of the keys he rejected."[13]

He quotes Dr. Dorner, "Montanism may be styled a democratic reaction on the part of the members of the church, asserting their universal prophetic and priestly rank against the concentration of ecclesiastical dignities and rights in the episcopate. In this respect, Montanism was a reaction of the substantial, real principle against the formal unity of the episcopate, which entrusted to the unworthy, and those who were destitute of the Spirit, power over those who were filled with the Spirit."[14]

Final Notes on the Montanists

Many of them suffered. Tertullian tells of many who were martyred. As in our quote from Dr. Christian, "The crown of life was martyrdom." This would not have been said unless many of them died. The Martyrs Mirror records some of their persecutions.

Some of them, no doubt, held to some things we would shy away from. That is true of some Baptists today. They were for the most part, churches of like principles with us today. We claim them in the line of our heritage.

NOTES ON CHAPTER 4

1 Ecclesiastical History, Introduction page VII.
2 Ecclesiastical History, pages 196-197.
3 Church History, pages 55-56.
4 Church History, page 56, footnote A.
5 History of the Church of God, page 367.
6 History of the Baptists, page 4.
7 A History of the Baptists, volume 1, pages 43-44.
8 A Short History of the Baptists, page 58.
9 A Short History of the Baptists, page 60.
10 A Short History of the Baptists, page 62.
11 The History of the Baptists, pages 175-176.
12 Baptist Church Perpetuity, page 69.
13 Baptist Church Perpetuity, page 73.
14 Baptist Church Perpetuity, page 76.

Chapter 5

THE NOVATIANISTS

Here is another group of our Baptist ancestors. Again, we do not claim kin with all of them any more than we claim kin with "all" of the people who go by the name Baptist today. We do claim that among them we find the true churches of our Lord Jesus Christ.

This group of our ancestors takes their name after a preacher in Rome who lived from A. D. 210-280. Neander says that Novatian was "an eminent presbyter, who had acquired celebrity as a theological writer."[1] Novatian composed many works. There are four that are extant. The two major ones are his work on the Trinity and his work on the Jewish meats. These are in the *Anti-Nicene Fathers*, volume 5. There are several works written against him that exist today. Cyprian, Bishop of Carthage wrote a lot against him.

It is to be noted that much of what is written about him in the history books came from his enemies. "The biography of Novatian belongs to the ecclesiastical history of the third century. He was, or is reputed to have been, the founder of the sect which claimed for itself the name of 'Puritan' (Cathari). For a long time he was in determined opposition to Cornelius, bishop of Rome, in regard to the admission of the lapsed and penitent into the church; but the facts of the controversy and much of our information in regard to Novatian are to be got only from his enemies, the Roman bishop and his adherents. Accordingly, some have believed all the accusations that have been brought against him, while others have been inclined to doubt them all."[2] This is a very honest statement.

For those who are interested in the charges made against him and those charges refuted, please read Neander, Vol. 1, pages 237-248 and W.A. Jarrel.[3] Anyone should be able to see that the best place to get the truth about someone would not be from their enemies. I like the words of Robert Robinson on this subject: "The character of the man ought no more to be taken from Cyprian, than his ought from the pagans, who by punning on his name called him Coprian, or the scavenger."[4]

The Novatian Rupture

J.M. Carroll, in the *Trail of Blood*, says that in A. D. 251, the loyal churches declared non-fellowship with the churches that had fallen into the errors that we have mentioned in chapter 2. This is known as the Novatian Rupture and was primarily over two things: church discipline and what constitutes the idea and essence of a true church. As we examine the matter of these two questions, we will see that J.M. Carroll was correct. Let us see what led to the division in A.D. 251. We begin with a quote from the historian Kurtz.

"In the Schism of Novatian, a Presbyter at Rome (251), the cause of dispute was an almost opposite character from that just described. Cornelius, Bishop of Rome, exercised a mild discipline; a practice opposed by a stricter party, under the presbyter Novatian. When Novatus of Carthage arrived at Rome, he joined the discontented party, although his own views on ecclesiastical discipline had been the very opposite of theirs, and incited them to separation. The strict party now chose Novatian as their bishop. Both parties appealed for recognition to the leading churches. Cyprian pronounced against Novatian, and contested the sectarian principles of his adherents, according to which the Church had not the right to assure forgiveness to the lapsed, or to those whom by gross sin, had broken their baptismal vows (though they admitted the possibility that, by the mercy of God, such persons might be pardoned). The Novatians also held that the Church, being a communion of pure persons, could not tolerate in its bosom any who were impure, nor readmit a person who had been excommunicated, even though he had undergone ecclesiastical discipline. On this ground the party called itself the cathari. Owing to the moral earnestness of their principles, even those bishops who took a different view from theirs were disposed to regard them more favourably; and almost through the whole Roman Empire. Novatian communities sprung up, of which remnants existed so late as the sixth century."[5]

You can see how this controversy relates around church discipline and the nature of the true church. Novatian and his followers believed a church was to be pure (hence Puritan or Cathari) and discipline was the only way to achieve it. Baptismal Regeneration and Infant Baptism would surely place into the church lost people and a pure church could not be maintained.

Gieseler

Next, we quote the German historian, Dr. John C. L. Gieseler. "The presbyter Novatian was dissatisfied with the choice of the bishop Cornelius at Rome (251) because Cornelius, in his opinion, had conducted himself with too great lenity toward the lapsed. In the controversy that now ensued, in which the Carthaginian presbyter Novatus proved particularly active in favor of Novatian, the latter returned to the old principle that none of the lapsed ought to be admitted to church communion. Hence arose a division in the church. Novatian was chosen bishop of his party at Rome. Though the other bishops, particularly Cyprian at Carthage, and Dionysius at Alexandria, stood on the side of Cornelius, yet many different countries joined the strict party. At first the Novatians (Cathari) declared themselves only against the readmission of the lapsi; but afterwards they fully returned to the old African notion, that all who had defiled themselves by gross sins after baptism should be forever excluded from the church, because the church itself would be tainted if they were received again. In accordance with this view they declared all other churches to have forfeited the rights of a Christian church; and baptized anew those who came over to them. This party was widely extended, and continued for a long time. In Phrygia they united with the remnant of the Montanists."[6]

Let us make a few observations from this quote, remembering that Gieseler follows Eusebus and others who would quickly side with Cyprian in this controversy. The charge that they were excluded forever from church fellowship is doubtful. They most probably demanded true repentance for having lapsed and watched those who were excluded for a long time. Even if they did (which is improbable) keep them out, that would be much better than allowing the impure to remain as members. This makes for weak churches as all in our day should know. It sounds like they were what all Baptists ought to be.

Gieseler says they were joined by others in other countries. This would mean there were others in our countries who already believed what the Novatianists believed. There were true churches already opposing the heretical churches. He said they united with the Montanists and we have already seen that they were Baptists. He said these Novatianists regarded themselves as the true churches and the others as false. Is that not what Baptists (true Baptists) believe today?

Origin of Novatianism

Albert Henry Newman has the following to say:

"Origin of Novatianism. So far as the Novatianist party was a new party, it originated as follows: During the Decian persecution, many Christians in all parts of the empire denied the faith. At the close of the persecution, it was a most important question with the churches how to deal with the multitudes party, which was at this time predominant at Rome, was in favor of readmitting them without much delay or ceremony. An influential party, led by Novatian, opposed this laxity, and when they failed to carry their point in the church, withdrew, Novatian becoming bishop of the protesting party. The Novatianists had the sympathy of a large element in the North African churches, and they soon formed there a strong organization. In North Africa and in Asia Minor they probably absorbed most of the Montanist party, which was still important. This was certainly the case in Phrygia, the original home of Montanism. Novatianist congregations persisted till the fifth century or later."[7]

Robert Robinson, in his work published in 1792, gives the following account: "The case in brief was this: Novatian was an elder in the church at Rome. He was a man of extensive learning, and held the same doctrine as the church did, and published several treaties in defence of what he believed. His address was eloquent and insinuating, and his morals were irreproachable. He saw with extreme pain the intolerable depravity of the church. Christians within the space of a very few years were caressed by one emperor, and persecuted by another. In seasons of prosperity many rushed into the church for base purposes. In times of adversity they denied the faith, and ran back to idolatry again. When the squall was over away they came again to the church with all their vices to deprave others by their examples. The bishops, fond of proselytes, encouraged all this, and transferred the attention of Christians from the old confederacy for virtue to vain shows at Easter, and other Jewish ceremonies, adulterated too with paganism. On the death of bishop Fabian, Cornelius, a brother elder, and a vehement partisan for taking in the multitude, was put in nomination. Novatian opposed him: but as Cornelius carried his election, and he saw no prospect of reformation, but on the contrary a tide of immorality pouring into the church, he withdrew, and a great many with him. Cornelius, irritated by Cyprian, who was just in the same condition through the remonstrances of virtuous men at Carthage, and who was exasperated beyond measure with one of his elders, named Nocatus, who had quitted Carthage, and had gone to Rome to espouse the cause of Novatian, called a council, and got a sentence of excommunication passed against Novatian. In the end, Novatian formed a church and was elected bishop. Great numbers followed his example, and all over the empire Puritan churches were constituted and flourished through the succeeding two hundred years. Afterward, when penal laws obliged them to lurk in corners, and worship God in private, they were distinguished by a variety of names and a succession of them continued until the reformation."[8]

The churches believing these doctrines were the true churches. The others were the false ones that developed into the Roman Catholic Church. Novatian, Novatus and others like them, did not invent those doctrines of church discipline and a pure church. They only ably expounded them. People believing the truth existed all over the empire so churches sprang up everywhere, ". . . which, on account of the severity of its discipline, was followed by many, and flourished until the fifth century, in the greatest part of those provinces which had received the gospel."[9] So writes Mosheim, the father of Modern Church History.

J. M. Cramp

We will look at one other general account of Novatian and the Novatian Rupture. We will hear the voice of J. M. Cramp, one of the finest Baptist historians:

"Novatian possessed such talent and zeal that he became a popular teacher. On the death of Fabiar, bishop of Rome, in the year 250, there was a strong desire that Novatian should succeed him, and he would have done so, had it not been for his known sentiments on one point. Lax habits of discipline, as he believed, had grown up, and were very mischievous in their tendencies. In the Decian persecution great numbers had apostatized who, in the return of tranquility, sought readmission into the churches. Novatian differed from his brethren on this subject. He held that apostasy was a sin which wholly disqualified an individual for restoration to Christian fellowship, and that it would be destructive to the purity of the church to readmit those who had so grossly fallen. God might pardon them. They might find a place in heaven. But the church must not be defiled, for it is a congregation of saints. Now, whatever opinion we may form respecting Novatian's particular theory, it is undeniable that the principle on which it rested was derived from the New Testament. Yet, it was too spiritual for the times. A majority declared in favor of Cornelius, who was duly installed bishop of Rome. Nevertheless, the minority would not yield. The time had come - so they argued - for a decided stand. The holiness of the church was in danger, and must be maintained at all hazards. Separation was better than corruption. They withdrew, formed a separate church, and invited Novatian to become their pastor. Others imitated their example in various parts of the empire, and Novatian churches sprang up in great abundance. They continued in existence more than three centuries. In all the principle towns and cities, these dissenting communities might be found. They were the "Puritans" of those days, and were so designated. There was a wholesome rivalry for some time between them and the "Orthodox" or "Catholic" body, each separating as a stimulus and a check to the other."[10]

Their Doctrines

We have noticed, at length, what the Novatian churches believed about church discipline and purity of the church. None can doubt but that they believed in a regenerated church membership. Since everyone at this early date (almost everyone) believed in and practiced immersion, they immersed for baptism. Since infant baptism was almost unheard of, they rejected it. From these observations alone we conclude they were Baptists.

Newman says, "Believing the general churches of the time to be apostate, they naturally rejected their ordinances, and rebaptized those who came to them from churches with which they did not affiliate."[11]

Vedder writes, "The Novatians were the earliest Anabaptists; refusing to recognize as valid the ministry and sacraments of their opponents, and claiming to be the true church, they were logically compelled to rebaptize all who came to them from the Catholic Church."[12]

Robinson had the following to say about them: "The Novatians said, If you be a virtuous believer, and will accede to our confederacy against sin, you may be admitted among us by baptism, or if any Catholick has baptized you before, by rebaptism: but mark this, if you violate the contract by lapsing into idolatry or vice, we shall separate you from our community, and, do what you will, we shall never readmit you. God forbid we should injure either your person, your property, or your character, or even judge the truth of your repentance, and your future state: but you can never be readmitted to our community without our giving up the best and only coercive guardian we have of the purity of our morals."[13]

We read in D. B. Ray's book: "The Novatians claimed no other standard of faith and practice except the Bible. Very little need be said on this point, as they have never been charged with appealing to any standard except the Scriptures. The Novatians were also called Paterines in after times; and they are known to have claimed the Scriptures alone as their rule of conduct. It is, therefore, taken for granted -unless proof to the contrary can be produce -that the Novatians possessed the Baptist characteristic that the Word of God alone is the rule of faith and practice."[14]

Reading these quotes from the pages of the church historians is much like reading a Baptist Confession of Faith. It seems, without doubt to me, that the Novatians believed in the local church as opposed to a universal, invisible church. What they believed about church purity and church discipline demands such a belief. Neander, in seeking to defend Novatian and take the edge off his rigid discipline, writes something that convinces me that the Novatianists held the local church view. "Hence was it, that Novatian, transferring the predicate of purity and unspotted holiness, which belongs to the invisible church appears, drew the conclusion, that every community which suffered unclean members to remain in it, ceased to be any longer a true church."[15]

Novatian transferred nothing. He believed a true church was composed of born-again people who had been baptized and were living holy lives. Folks, that is what a church is -nothing more or nothing less or nothing else. That is what true Baptists believe today, yesterday and tomorrow.

Persecuted

The Novatianists, like all of our Baptist ancestors, suffered for their strong beliefs. William Manius Nevins writes of them: "At the conclusion of the fourth century, the Novatians had three, if not four, churches in Constantinople: they also had churches at Nice, Nicomedia, and Cotivetus, in Phrygia, all of them large and extensive bodies, besides which they were very numerous in the western empire. There were several churches in Alexandria in the fifth century. Here Cyril, ordained bishop of the Catholics, shut up the churches of the Novatians. They awakened the anger of the Catholics because they rebaptized all who came to them from the Catholics. An edict was issued in 413 by the emperors Theodosius and Honorius, declaring, that all persons rebaptized, and the rebaptizers should both be punished with death. Accordingly, Albanus, a zealous minister, with others, was punished with death for baptizing. As a result of the persecution at this time, many abandoned the cities and sought retreats in the country and valleys of the Piedmont, where later they were called Waldenses."[16]

Concerning the edict of Theodosius, persecution and Baptist perpetuity, I should like to give the following quote from van Braght: "A.D. 413 -As those Christians greatly increased, who valued only the baptism which is administered upon faith, and, consequently rebaptized (as not having been baptized aright) those who had been baptized by unbelievers or in infancy, when they attained to the true faith, the Emperor Theodosius, A.D. 413, issued an edict against the Anabaptists, commanding they should be put to death.

"But lest anyone should think that the people who, under the name Anabaptists, where threatened with death by the Emperor Theodosius, held, with regard to the point, views different from those maintained by the Baptists of the present day, who are likewise called Anabaptists, it is expedient to mention what was said about their views by the inquisitor of Leeuwaerden, in opposition to one of our latest martyrs, namely, Jagues d' Auchi. When Jagues wanted the inquisitor, who appealed to the Emperor's edict, to prove that the said edict was just or founded on holy Scripture, the inquisitor made this reply to him: 'I believe you think that all our fathers were deceived, and that your sect is saved: what do you say? It is now 1200 or 1300 years since the Emperor Theodosius issued an edict, that the heretics should be put to death, namely, those who were rebaptized like your sect.'

"When, therefore, the inquisitor says that they 'were rebaptized like your sect' he certainly indicates thereby, that they were people like Jagues d' Auchi was, and consequently, like the Anabaptists who at that time, namely, A.D. 1558, gave their lives for the truth."[17]

How very clear is this, then, that the Novatians were Baptists. How clear that they continued on as Anabaptists. Martyrs' Mirror was published in 1660. van Braght gives the whole of the inquisition of d' Auchi and his martyrdom on pages 591-611 of his book. Let me repeat one more time, "Everyone should buy and read *Martyrs Mirror*." Herald Press of Scottsdale, Pa., has reprinted it. C. H. Spurgeon: "Novatian held that apostasy was a sin which disqualified them from again entering into church fellowship, and to secure a pure community, he formed a separate church, which elected him for its pastor. The purer churches multiplied, and continued in existence for more than three centuries, the members being everywhere looked upon as Puritans and Dissenters. They were Anabaptists, baptizing again all who had been immersed by the orthodox and corrupt church. The Novatianists, then, were Baptists."[18]

NOTES ON CHAPTER 5

1 *History of the Christian Religion and Church, Volume I, page 237.*
2 *The Anti-Nicene Fathers, Volume 5, page 608.*
3 *Baptist Church Perpetuity or History, pages 77-78.*
4 *Ecclesiastical Researchers, page 126.*
5 *Church History, pages 134-135.*
6 *A Compendium of Ecclesiastical History, Volume 1, pages 284-285.*
7 *A Manual of Church History, Volume 1, page 207.*
8 *Ecclesiastical Researches, pages 126 and 127.*
9 *Church History, page 74.*
10 *Baptist History, pages 55-57.*
11 *A Manual of Church History, Volume 1, page 207.*
12 *Short History of the Baptists, page 64.*
13 *Ecclesiastical Researchers, pages 127-128.*
14 *Baptist Succession, page 315.*
15 *History of the Christian Religion and Church, Volume 1, page 247.*
16 *Alien Baptism & the Baptists, page 49.*
17 *Martyrs Mirror, page 190.*
18 *The Sword & the Trowel, Vol. 2, page 92.*

Chapter 6

CONSTANTINE THE GREAT

The Roman Catholic Church is a developing body. She is not today what she was years ago. As the ages have come and gone she has called councils where different doctrines have been added and some have been subtracted. She is truly the product of evolutionary thought. Just when did this antichristian institution begin? Different writers give different men and different dates as the beginning of the Roman Catholic Church. For example, J. T. Odle, in his *Church Member's Handbook*, page 16, lists Gregory as the founder and 590 as the beginning date. Dr. Boettner says: "The papacy really began in the year 590, with Gregory I, as Gregory the Great, who consolidated the power of the bishopric in Rome and started that church on a new course."[1] On page 125 of the same book Dr. Boettner says: "In Italy the term 'pope' came to be applied to all bishops as a title of honor, and then to the bishop of Rome exclusively as the universal bishop. It was first given to Gregory I by the wicked emperor Phocas, in the year 604. This he did to spite the bishop of Constantinople, who had justly excommunicated him for having caused the assassination of his (Phocas') predecessor, emperor Mauritus. Gregory, however, refused the title, but his second successor, Boniface III (607) assumed the title, and it has been the designation of the bishops of Rome ever since." Thus, many date Catholicism as beginning with Gregory the Great.

Leo I and Boniface III

Some date the origin of Catholicism with Leo the Great A.D. 440-461. He first asserted the universal episcopate of the Roman bishop. He said the church was built on Peter. "According to him the church is built upon Peter, in pursuance of the promise of Matt. 16:16-19. Peter participates in everything which is Christ's: what the other apostles have in common with him they have through him. The Lord prays for Peter alone when danger threatens all the apostles, because his firmness will strengthen the others. What is true of Peter is true also of his successors. Every other bishop is charged with the care of his own special flock, the Roman with that of the whole church. Other bishops are only his assistants in this great task. Through the see of Peter, Rome has become the capital of the world in a wider sense than before. For this reason, when the earth was divided among the apostles, Rome was reserved to Peter, that here, at the very center, the decisive triumph might be won over the earthly wisdom of philosophy and the power of the demons; and thus from the head the light of truth streams out through the whole body. In Leo's eyes the decrees of the council of Chalcedon acquired their validity from his confirmation. The wide range of this theory justifies the application to him of the title of the first pope."[2] Leo also began to acquire power over the Roman Emperor. Thus the bloody woman begins to take reigns and ride the beast that had seven heads and ten horns! It is easy to see, then, why some date Catholicism as beginning with Leo.

Because Boniface III acquired the title of "Universal Bishop," some date Catholicism from him. And so it could be said of others who helped to mold the Harlot into what she is today. Leo and Boniface and Gregory certainly did their part.

Flavius Valerius Constantinus
A. D. 306-337

It is my opinion that the dubious honor of being the founder of Catholicism should go to Constantine the Great. He, more than anyone else, put into the pot the ingredients to brew the Roman Catholic hierarchy. He laid the ground-work necessary to make possible the usurpations of Leo, Gregory, Boniface and all the popes after them.

As best as this writer can tell, he is the first, under the name of religion, to persecute our Baptist ancestors. He persecuted the Donatists as we shall presently see. Not much has been written about him that I know of from Baptist circles. A full book about him from our point of view would fill a great need. Whether he did all that he did willfully, ignorantly or both, God knows and we form our opinions. Whichever, he certainly was a tool in the hands of Satan, used effectually to build the devil a church with which to persecute the true churches of our Lord Jesus Christ.

His Early Life

His father was a military man whose career moved him into the political arena. His mother, Helena, was a concubine of his father's. His father separated from Helena and married Flavia Maximiana Theodora, stepdaughter of Maximianus; the Augustus of the West. "That his second wife may perhaps have influenced him religiously is fairly supposable, since she, at all events, as appears from a coin which has remained heretofore unnoticed, was a Christian."[3]

His father was favorable to Christians and protected them whenever he could. Constantine may have gotten his spirit of toleration of Christians from his father. He loved his mother, Helena. He later raised statues of her all over the empire, struck coins with her image and named cities after her. That Helena was a very religiously superstitious person we will see. She, too, had an effect on Constantine.

Constantine's Supposed Conversion

Around Constantine's conversion there are great clouds of doubt. The only account we have of it comes from Eusebius' *Life of Constantine*. Following is a lengthy quote from Neander:

"In the next following years, after Constantine, as his father's successor, he had been proclaimed Augustus, in 306, by the legions in Britain, he appears to have been still attached to the pagan forms of worship, When, in the year 308, after the successful termination of the war with that Maximianus Herculius who had a second time set himself up as emperor, he received the unexpected intelligence that the Franks, against whom he was just commencing a campaign, had ceased from their hostile demonstrations, he gave public thanks in a celebrated temple of Apollo, probably at Autun, (Augustodunum,) and presented a magnificent offered to the god. ' From this circumstance we may gather, not only that Constantine still professed an attachment to the old heathen ceremonies, but also that he did not belong to the class of warriors and princes who make no account of the religious interest, and who, strangers to all emotions and impulses of that nature, have an eye only to the human means of prosecuting their undertakings. He believed himself to be indebted for his good fortune to the protection of a god.

It was not until after his victory over the tyrant Maxentius, that Constantine publicly declared in favor of the Christians. The question here presents itself, whether, as we must suppose according to one of the traditions, it was this victory itself, in connection with the extraordinary circumstances preceding it, which gave this new and decided direction, not to the public conduct only, but also to the religious opinions of the emperor.

According to Eusebius, the way in which this important change was brought about, was as follows: - Maxentius, in making his preparations for the war, had scrupulously observed all the customary ceremonies of Paganism, and was relying for success on the agency of supernatural powers. Hence Constantine was the more strongly persuaded that he ought not to place his whole confidence in an arm of flesh. He resolved in his mind, to what god it would be suitable for him to apply for aid. The misfortunes of the last emperors, who had been so zealously devoted to the cause of Paganism, and the example of his father, who had trusted in the one true and almighty God alone, admonished him that he also should place confidence in no other. To this God, therefore, he applied, praying that he would reveal himself to him, and lend him the protection of his arm in the approaching contest. While thus praying, a short time after noon, he beheld, spread on the face of the heavens, a glittering cross, and above it the inscription: "By this conquer." The emperor and his whole army, now just about to commence their march toward Italy, were seized with awe. While Constantine was still pondering the import of this sign, night came on; and in a dream Christ appeared to him, with the same symbol which he had seen in the heavens, and directed him to cause a banner to be prepared after the same pattern, and to use it as his protection against the power of the enemy. The emperor obeyed: he caused to be made, after the pattern he had seen, the resplendent banner of the cross, (called the Labarum,) on the shaft of which was affixed, with the symbol of the cross, [a] monogram of the name of Christ. He then sent for teachers of whom he inquired concerning the God that had appeared unto him, and the import of the symbol. This gave them an opportunity of instructing him in the knowledge of Christianity."[4]

If this account is true, then a real miracle took place. I, for one, do not believe that a miracle took place. One should be careful how one interprets things seen in the sky. Brother Clarence Walker used to tell us of a man who believed God had called him to preach. He told Bro. Walker he saw clouds in the sky form the letters G.P.C. He interpreted that to mean he was to Go Preach Christ. After talking with him Bro. Walker, believing God had not called the man, said, "Young man those letters meant Go Plow Corn!" No doubt Bro. Walker was right.

Religion United to the State

Constantine's embracing so-called Christianity united the power of Rome to the false churches. Those churches which had embraced the errors of the Episcopal Church Government, Baptismal Regeneration and Infant Baptism were the ones who flocked to Constantine. Thus formed the most unholy alliance ever made. It was the death knell to millions of Baptists from that day forward.

Let us see what Dowling says upon this subject: - "It was owing to forgetfulness or disregard of the important principle, mentioned at the close of the last chapter, vix., that Christ's kingdom is not of this world, that the emperor Constantine, soon after his remarkable, and as some suppose, miraculous conversion to Christianity in the year 312, took the religion of Christ to.the unhallowed embraces of the state, assumed to unite in his own person the civil and ecclesiastical dominion, and claimed the power of convening councils and presiding in them, and of regulating the external affairs of the church. The account of Constantine's conversion, which is related by Eusebius in his life of the Emperor, by whom the particulars were communicated to the historian, is as follows: (Eusebius, vita Const., lib. i., chapter 28., and c.) At the head of his army, Constantine was marching from France into Italy, oppressed with anxiety as to the result of a battle with Maxentius, and looking for the aid of some deity to assure him of success, when he suddenly beheld a luminous cross in the air, with the words inscribed thereon, "BY THIS OVERCOME." Pondering on the event at night, he asserted that Jesus Christ appeared to him in a vision, and directed him to make the symbol of the cross his military ensign. Different opinions have been entertained relative to the credibility of this account. Dr. Milner receives it, though in evident inconsistency with his creed; Mosheim supposes, with the ancient writers, Sozomen and Rufinus, that the whole was a dream; Gregory, Jones, Haweis, and others reject it altogether, and Professor Gieseler, with his usual accuracy and good sense, reckons it among "the legends of the age, which had their origin in the feeling that the final struggle was come between Paganism and Christianity." For my part, I have no hesitation in regarding the whole as a fable. It was not until many years after it was said to have occurred, that Constantine related the story to Eusebius, and in all probability he did it then by the instigation of his superstitious mother, Helena, the celebrated discoverer of the wood of the true cross (?) at Jerusalem, some 250 years after the total destruction of that city, and all that it contained, and the disappearance of the identity of its very foundations, under the ploughshare of the Roman conqueror Vespasian. The subsequent life of Constantine furnished no evidence that he was a peculiar favorite of Heaven; and the results of is patronage of the church, eventually so disastrous to its purity and spirituality, are sufficient to prove that God would never work a miracle to accomplish such a purpose."[5]

The Edict of Milan 313 A. D.

It is no small wonder that many felt Constantine to be their Champion. All had suffered much at the hands of the emperors under severe persecution. Constantine and Licinius issued the famous Edict of Milan which was an edict of toleration. From Eusebius, I give the Edict in its entirety:

"As we long since perceived that religious liberty should not be denied, but that it should be granted to the opinion and wishes of each one to perform divine duties according to his own determination, we had given orders, that each one, and the Christians among the rest, have the liberty to observe the religion of his choice, and his peculiar mode of worship. But as there plainly appeared to be many and different sects added in that edict, in which this privilege was granted them, some of them perhaps, after a little while, on this account shrunk from this kind of attention and observance. Wherefore, as I, Constantine Augustus, and I, Licinius Augustus, came under favourable auspices to Milan, and took under consideration all affairs that pertained to the public benefit and welfare, these things among the rest appeared to us to be most advantageous and profitable to all. We have resolved among the first things to ordain, those matters by which reverence and worship to the Deity might be exhibited. That is how we may grant likewise to the Christians, and to all, the free choice to follow that mode of worship which they may wish. That whatsoever divinity and celestial power may exist, may be propitious to us and to all that live under our government. Therefore, we have decreed the following ordinance, as our will, with a salutary and most correct intention, that no freedom at all shall be refused to Christians, to follow or to keep their observances or worship. But that to each one power be granted to devote his mind to that worship which he may think adapted to himself. That the Deity may in all things exhibit to us his accustomed favour and kindness. It was just and consistent that we should write that this was our pleasure. That all exceptions respecting the Christians being completely removed, which were contained in the former epistle, that we sent to your fidelity, and whatever measures were wholly sinister and foreign to our mildness, that these should be altogether annulled; and now that each one of the Christians may freely and without molestation, pursue and follow that course and worship which he has proposed to himself: which, indeed, we have resolved to communicate most fully to your care and diligence, that you may know we have granted liberty and full freedom to the Christians, to observe their own mode of worship; which as your fidelity understands absolutely granted to them by us, the privilege is also granted to others to pursue that worship and religion they wish. Which it is obvious is consistent with the peace and tranquility of our times; that each may have the privilege to select and to worship whatsoever divinity he pleases. But this has been done by us, that we might not appear in any manner to detract any thing from any manner of religion, or any mode of worship. And this, we further decree, with respect to the Christians, that the places in which they were formerly accustomed to assemble, concerning which also we formerly wrote to your fidelity, in a different form, that if any persons have purchased these, either from our treasury, or from any other one, these shall restore them to the Christians, without money and without demanding any price, without any superadded value, or augmentation, without delay, or hesitancy. And if any have happened to receive these places as presents, that they shall restore them as soon as possible to the Christians, so that if either those that purchased or those that received them as presents, have any thing to request of our munificence, they may go to the provincial governor as the judge; that provision may also be made for them by our clemency. All which, it will be necessary to be delivered up to the body of Christians, by your care, without any delay. And since the Christians themselves are known to have had not only those places where they were accustomed to meet, but other places also belonging not to individuals among them, but to the right of the whole body of Christians, you will also command all these, by virtue of the law before mentioned, without any hesitancy, to be restored to these same Christians, that is to their body, and to each conventicler respectively. The aforesaid consideration, to wit, being observed; namely, that they who as we have said restore them without valuation and price, may expect their indemnity from our munificence and liberality. In all which it will be incumbent on you, to exhibit your exertions as much as possible, to the aforesaid body of Christians, that our orders may be most speedily accomplished, that likewise in this, provision may be made by our clemency, for the preservation of the common and public tranquility. For by these means, as before said, the divine favour with regard to us, which we have already experienced in many affairs, will continue firm and permanent at all times. But that the purpose of this our ordinance and liberality may be extended to the knowledge of all, it is expected that these things written by us, should be proposed and published to the knowledge of all. That this act of our liberality and kindness may remain unknown to none."[6]

Changes in the False Churches

The false churches flocked to him and he became their head. Through his efforts these false churches were reconstructed into one whole over which he presided. "Soon after Constantine professed conversion to Christianity, he undertook to remodel the government of the church, so as to make it conform as much as possible to the government of the state. Hence the origin of the dignities of patriarchs, etc., intended by the Emperor to correspond with the different secular offices and dignities, connected with the civil administration of the empire. Taking these newly constituted dignitaries of the church into his own special favor, he loaded them with the wealth and worldly honors, and richly endowed the churches over which they presided, thus fostering in those who professed to be the followers and ministers of Him who was 'meek and lowly of heart' a spirit of worldly ambition, pride, and arvice. And thus was the let on hinderance to the progress of corruption, and the revelation of'the man of sin' spoken of by Saint Paul in the remarkable prediction already referred to, in a great measure removed."[7]

It is easy to see from the words of Dowling, how the struggle among the bishops for power came about. In a quest for wealth, power and fame one bishop must become the "universal bishop." One must become "pope."

That the readers of this notebook not think that Dowling was not "telling it like it is" let us see a few letters of Constantine himself:

Copy of an Epistle in which the Emperor grants money to the churches:

"Constantine Augustus to Caecilianus bishop of Carthage. As we have determined, that in all the provinces of Africa, Numidia and Mauritania, something should be granted to certain ministers of the legitimate and most holy catholic (universal) religion, to defray their expenses, I have given letters to Ursus, the most illustrious lieutenant-governor of Africa, and have communicated to him, that he shall provide, to pay for your authority, three thousand follies ($10,000.00)

After you shall have obtained this sum, you are to order these monies to be distributed among the aforesaid ministers, according to the abstract addressed to thee from Hosius. But if thou shall learn, perhaps, that any thing shall be wanting to complete this my purpose with regard to all, thou art authorized, without delay, to make demands for whatever thou mayest ascertain to be necessary, from Heraclides, the procurator of our possessions. And I have also commanded him when present, that if thy authority should demand any monies from him, he should see that it should be paid without delay. And as 1 ascertained that some men, who are of no settled mind, wish to divert the people from the most holy catholic (universal) church, by a certain pernicious adulteration, 1 wish thee to understand that I have given, both to the proconsul Anulinus and to Patricius, vicar-general of the praefects, when present, the following injunctions; that among all the rest, they should particularly pay the necessary attention to this, nor should by any means tolerate that this should be overlooked. Wherefore, if thou seest any of these men persevering in this madness, thou shalt, without any hesitation, proceed to the aforesaid judges, and report it to them, that they may animadvert upon them, as I commanded them, when present. May the power of the great God preserve thee many years."

The Privileges and Immunities of the Clergy

Copy of an Epistle in which the Emperor commands that the prelates of the churches should be exempt from performing service in political matters:

"Health to thee, most esteemed Anulinus. As it appears from many circumstances, that when the religion was despised, in which the highest reverence of the heavenly majesty is observed, that our public affairs were beset with great dangers, and that this religion, when legally adopted and observed, afforded the greatest prosperity to the Roman name, and distinguished felicity to all men, as it has been granted by the divine beneficence, we have resolved that those men who gave their services with becoming sanctity, and the observance of this law, to the performance of divine worship, should receive the recompence for their labours, oh most esteemed Anulinus; wherefore it is my will that these men, within the province, entrusted to thee in the Catholic church, over which Caecilianus presides, who give their services to this holy religion, and whom they commonly call clergy, shall be held totally free, and exempt from all public offices, to the end that they may not by any error or sacrilegious deviation, be drawn away from the service due to the Divinity, but rather may devote themselves to their proper law, without molestation. So that, whilst they exhibit the greatest possible reverence to the Deity, it appears the greatest good will be conferred on the state. Farewell, most esteemed and beloved Anulinus."[8]

Unity Among All Churches

Constantine was possessed with great energy and determination. All of those energized by Satan have been. He was determined that everyone agree with him. He set about to bring unity among all the bishops and churches. Can you not see how this begins and leads to the Universal Church of Rome?

He commanded councils to be called for this very purpose. Let us read two of his letters for this purpose from Eusebius:

Copy of the Emperor's Epistle, in which he ordains a council of bishops to be held at Rome, for the unity and peace of the church:

"Constantine Augustus, to Miltiades bishop of Rome, and to Marcus. As many communications of this kind have been sent to me from Anulinus, the most illustrious proconsul of Africa, in which it is contained that Caecilianus, respects, by his colleagues in Africa; and as this appears to be grievous, that in those provinces which divine Providence has freely entrusted to my fidelity, and in which there is a vast population, the multitude are found inclining to deteriorate, and in a manner divided into two parties, and among others, that the bishops were at variance; 1 have resolved that same Caecilianus, together with ten bishops, who appear to accuse him, and ten others, whom he himself may consider necessary for his cause, shall sail to Rome. That you, being present there, as also Reticius Maternus, and Marinus, your colleagues, whom I have commanded to hasten to Rome for this purpose, may be heard, as you may understand most consistent with the most sacred law. And, indeed, that you may have the most perfect knowledge of these matters, I have subjoined to my own by Anulinus, and sent them to your aforesaid colleagues. In which your gravity will read and consider in what way the aforesaid cause may be most accurately investigated and justly decided. Since it neither escapes your diligence, that I show such regard for the holy catholic church, that I wish you, upon the whole, to leave no room for schism or division. May the power of the great God preserve you many years, most esteemed."

Copy of the Epistle in which the Emperor commanded another council to be held, for the purpose of removing all the dissension of the bishops:

"Constantine Augustus to Chrestus bishop of Syracuse. As there were some already before who perversely and wickedly began to waver in the holy religion and celestial virtue, and to abandon the doctrine of the catholic (universal) church, desirous, therefore, of preventing such disputes among them, I had thus written, that this subject, which appeared to be agitated among them, might be rectified, be delegating certain bishops from Gaul, and summoning others of the opposite parties from Africa, who are pertinaciously and incessantly contending with one another, that by a careful examination of the matter in their presence, it might thus be decided. But since, as it happens, some, forgetful of their own salvation, and the reverence due to our most holy religion, even now do not cease to protract to the decision already promulgated, and asserting that they were very few that advanced their sentiments and opinions, or else that all points which ought to have been first fully discussed not being first examined, they proceeded with too much haste and precipitancy to give publicity to the decision. Hence it has happened, that those very persons who ought to exhibit a brotherly and peaceful unanimity, rather disgracefully and detestably are at variance with one another, and thus give this occasion of derision to those that are without, and whose minds are averse to our most holy religion. Hence it has appeared necessary to me to provide that this matter which ought to have ceased after the decision was issued by their own voluntary agreement, now, at length, should be fully terminated by the intervention of many.

"Since, therefore, we have commanded many bishops to meet together from different remote places, in the city or Aries, towards the calends of August, I have also thought proper to write to thee, that taking the public vehicle from the most illustrious Latronianus, corrector of Sicily, and taking with thee two others of the second rank, which thou mayest select, also three servants to afford you services on the way; I would have you meet them within the same day at the aforesaid place. That by the weight of your authority, and the prudence and unanimity of the rest that assemble, this dispute, which has disgracefully continued until the present time, in consequence of certain disgraceful contentions, may be discussed, by hearing all that shall be alleged by those who are now at variance, whom we have also commanded to be present, and thus the controversy be reduced, though slowly, to that faith, and observance or religion, and fraternal concord, which ought to prevail. May Almighty God preserve thee in safety many years."[9]

Since the true churches. Baptist churches, would and did oppose such unity, they ran into trouble with Constantine. As a result, he persecuted them severely as we shall see when we study the Donatists.

Constantine's Life

Constantine's life, after his supposed conversion, does not bear resemblance to that of a dedicated Christian. His ultimate salvation, of course, rests with God and not with us. However, we are to know people by their fruit. Neander remarks: "Constantine, instigated by the calumnious representations of his second wife, Fausta, had in a paroxysm of anger, caused his son, the Caesar Crispus, step-son of Fausta, to be put to death. Reproached for this act by his mother Helena, and convinced afterwards himself that he had been falsely informed, he had added another crime to this by a cruel revenge on Fausta, whom he caused to be thrown into the glowing furnace of a bath. Suspicious jealously had misled him to order the execution of his nephew, a hopeful prince, the son of the unfortunate Licinius; and several others, connected with the court, are said to have fallen victims to his anger or his suspicion."[10] Much more could be added but this will allow you to see his true character.

Constantine's Baptism

When Constantine inquired about Christianity from the irregular churches, he was, no doubt, told of Baptismal Regeneration. "When this hierarchy was created, Constantine, who was made its head, was not at that time a Christian. He had agreed to become one. But as the erring or irregular churches which had gone with him into this organization had come to adopt the error of Baptismal Regeneration, a serious question arose in the mind of Constantine, 'If I am saved from my sins by baptism, what is to become of my sins which I may commit after I am baptized?' He raised a question which had puzzled the world in all succeeding generations. Can baptism wash away yet uncommitted sins? Or, are the sins committed prior to baptism washed away by one method (that is, baptism), and sins committed subsequent to baptism washed away by another method?"[11]

J. M. Cramp says the following: "And great numbers followed the example of Constantine, who deferred his baptism until the latest possible period, that all his sins might be washed away at once, as he, poor man, vainly imagined they would be, by the administration of the ordinance."[12]

Neander: "It is most probable that, carrying his heathen superstition into Christianity, he looked upon baptism as a sort of rite for the magical removal of sin, and so delayed it, in the confidence that, although he had not lived an exemplary life, he might yet in the end be enabled to enter into bliss, purified from all his sins. He was doubtless sincere, therefore, when, on receiving baptism, he said, as Eusebius reports, that from thenceforth, if God spared him his life, he would devote himself to God's worthy laws of life."[13]

Conclusion

There is so much that needs to be said about Constantine but this chapter has run too far. However, enough has been said to show why this writer prefers to date the Roman Catholic Church with Constantine.

Please remember: There were hundreds of true churches that had nothing to do with the organization of the hierarchy under Constantine. They opposed it, thus becoming guilty of treason against the Roman Empire. Many lost their lives as Satan now, under the name of religion, wields the sword of the state against our Baptist ancestors.

NOTES ON CHAPTER 6

1 Roman Catholicism, page 126.
2 The New Schaff-Hergoz Religion Encyclopedia, Vol. 6, pages 449-450.
3The New Schaff-Hergoz Religion Encyclopedia, Vol. 3, page 250.
4 History of the Christian Religion and Church, Vol. 2. pages 6-8.
5 History of Romanism, pages 30-31.
6 Ecclesiastical History, pages 426-428.
7 History of Romanism, page 31.
8 Ecclesiastical History of Eusebius, pages 431-433.
9 Ecclesiastical History of Eusebius, pages 429-431.
10 History of the Christian Religion and Church, Vol. 2, page 29.
11 The Trail of Blood, pages 16-17.
12 Baptist History, page 44.
13 History of the Christian Religion and Church, Vol. 2, page 29.

Chapter 7

THE DONATISTS

We come now in our Notebook to the study of another group of our Baptist ancestors. Within the group called "Donatists" we find the true churches of our Lord Jesus Christ. Among them we find the doctrines that Christ gave to His church. We also find them suffering much for their beliefs at the hands of the Catholics who now had the sword of State behind them. They take their name from one Donatus, bishop of Casae Nigiae in Numidia, an able leader among them. While they were located primarily in North Africa, they were scattered everywhere.

James Wharey, a Presbyterian gives the following sketch of them as to their origin, persecution and peculiarities:

"In the year 311 arose the sect of the Donatists, so called from Donatus their leader. This schism had its rise as follows. Mensurius, the deacon, was elected to the vacant chair, by the people and clergy of Africa proper, and consecrated without the concurrence of the Numidian bishops, who ought, according to custom, to have been present. This gave great offence to the Numidians, who held a meeting, deposed Caecilian and in his room, consecrated Majorinus, bishop of Carthage. Hence the Carthaginian church was divided into two factions, headed by two bishops. This schism spread all over Africa, most cities having two bishops, one taking sides with Caecilian, the other with Majorinus. The Donatists were condemned by several special councils, held by order of the emperor, and finally by the emperor himself; who, provoked by their continued contumacy and reproaches, deprived them of their churches, sent their seditious bishops into banishment, and punished some of them with death. This produced very violent tumults and commotions in Africa. Amongst these commotions arose the Circumcelliones, so called because they were accustomed to hover round the cellae, or cottages of the peasants, without any fixed habitations. They were "a furious, headlong, sanguinary set, composed of the peasantry and rustic populace, who espoused the cause of the Donatists, defended it by the force of arms, and roaming through the providence of Africa, filled it with slaughter, rapine and burnings, and committed the most atrocious crimes against the adverse party."

It does not appear, however, that the Donatist bishops, especially the better sort of them, excited or approved of the violent and irregular proceedings, which brought great reproach upon their cause. The sect was greatly weakened toward the end of the century, as well as by a schism that arose among themselves, as by the activity and zeal of Augustine against them. The Donatists were in the main orthodox, but held no communion with any not of their party. They re-ordained and re-baptized such as came over to them."[1]

J. M. Cramp

The Baptist historian, J. M. Cramp says: "The Donatists first appeared in the early part of the fourth century. A dispute against an election to a bishopric was the occasion of their separation from the catholic church. Caecilian was chosen bishop of Carthage in a somewhat irregular manner and hastily ordained. Among those who officiated at his ordination was Felix, bishop of Aptunga. This man was said to be a traditor, that is, one who had delivered up copies of the Scriptures to the civil authorities during the Diocletian persecution. His concurrence in the ordination was thought by some to vitiate the service. They refused to regard Caecilian as a regularly appointed bishop. A secession took place, which spread rapidly and extensively, so that, in a short time the Donatist churches in Africa were nearly equal in number to those of the hitherto dominant party."[2]

It is wrong to suppose that any one incident gave birth to either the Montanists, Novatianists or the Donatists. Numerous disagreements already existed. It is right to suppose that one incident was the straw that broke the camel's back, so to speak. These people, as a group, did not originate with Donatus. They simply were called after his name because he was a leader of great ability and gave voice to what they believed. Neander says: "They (the Donatists) declared that they called themselves after the name of Donatus, not as the founder of a new church, but as one of the bishops of the ancient church derived from Christ."

Identified with The Novatians

Almost all of the church historians tell us the Donatists were of the same opinion and practice as the Novatians at whom we have already looked. Neander says, "This schism may be compared in many respects with that of Novatian in the proceeding period. In this, too, we see the conflict, for example, of Separatism with Catholicism..."[3]

William Jones, using Dr. Lardner as a source, says, "The Donatists appear to have resembled the followers of Novatian more than any other class of professors in that period of the church, of whom we have any authentic records..."[4]

D. B. Ray writes, "The Donatists of Africa possessed the same peculiarities with the Novatians, and, on this account, may be called the Novatians of Africa."[5]

A. H. Newman gives the following: "The Donatists follow in the same general line with the Montanists and the Novatianists."[6]

G. H. Orchard: "The Donatists and the Novatianists very nearly resembled each other in doctrines and discipline..."[7]

In our chapter on the Novatianists we showed their relationship to the Montanists. These three groups, Montanists, Novatianists and Donatists believed and practiced the same things. They were Baptists. We come now to take up their doctrinal beliefs.

The Church

What the Donatists believed about the church identifies them as the Lord's churches and separates them from the Catholic church. We have ample proof from the historians that these Donatists believed in a pure church - a regenerated church membership. They believed strongly in a strong church discipline and a strict baptism. These things prove they believed that the church was a local group of baptized believers and not something universal and invisible.

Let us quote Hagenbach: "Two causes contributed to determine the doctrine about the church: 1. The external history of the church itself, its victory over paganism, and its rising power under the protection of the state. 2. The victory of Augustianism over the doctrines of the Pelagians, Manicheans, and Donatists, which in different ways threatened to destroy ecclesiastical unity. The last mentioned puritanic period, maintained that the church was composed only of saints."[8]

It is easy to see that Hagenbach was no friend to Baptist truth. To assume Augustine defeated the Donatists would be to assume there are no Baptists today. He does show how Augustine helped to develop Catholicism. He is quoted merely to show that the Donatists, like the Novatians, believed in a regenerated church membership.

Thomas Armitage said, "In this region the inner dependence of the churches had been more firmly maintained than in many other places, and the late encroachments upon it had aroused the churches to a determined defense. Merivale says of the Donatists: 'they represented the broad principle of the Montanists and Novatianists, that the true church of Christ is the assembly of really pious persons only, and admits of no merely nominal membership.' They dreaded any form of un-Christian membership which eats out the spiritual fellowship of a Gospel Church."[9]

J. M. Cramp writes: "The Donatists pleaded for purity. They maintained that Christian churches should consist of godly persons and no others, and that in all the arrangements made for their management that important principle should be kept in view. They followed the example of the Novatians in rebaptizing those who joined them from other churches. They baptized new converts on a profession of faith, as a matter of course, for that was the practice of all churches."[10]

Separation of Church and State

Their correct view of the church led them to the true belief of separation of church and state. Kurtz writes: "Like the Novatians, they insisted on absolute purity in the church, although they allowed that penitents might be readmitted to " the communion of the church. Their own churches they regarded as pure while they denounced the Catholics as schismatics, who had no fellowship with Christ, and whose sacraments were therefore invalid and null. On this ground, they rebaptized their proselytes. The part which the state took against them , and prevailing confusion between the visible and invisible church, led them to broach the view that State and Church -the Kingdom of God and that of the world -had nothing in common, and that the state should not in any way take notice of religious questions." [11]

According to Neander "the bishop Donatus of Carthage repelled the advances of the imperial officer with the remark: 'What had the emperor to do with the church?' ...In their sermons, the Donatists' bishops spoke of the corruption of the church, which had originated in the confusion of the church and state."[12]

Landmark Baptists of today believe exactly alike with these Donatists of old on this subject. Surely, we see clearly our ancestors of truth here.

Baptism

We have already noticed much of the Donatist belief concerning baptism. David Benedict wrote *The History of the Baptists* with which most are familiar. He also wrote *A History of the Donatists* with which most are not familiar. It is a very good book and a very rare one. In that book he searched out the beliefs of the Donatists from the writings of their opponents, especially Augustine -the arch-enemy of the Donatists. The Donatists wrote much against the Catholics which Augustine attempted to answer. He has gathered many quotations from Petillian, a Donatist, against the Catholics. These were gathered from among the writings of Augustine. Let us read a few that will tell us what they believed about baptism.

"They who throw against us a two-fold baptism under the name of baptism, have polluted their own souls with a criminal bath."

"He who accused me of baptizing twice, does not himself truly baptize once."

"We by our baptism put on Christ; you by your contagion put on Judas the traitor."

"The character of a baptizer must be well known."

"The apostle Paul says there is one Lord, one faith, and one baptism; this one baptism we openly profess, and it is certain that they who think there are two, are insane."[14]

A further quote of Petillian by Benedict: "Come to the true church, O ye people, and flee away from all traitors, if you are not willing to perish with them. I baptize their members, as having an imperfect baptism, and as in reality unbaptized. They will receive my members, but far be it from being done, as truly baptized, which they would not do at all, if they could discover any faults in our baptism. See, therefore, that the baptism which I give you may be held so holy that not any sacrilegious enemy will have dared to destroy it."

How about that? This Donatist preached our sermon before we ever had it. Thank God for Benedict's *History of the Donatists*! How sad that we hear Augustine praised in so many Baptist churches today. He was the enemy of truth and the cause of thousands of Donatists (and Baptists later on) being martyred. Benedict lists several writers from among the Donatists who opposed him. Get his book if possible. Mine is not for sale.

Thus, we have seen that the Donatists were Baptists under a different name. We have observed this true by their connection with the Novatianists and Montanists. We have observed it true by their doctrinal beliefs.

Donatist Persecution

If the Donatists were true churches of our Lord, holding fast the truths He gave to His churches, they would certainly fall under the persecution of Satan. Do we find them suffering persecution?

Let us hear Orchard first: "The disputes between the Donatists and the Catholics were at their height, when Constantine became fully invested with imperial power, A.D. 314. The Catholic party solicited the services of the emperor, who, in answer, appointed commissions to hear both sides, but this measure not giving satisfaction, he even condescended to hear the parties himself; but his best exertions could not effect a reconciliation. The interested party that Constantine took in the dispute led the Donatists to inquire, 'What has the emperor to do with the church? What have Christians to do with kings? Or what have bishops to do at court?' Constantine, finding his authority questioned and even set at naught by these Baptists, listened to the advice of his bishops and court, and deprived the Donatists of their churches. This persecution was the first which realized the support of a Christian emperor, and Constantine sent so far as to put some of the Donatists to death."[16]

Kurtz writes: "In 414 the Emperor deprived them of their

civil rights, and in 415 forbade their religious meetings under pain of death."[17] First one emperor gave them toleration and the next persecuted them.

We must return to Benedict for the fullest account of these persecutions.

"In the year 340, the emperor directed his two commissioners, Ursacius and Leontius, to endeavor by the distribution of money under the name of alms to win over the Donatist churches; and as the said emperor at the same time issued an edict whereby he called upon the North African Christians to return back to the unity of the church which Christ loved, it was the less possible that the object of these measures should remain concealed from the Donatist bishops.

On the failure of this covert scheme for gaining the Donatists, forcible measures were the next resort. The Donatists now were to be deprived of their churches, and they were actually fallen upon by armed troops while assembled in them for the worship of God. Hence followed the effusion of blood, and the martyrdoms of which the Donatists so often complained of their adversaries. Those who fell victim to these persecutions, says Neander, were honored by their party as martyrs, and the annual celebration of the days of their death furnished new means of enkindling the enthusiasm of the Donatist party. In the time under consideration Gratius had succeeded Caecilian as bishop of Carthage. Both he and the emperor Constantius, says Robinson, persecuted the Donatists with great severity."[18]

Listen to how Optatus, a Catholic who wrote against the Donatists, justified the Macarian War of 347 A.D. against the Donatists, in which many Donatists were slaughtered: "Optatus argued that the killing of the Donatists by Macarius (so-called Christian emperor) in his war against them for heresy, was sanctioned by Moses killing three thousand for worshiping the golden calf, and Phinehas and Elijah for those they killed. Macarius, said Optatus, did not persecute like the heathen emperors, whose policy was to drive the Christians out of their churches, while that of Macarius was to drive the Donatists into the Catholic churches, where they might worship God together in the spirit of peace and unity." [19]

The Catholics have always, when they had the power, killed the Baptists, claiming while doing it that they were doing God a service. "In the record of a council in Carthage in 404 we find the following statement: 'it is now full time for the emperor to provide for the safety of the Catholic church, and prevent these rash men from terrifying the weak people, whom they cannot seduce. We think it is as lawful for us to ask assistance against them, as it was for Paul to employ a military force against the conspiration of factious men.' This is a new version of the conduct of the apostle Paul in the case here referred to." [20]

Benedict and others tell us we are indebted to Augustine for the history of these councils for this time. At that time, even though young in the episcopal office, he was evidently their principal manager. The law of infant baptism in 416 A.D., enacted at a council at Mela, had Augustine behind it. It specifically accursed all those who denied forgiveness to accompany infant baptism. In 413 A.D. the emperors Theodosius and Honorius, issued an edict "declaring that all persons rebaptized and the rebaptizers should be both punished with death. Accordingly, Albanus, a zealous minister, with others, was punished with death, for rebaptizing. The edict was probably obtained by the influence of Augustine, who could endure no rival..." [21] It seems to me that the main one who led in the persecution and death of many Donatists was Augustine. How I hate to hear Baptists brag on this man!

The Donatists on Persecution

The Donatists wrote much about their own persecution when they attacked Augustine. Benedict gives quotations from the Donatist Gaudentius: "All who live godly in Christ Jesus shall suffer persecution. The time will come when whosoever killeth you will think he doeth God service. Our enemies boast of being in peace and unity, but their peace is gained by war, and their union is stained with blood. For the teaching of the people of Israel the omnipotent God sent prophets; he did not enjoin this service on kings; the Lord Christ, the Saviour of souls, sent fishermen, not soldiers for the propagation of His gospel; He Who alone can judge the quick and the dead has never sought the aid of a military force." [22]

Conclusion

We could and would like to add more on the Donatists, our faithful unto death Baptist ancestors. But we most move on to the Baptists of other ages and places. How I pray that this brief bit of history might move you, the student, into a more detailed study of the people called Donatists.

NOTES ON CHAPTER 7

1 *Sketches of Church History, pages 68-69.*
2 *Baptists History, pages 59-60.*
3 *History of the Christian Religion and Church, Volume 1, page 208.*
4 *History of the Christian Church, page 222.*
5 *Baptist Succession, page 328.*
6 *A Manual of Church History, Volume 1, page 208.*
7 *A Concise History of Baptists, page 87.*
8 *Text Book on the History of Doctrines, Volume I, page 352.*
9 *The History of the Baptists, Volume 1, page 200.*
10 *Baptist History, page 60.*
11 *Church History, page 246.*
12 *History of the Christian Religion and Church, Volume, 2, page 195.*
13 *History of the Christian Religion and Church, Volume 2, page 191.*
14 *History of the Donatists, page 49.*
15 *History of the Donatists, page 56.*
16 *A Concise History of Baptists, pages 87-88.*
17 *Church History, page 246.*
18 *History of the Donatists, page 32.*
19 *History of the Donatists, page 36.*
20 *History of the Donatists, page 38.*
21 *Orchard, A Concise History of the Baptists, pages 60-61.*
22 *History of the Donatists, page 60.*

Chapter 8

PATERINS, PURITANS, CATHARI

Throughout our Baptist history, from the time of Christ until now, we have been called by many names. The majority of these names have been given to us by our enemies. Many of these names show up on The Trail of Blood chart by J. M. Carroll. Often, there is no explanation concerning the names in his booklet. In this chapter we will look at some of these names and seek to give you a little information concerning them.

Paterins (Patarenes)

This is a name by which our Baptist forefathers in Italy were called. Let us look at a lengthy quote from William Jones:

"Much has been written on the etymology of the word PATERINE; but as the Italians themselves are not agreed on the derivation, it is not likely foreigners should be able to determine it. In Milan, where it was first used, it answered to the English words, vulgar, illiterate, low-bred; and these people were so called, because they were chiefly of the lower order of men; mechanics, artificers, manufactures and others, who lived of their honest labour. GAZARI is a corruption of Cathari, puritans; and it is remarkable, that in the examination of these people, they are not taxed with any immoralities, but were condemned for the speculations, or rather virtuous rules of action, which all in power accounted heresies. They said a Christian church ought to consist of only good people; a church had no power to frame any constitutions; it was not right to take oaths; it was not lawful to kill mankind; a man ought not to be delivered up to officers of justice to be converted; the benefits of society belonged alike to all the members of it; faith without works could not save a man; the church ought not to persecute any, even the wicked: -the law of Moses was no rule to Christians; there was no need of priests, especially the wicked ones; the sacraments, an orders, and ceremonies of the church of Rome were futile, expensive, oppressive, and wicked; with many more such positions, all inimical to the hierarchy.

As the Catholics of those times baptized by immersion, the Paterines, by what name soever they were called, as Manichaeans, Gazari, Josephists, Passigines, & c. made no complaint of the mode of Baptizing, but when they were examined, they objected vehemently against the baptism of infants, and condemned it as an error. Among other things, they said, that a child knew nothing of the matter, that he had no desire to be baptized, and was incapable of making any confession of faith, and that the willing and professing of another could be of no service to him. "Here then," says Dr. Allix, very truly, "we have found a body of men in Italy, before the year one thousand twenty-six, five hundred years before the reformation, who believed contrary to the opinions of the church of Rome, and who highly condemned their errors." Atto, bishop of Verceulli, had complained of such people eighty years before and so had others before him, and there is the highest reason to believe that they had always existed in Italy. It is observable that those who alluded to by Dr. Allix were brought to light by mere accident. No notice was taken of them in Italy, but some disciples of Gundulf, one of their teachers, went to settle in the low countries, (Netherlands) and Gerard, bishop of Cambray, imprisoned them, under pretence of converting them.

From the tenth to the thirteenth century, the dissenters in Italy continued to multiply and increase; for which several reasons may be assigned. The excessive wickedness of the court of Rome and the Italian prelates was better known in Italy than in other countries. There was no legal power in Italy in these times to put dissenters to death. Popular preachers in the church, such as Claude of Turin, and Arnold of Brescia, increased the number of dissenters, for their disciples went further than their masters. The adjacency of France and Spain, too, contributed to their increase, for both abounded with Christians of this sort. Their churches were divided into sixteen compartments, such as the English Baptists would call associations. Each of these was subdivided into parts, which would be here termed churches or congregations. In Milan, there was a street called Pataria, where it is supposed they met for divine worship. At Modena, they assembled at the water-mills. They had houses at Ferrara, Brescia, Viterbe, Verona, Vicenza and several in Rimini, Romandiola, and other places. Reinerius says, in 1259 the Paterine church of the Alba consisted of above five hundred members; that Concorezzo, of more than fifteen hundred; and that of Bagnolo, of about two hundred. The houses where they met seem to have been hired by the people, and tenanted by one of the brethren. There were several in each city, and each was distinguished by a mark known by themselves. They had bishops or elders, pastors and teachers, deacons and messengers; that is, men employed in traveling to administer to the relief and comfort of the poor and the persecuted. In times of persecution they met in small companies of eight, twenty, thirty, or as it might happen; but never in large assemblies, for fear of the consequences.

The Paterines were decent in their deportment, modest in their address and discourse, and their morals irreproachable. In their conversation there was no levity, no scurrility, no detraction, no false-hood, no swearing. Their dress was neither fine nor mean. They were chaste, and temperate, never frequenting taverns, or places of public amusement. They were not given to anger and other violent passions. They were not eager to accumulate wealth, but content with the necessities of life. They avoided commerce, because they thought it would expose them to the temptation of collusion, falsehood, and oaths, choosing rather to live by labour or useful trades. They were always employed in spare hours, either by giving or receiving instruction. Their bishops and officers were mechanics, weavers, shoemakers, and others, who maintained themselves by their industry.

About the year 1040, the Paterines had become very numerous at Milan, which was their principal residence, and here they flourished at least two hundred years. They had no connection with the (Catholic) church; for they rejected not only Jerome of Syria, Augustine of Africa, and Gregory of Rome, but Ambrose of Milan; considering them, and all other pretended fathers, as corrupters of Christianity. They particularly condemned pope Sylvester, as Antichrist. They called (the adoration of) the cross the mark of the beast. They had no share in the state, for they took no oaths and bore no arms. The state did not trouble them, but the clergy preached, prayed and published books against them with unabated zeal. About the year 1176, the archbishop of Milan, an old infirm man, while preaching against them with great vehemence, dropped down in a fit, and expired as soon as he had received extreme unction! About fourteen years afterwards, one Bonacursi, who pretended he had been one of these Paterines, made a public renunciation of his opinions, and embraced the Catholic faith, filling Milan with fables, as all renegadoes do. He reported that cities, suburbs, towns, and castles, were full of these false prophets -that this was the time to suppress them, and that the prophet Jeremiah had directed the Milanese what to do, when he said, "Cursed be he that keepeth back his sword from blood!!" Advice which we shall presently see was but too implicitly followed."[1]

Etymology

Dr. Jones said that much had been written on the etymology of the word "Paterine." I have found this word spelled "Patarenes" in some of the histories. Concerning the etymology let us see what some have said about it.

Let us begin with Orchard: "Socrates states that, when the church was taken under the fostering care of Constantino, and on his party, using severe measures against the dissenters, the dominant party called themselves the Catholic church; but the oppressed and suffering party was known by the name, the church of martyrs. In a previous section, we have given the outlines of these suffering people, under the denomination of Novatianists, and endeavored to trace their history till penal laws compelled them to retire into caves and dens to worship God. While oppressed by the Catholic party, they obtained the name of Paterines; which means sufferers, or what is synonymous with our modern acceptation of the word martyrs, and which indicated an afflicted and poor people, trusting in the name of the Lord; and which name was, in a great measure, restricted to the dissenters of Italy, where it was as common as the Albigenses in the south of France, or Waldenses in Piedmont."[2]

Augustus Neander gives it a slightly different slant: "The whole population of Milan was separated into two hotly contending parties. This controversy divided families; it was the one object which commanded universal participation. The popular party, devoted to Ariald and Landulph, was nick-named Pataria, which in the dialect of Milan signified a popular faction; and as a heretical tendency might easily grow out of, or attach itself to, this spirit of separation, so zealously opposed to the corruption of the clergy, it came about that, in the following centuries, the name Patarenes was applied in Italy as a general appellation to denote sects contending against the dominant church and clergy, -sects which, for the most part, met with great favor from the people."[3]

Again, Neander says, "The name Patarenes, which, signifying in the first place a union of the people against the corrupt clergy, passed over into an appellation of the Catharists, may serve as an illustration."[4]

Hassell lists them right along with the other Baptists of the other ages. "Among the persecuted people of God have been the Novatians, Donatists, Cathari, Paterines, Paulicians, Petrobrusians, Henricans, Arnoldists, Albigenses, Waldenses, Lollards, Mennonites and Baptists, nearly all of whom were occasionally designated Anabaptists or Re-Baptizers by their enemies, because they disregarded infant or unregenerate baptism, and baptized all adults, whether previously baptized or not, who, upon a credible profession of faith, applied to them for membership in their churches -thus insisting upon a spiritual or regenerate church membership, the First and Most Important Mark of the Apostolic Church."[5]

Paterines Were Baptists

This will be all the information we will give on the Paterines. It should be easy to see, from the historical quotations, that they held to Baptist doctrine and that their stand made many of them martyrs. They were suffering churches united in their opposition to a corrupt clergy of the Catholic church. That takes in both Orchard's and Neander's ideas of the etymology of Paterines.

Puritans

The name Puritan appears on J.M. Carroll's chart in the Trail of Blood. This has nothing to do whatsoever with the Puritans of England and New England. These were non-conformists of the church of England. They flourished in the 17th century. These were not Baptists even though the Reformed (?) Baptists (?) of our day praise them so highly.

As best as I can tell, "Puritan" comes from the word "Cathari." The last word means "the pure." There is very little use of the word "Puritan" in the histories referring to the early Baptists. However, the word "Cathari" is often used so most of our information will be concerning them.

The Novatians were the first to be called Puritan (Cathari). Jones writes: "In the end Novatian formed a church and was elected bishop. Great numbers followed his example, and all over the empire Puritan churches were constituted and flourished through the succeeding two hundred years... They call Novatian the author of the heresy of puritanism, and yet they know that Tertullian had quitted the church nearly fifty years before, for the same reason.

The doctrinal sentiments of the Novatians appear to have been very scriptural, and the discipline of their churches rigid in the extreme. They were the first class of Christians who obtained the name of (Cathari) Puritans, an appellation which doth not appear to have been chosen by themselves, but applied to them by their adversaries; from which we may reasonably conclude that their manners were simple and irreproachable."[6]

Of the Novatianists Orchard writes: "The churches thus formed upon a plan of strict communion and rigid discipline, obtained the reproach of Puritans; they were the oldest body of Christian churches, of which we have any account, and a succession of them, as we shall prove, has continued to the present day."[7]

Cathari

This is the Greek word meaning, according to Thayer, "clean, pure." That is the meaning of Puritan. As Constantine changed the government of the false churches when he took the reins of it, other changes naturally followed. He desired to make the church inclusive. By that I mean he wanted everybody in the empire to be in "the church." If the "church" is to include everyone in a given locality then, the world and the church are the same. The church is no longer in the world but not of the world. Constantine's inclusive church (all citizens are to be church members) would lead to a non-distinction between the church and the world. Logically, this is exactly what Catholicism is.

The Novatianists and the Donatists began to withdraw and to speak of the Catholic church as the fallen church for this reason. Quite naturally the "fallen church" would seek to discredit these whom she labeled heretics.

Leonard Verdiun's book The Reformers and Their Stepchildren is one of the greatest aids to the serious student of Baptist history ever written. Listen to what he says about the term Cathari. "The fallen church in her effort to discredit the heretic, who was incessantly nagging her concerning her conductal averagism, dug up an old term of reproach, the name by which an ancient dualistic heretic had been known, the name Cathar, a word meaning cleansed."[8] He wrote this in connection with the Donatists.

Widely Applied

Cathari was a name widely applied to those who opposed the corruption in the church of Rome in all ages. It was applied to the Albigenses. Jacques Madaule (no friend to the Baptists at all) has much to say about the Cathari that is very useful. Following are some quotes in the chapter of his book that is titled The Cathars:

"Admittedly the Cathars re-echoed the attacks against the church of Rome, which they viewed as the church of the Devil or of the Antichrist... The Cathars, on the other hand, refused any kind of legitimacy to the Roman church. Though the prelate's evil ways might bear witness to her error, they were not its cause. The church, in the Catharist view, had taken a wrong turning with Pope Sylvester at the beginning of the fourth century, after the edict of Milan (313) by which her position had been radically altered: from the persecuted church she had become the official church. Dante, too, dated the church's misfortunes and deviations were in the moral order only, whereas for the Cathars (who claimed links with the early Christians) they were in the doctrinal order."[9]

The Catharist Doctrine

Madaule writes: "The immediate origins of the movement are easy enough to trace; the more distant ones are less clear. We cannot help being struck- as Jean Guiraud, though a very Catholic historian, has brought out excellently in his History or the Inquisition - by the astonishing resemblance between the Catharist ritual and the ceremonies of the early church; so it would seem that the Cathars' claim to be the true

Christians, preserving the purity and simplicity of the early church, was not entirely fanciful."[10]

Let me introduce a quote from Armitage. He quotes Everine, a Roman Catholic; which really is a good source of information for anyone studying the Cathari:

"Amongst the Cathari, however, we find a Baptist Body at Cologne and Bonn. Whence they came we are not informed; but they appeared in 1146, and Everine gives a full account of them in writing to Bernard, of whom he seeks aid in their suppression. He says that they had been recently discovered, and that two of them had openly opposed the Catholic clergy and laity in their assembly; the archbishop and nobles being present. The 'heretics' asked for a day of disputation, when re-enforced by certain of their number they would maintain their doctrines from Christ and the Apostles; and unless they were properly answered they would rather die than give up their principles. Upon this they were seized and burnt to death. Everine expresses his astonishment that they endured the torment of the stake not only with patience, but with joy; and asks how these members of Satan could suffer with such constancy and courage as were seldom found amongst the most godly. He then describes their heresy.

They professed to be the true Church, because they followed Christ, and patterned after the Apostles; they sought no secular gain or earthly property, but were the poor in Christ, while the Roman Church made itself rich. They accounted themselves as sheep amongst wolves, fleeing from city to city, enduring persecution with the ancient martyrs, although they were living laborious, holy and self-denying lives. They charged their persecutors with being false apostles, with adulterating the word of God, with self-seeking, and the pope with corrupting the Apostle Peter's chair. He says: 'They do not hold the baptism of infants, alleging that passage of the Gospel, "He that believeth and is baptized shall be saved."' They rejected the intercession of saints, and they called all observances in the Church which Christ had not established superstitions. They denied the doctrine of purgatorial fire after death, and believed that when men die they go immediately to heaven or to hell. He therefore beseeches the 'holy father' to direct his pen against 'these wild beasts,' and to help him to 'resist these monsters.' He then says some of them 'Tell us that they had great numbers of their persuasion scattered almost everywhere, and that amongst them were many of our clergy and monks. And as for those who were burnt, they in the defense they made for themselves told us that this heresy had been concealed from the time of the martyrs -and that it had existed in Greece and other countries.' All this he evidently believed."[11]

The Cathari Were Baptists

By their doctrine and sufferings we identify with them as Baptists. Puritan or Cathari was just a name that described them. It was applied to most of the different Baptist groups. Vedder writes: "In the East they were long known as Paulicians, in Italy as the Paterines, in Bulgaria as Bogomils, in Southern France as Albigenses, and in all these places as Cathari."[12]

NOTES ON CHAPTER 8

1 History of the Christian Church, pages 281-283.
2 A Concise History of Baptists, pages 141-142.
3 History of the Christian Church, Volume 3, page 393.
4 History of the Christian Religion and Church, Volume 4, page 592.
5 History of the Church of God, page 299.
6 History of the Christian Church, page 181.
7 A Concise History of the Baptists, page 55.
8 The Reformers and Their Stepchildren, page 97.
9 The Albigensian Crusade, page 31.
10 The Albigensian Crusade, page 32.
11 History of the Baptists, Volume 1, pages 280-281.
12 A Short History of the Baptists, page 102.

Chapter 9

THE PAULICIANS

Another group of our Baptist ancestors were called Paulicians. That there were some radicals among them we do not deny. Nor do we deny that there are radicals among the people called Baptists today. We again maintain that among the Paulicians we find the true churches of Jesus Christ just as we find the true churches of our day among the people called Baptists.

In my research of the Paulicians it was found that the charges of heresy against them came from two men, Photius and Siculus. A great number of historians have followed these two men. These two men were Roman Catholics and bitter enemies of the Paulicians. I tell you of these two men before giving the history of the Paulicians, so the student may beware of those church historians who follow the prejudices of these two "enemies of truth."

Photius

First we will see who Photius was and the kind of person he was. Thomas Armitage has this to say about him:

"Photius possessed great ability, but he was an interested party in his own evidence, and we may fairly question how far he is entitled to absolute credence. As Patriarch of Constantinople, no one was more interested than he in crushing the Paulicians. He was a layman, a great diplomat, and headed one of the most scandalous dissensions of his times. In five days he hurried himself through the five necessary orders, to become Patriarch on the sixth day, thrusting himself into the place of Ignatius, son of Michael I., a man of blameless character, who was deposed because he refused to put the Empress out of the way of plotting Bardas by forcing her into a nunnery. But Pope Nicolas I., by the advice of a synod held at Rome, deposed Photius as an usurper, A.D. 862. In turn, Photius excommunicated the pope, but Gass says that another synod deposed Photius in 867 as 'a liar, adulterer, parricide and heretic.' He was restored to the patriarchate on the death of Ignatius, but was degraded and banished by the Emperor Leo in 886 for political intrigue and embezzlement of the public money. Thus is the chief witness on whose word the Paulicians are condemned."[1]

Siculus

Armitage gives the following: "Peter Siculus is not so well-known; but he was a nobleman under Basil when that emperor drifted into a war with the Paulicians. He was sent to Fabrica, a Paulician town, to negotiate an exchange of prisoners, remaining there from seven to nine months under restraint, within an enemy's lines of sufferance. After this, he pretends to write their history as a sect. But they were split up into several sects, and how could he learn the history of them all in that place and time? They were scattered, according to Gibbon, 'through all the regions of Pontus and Cappadocia,' and made up of 'the remnant of the Gnostic sects,' with many converted Catholics, and 'those of the religion of Zoroaster.' This was the training he received from writing a history of the Paulicians, under the absurd notion that they were followers of Manes. Gass remarks that Photius wrote his book before A.D. 867, and Siculus wrote his after 868, the latter having a 'curious resemblance' to the former, from which Siculus 'borrowed.' Gibbon charges him with 'much prejudice and passion' in defining 'the six capital errors of the Paulicians.' Now, on common legal principles, what is the value of these two witnesses?

Had they full knowledge of the subject to which they deposed? Were they disinterested and unbiased? And did their testimony harmonize? On the first of these questions we have scant knowledge. As to the second, no more partial witnesses could be chosen, one being patriarch of that religion which the Paulicians opposed, the other ambassador to a prince who was seeking their lives. And as to the third, their testimony conflicts in many points, and bears the marks of ill-will. They openly take the place of accusers rather than of witnesses, and treat them as enemies whom they would destroy. Photius makes no attempt to disguise his hatred, but bluntly titles his book 'against' them. Then, Siculus is so violent in his denunciation that he spends his strength and space in scorning what they denied, rather than in stating what they held, his deepest grievance being, that they rejected so much that he avowed. That whole animus of their design and drift is seen in their unblushing effort to stigmatize them as Manichaeans."[2]

Please remember that the charges of heresy against the Paulicians, made by many historians, come from this original source. For them to write the Paulician story would be like Satan writing the true gospel.

Origin, Doctrine, Persecution

Of all the historians, Baptists and otherwise, Joseph Milner gives the best short history of them. This is a very useful source since Joseph Milner was a member of the Church of England. He was no friend to Baptists as all know who are acquainted with his history. I give here a very long quote from him.

"About the year 660, a new sect arose in the East, the accounts of which are far more scanty than a writer with real Church history would wish. Constantine, a person who dwelt in Mananalis, an obscure town in the neighborhood of Samosata, entertained a deacon, who having been a prisoner among the Mahometans, had returned from captivity, and received from the same deacon, the gift of the New Testament in the original language. So early had the laity begun to think themselves excluded from the reading of the sacred volume; and the clergy, both in the East and the West, encouraged this apprehension. The growing ignorance rendered by far the greatest part of the laity incapable of reading the Scriptures. I do not find any ecclesiastical prohibitory decree in these times, nor was there much occasion for it. But Constantine made the best use of the deacon's present. He studied the sacred oracles, and exercised his own understanding upon them. He formed to himself a plan of divinity from the New Testament; and, as St. Paul is the most systematical of all the Apostles, Constantine very properly attached himself to his writings with peculiar attention, as indeed every serious theologian must do. He will find, no doubt, the same truths interspersed through the rest of the sacred volume and a wonderful unity of design and spirit breathing through the whole; but, as it pleased God to employ one person more learned than the rest, it is highly proper, that the student should avail himself of this advantage. That Constantine was in possession of the genuine text was acknowledged universally. A remarkable circumstance! which shows the watchful providence of God over the Scriptures! - Amidst a thousand frauds and sophisms of the times, no adulteration of them was ever permitted to take place.

"The enemies of the Paulicians give them the name from some unknown teacher, but there seems scarcely a doubt, that they took the name from St. Paul himself. For Constantine gave himself the name of Sylvanus; his disciples were called, Titus, Timothy, Tychicus, the names of the Apostle's fellow-labourers; and the names of the Apostolic Churches were given to the congregations formed by their labourers in Armenia and Cappadocia. - Their enemies called them the Gnostics or Manichees; and confounded them with those ancient sectaries, of whom it is probable that there were then scarcely any remains. It has been too customary to connect different and independent sects into one; and to suppose, that every new phenomenon in religion is nothing more than the revival of some former party. This is frequently the case, but not always. In the present instance, I see reason to suppose the Paulicians to have been perfect originals, in regard to any other denomination of Christians. The little, that has already been mentioned concerning them, carries entirely this appearance; and I hope, it may shortly be evident, that they originated from a heavenly influence, teaching and converting them; and that, in them, we have one of those extraordinary effusions of the Divine Spirit, by which the knowledge of Christ and the practice of godliness is kept alive in the world.

"The Paulicians are said to have rejected the two epistles of St. Peter. We know nothing of these men, but from the pens of their enemies. Their writings and the lives of their eminent teachers are totally lost. In this case, common justice requires us to suspend our belief; and, if internal evidence militates in their favour, a strong presumption is formed against the credibility of a report, raised to their disadvantage. This is the case in the present instance, for there is nothing in St. Peter's writings that could naturally prejudice against those writings persons who cordially received the epistles of St. Paul. There is, on the other hand, the most coincidence of sentiment and spirit between the two Apostles; and, in the latter epistle of St. Peter, toward the end, there is very remarkable testimony to the inspired character and divine wisdom of St. Paul. That this sect also despised the whole of the Old Testament is asserted, but on grounds which seem utterly unwarrantable. For, they are said to have done this as Gnostics and Manichees, though they steadily condemned the Manichees, and complained of the injustice which branded them with that odious name. They are also charged with holding the eternity of matter, and the existence of two independent principles; and with denying the real sufferings and real flesh of Christ. It seems no way was found so convenient to disgrace them as by the charge of Manicheism. But I cannot believe that they held these tenets; not only because they themselves denied the charge, but also because they unquestionably held things perfectly inconsistent with such notions. Is it possible, that rational creatures, men endued with common understanding, could agree to revere the writings of St.

Paul, and to consider them as divinely inspired, and at the same time to condemn those of the Old Testament?

"The pious, intelligent, reader, who is moderately versed in Scripture, does not need to be told, that the Apostle is continually quoting the Old Testament, expounding and illustrating, and building his doctrines upon it; in short, that the New Testament is so indissolubly connected with the Old, that he, who despises the latter, cannot really, whatever he may pretend, respect the former as divine; and that this observation holds good in regard to all the writers in the New Testament, and to St. Paul more particularly. It is allowed also, that the Paulicians held the common orthodox doctrine of the Trinity, with the confession and use of which the whole apparatus of the Manichean fable seems incompatible. Let the reader reflect only on the light in which the manicheism appeared to Augustine of Hippo, after he became acquainted with St. Paul, and he will probably form a just estimate of this whole subject.

"This people also were perfectly free from the image-worship, which more and more pervaded the East. They were simply scriptural in the use of sacraments: they disregarded relics, and all the fashionable equipage of superstition; they knew no other Mediator but the Lord Jesus Christ.

"Sylvanus preached with great success. Pontus and Cappadocia, regions once renowned for Christian piety, were again enlightened through his labours. He and his associates were distinguished from the clergy of that day, by their scriptural names, modest titles, zeal, knowledge, activity and holiness. Their congregations were diffused over the provinces of Asia Minor: six of the principal churches were called by the names of those to whom St. Paul addressed his epistles; and Sylvanus resided in the neighborhood of Colonia in Pontus. Roused by the growing importance of the sect, the Greek emperors began to persecute the Paulicians with the most sanguinary severity; and under Christian forms and names, they reacted the scenes of the Galerius and Maximin. "To their other excellent deeds," says the bigoted Peter, the Sicilian, "the divine and orthodox emperors added this virtue, that they ordered the Montanists and Manicheans to be committed to the flames: also, that if any person was found to have secreted them, he was to be put to death, and his goods to be confiscated." False religion, in all ages, hates the light, and supports herself by persecution, not by instruction; while the real truth as it is in Jesus always COMES TO THE LIGHT of Scripture, and exhibits the light plainly to the world by reading and expounding the sacred volume, whence alone she derives her authority.

"A Greek officer, named Simeon, armed with imperial authority, came to Colonia and apprehended Sylvanus and a number of his disciples. Stones were put into the hands of these last, and they were required to kill their pastor, as the price of their forgiveness. A person named Justus was the only one of the number who obeyed; and he stoned to death the father of the Paulicians, who had laboured twenty-seven years. Justus signalized himself still more by betraying his brethren; while Simeon, struck, no doubt, with the evidences of divine grace apparent in the sufferers, embraced, at length, the faith which he came to destroy, gave up the world, preached the Gospel, and died a martyr. For a hundred and fifty years these servants of Christ underwent the horrors of persecution, with Christian patience and meekness; and if the acts of their martyrdom, their preaching, and their lives, were distinctly recorded, there seems no doubt, but this people would appear to have resembled them, whom the Church justly reveres as having suffered in the behalf of Christ during the three first centuries. During all this time the power of the Spirit of God was with them; and they practiced the precepts of the 13th chapter of Romans, as well as believed doctrinal chapters of the same epistle. The blood of the martyrs was, in this case, as formerly, the seed of the Church: a succession of teachers and congregations arose, and a person named Sergius, who laboured among them thirty-three years, is confessed by the bigoted historians to have been a man of extraordinary virtue. The persecution had, however, some intermissions, till at length, Theodora, the same Empress, who fully established image-worship, exerted herself beyond any of her predecessors against them. Her inquisitors ransacked the lesser Asia, in search of these sectaries; and she is computed to have killed by a gibbet, by fire, and by sword, a hundred thousand persons.

"We have brought down the scanty history of this people to about the year of 845. To undergo a constant scene of persecution with Christian meekness, and to render both to God and to Caesar their dues all the time, at once require and evidence the strength of real grace. Of this the Paulicians seem to have been possessed till the period just mentioned. They remembered the injunction of Revelation xiii. 10: "He that killeth with the sword, must be killed with the sword: here is the faith and patience of the Saints." "Let Christians believe, rejoice in God, patiently suffer, return good for evil, and still obey those whom God hath set over them. These weapons have ever been found too hard for Satan: the Church has grown exceedingly, wherever they were faithfully handled: and the power of the Gospel has prevailed."[3]

Paulicians Were Baptists

In giving the principles of the Paulicians, Orchard quotes several authorities: "In these churches of the Paulicians, the sacraments of baptism and the Lord's Supper, they held to be peculiar to the communion of the faithful; i.e., to be restricted to believers" (Jones).

"The Paulicians or Bogomilians baptized and re-baptized adults by immersion" (Robinson).

"It is evident", says Mosheim, "they rejected the baptism of infants. They were not charged with any error concerning baptism."

"These people were called Acephali, or headless (from having no distinct order of clergy, or presiding person in their assemblies) and were hooted in councils for re-baptizing in private houses, says Robinson, and holding conventicles; and for calling the established church a worldly community, and re-baptizing such as joined their churches."[4]

Persecuted

The truth, held and contended for, always brings about persecution and a trail of blood. The Paulicians were persecuted. Listen to George Park Fisher: "The Paulicians were persecuted by a succession of Greek sovereigns. It is said that under Theodore not less than one hundred thousand of them were put to death in Grecian Armenia."[5]

John T. Christian writes: "After the year 1000 the Paulicians began to make their appearance in England. In 1154 a body of Germans migrated into England, driven into exile by persecution. A portion of them settled in Oxford. William Newberry (Rerum Anglicarum, 125: London, 1667) tells of the terrible punishment meted out to the pastor Gerhard and the people. Six years later another company of Paulicians entered Oxford. Henry II ordered them to be branded on the foreheads with hot irons, publicly whipped through the streets of the city, to have their garments cut short at the girdles, and be turned into the open country. The villages were not to afford them any shelter or food, and they perished a lingering death from cold and hunger (Moore, *Earlier and Later Nonconformity in Oxford*, 12)."[6]

NOTES ON CHAPTER 9

1 A History of the Baptists, Volume 1, pages 280-281.
2 A History of the Baptists, Volume 1, pages 235-236.
3 The History of the Church of Christ, Volume 1, pages 571-573.
4 A Concise History of the Baptists, page 130.
5 History of the Christian Church, page 162.
6 A History of the Baptists, Volume 1, page 182.

Chapter 10

DEVELOPMENTS IN
THE HIERARCHY

Earlier, in this Notebook, we have said that the Roman Catholic Church is a developing institution. It was and is being built by Satan himself. Truth never changes. Error must always change and develop for one lie necessitates another. In this lesson we wish to notice some changes and developments in this anti-Christ system.

There is good reason for doing this in a study of Baptist history. When Constantine embraced false Christianity, he reshaped it after the model of Roman Empire government. This meant that the power of the State was behind the unholy church. When anyone opposed the teachings of this unholy church they were guilty of treason against the empire. This meant that, when caught, the offenders must recant or die. Millions died. When the different dogmas were incorporated by the Roman Church, they were opposed by the Montanists, Novatians, Donatists, Cathari, Paterines, Albigenses, Paulicians and all other true churches by whatever name they were called. This brought down the sword of the Beast upon them. So we review some of these developments because they directly affected our ancestors.

The Sign of the Cross

"The symbolic act known as the sign of the cross appears very early, signifying, of course, Christ's death on the cross; but inevitably importance came to be attached to the mere act and it was believed to be helpful in receiving the blessing and efficacy of this holy event and of the exalted Christ. As early as about the middle of the second century a superstitious conception and application had so far developed that the popular faith of the church, not without support from theology, sought by performing the act a powerful device against the will of demons, by whom people imagined themselves beset and threatened. The expedient was also applied in case of sickness and other perils, before battle and elsewhere. The sign was usually made on the forehead, but also on others parts of the body, which were supposed to need its protective operation. The sign is also used contemporaneously in public worship as conferring a blessing or consecration and protection against the ungodly world. Its supposed efficacy comes to light especially in exorcism."[1] The exact date of its beginning is not known. Most of the writers list this dogma, along with Prayers for the Dead, at about 300 A.D. Dr. Loraine Boettner, in his excellent book, quotes a Roman Catholic authority: "It may be safely assumed that only after the edict of Milan, A.D. 312, was the cross used as a permanent sign of our redemption. De Rossi (a Roman Catholic archaeologist) states positively that no monogram of Christ, discovered in the Catacombs or other places, can be traced to that period anterior to the year 312 (*The American Ecclesiastical Review*, p. 275, Sept. 1920)."[2] It would seem to me that Constantine (author of the edict of Milan) and his supposed vision of the fiery cross in the sky was responsible for this superstition. At any rate, the true churches would preach against such ignorance and thus incur the wrath of the State-Church.

Wax Candles

A. A. Davis says this began about 320 A. D.[3] All the historians say this began very early. The Roman Church keeps these wax candles constantly burning before the shrines and images of their saints. This custom was incorporated from paganism. "The primitive writers frequently expose the folly and absurdity of this heathenish custom. 'They light up candles to God,' says Lactantius, 'as if he lived in the dark; and do not they deserve to pass for madmen, who offer lamps to the author and giver of light?'" This quote is from John Dowling.[4] When our Baptist ancestors preached against such superstition, and they did, they angered the State. Dear reader, such superstition was nonsense and it still is.

Mother of God

The phrase "Mother of God" began in the Council of Ephesus, called by Theodosius II and Valentian III in 431 A. D. At this council there were 250 bishops present. The phrase occurs in the Creed of Chalcedon, adopted in 451 A. D. Mariolatry, the veneration and worship of Mary, has grown over the years. "As we have seen the expression 'Mother of God,' as set forth in the decree of the Council of Ephesus gave impetus to Mary worship, although the practice did not become general until two or three centuries later. From the fifth century on the Mary cult becomes more common. Mary appears more frequently in paintings, churches were named after her, and prayers were offered to her as an intercessor."[5] The Catholic teaching about Mary develops. Boettner writes: "The doctrine of the 'Immaculate Conception' teaches that Mary herself was born without sin, that from the very first moment of her existence she was free from the taint of original sin. It holds that while all the rest of mankind is born into an inheritance of original sin, Mary alone, by a special miracle of God, was excepted. The original decree setting forth this doctrine was issued by Pope Pius IX, on December 8, 1854, and reads as follows: 'We declare, pronounce and define that the Most Blessed Virgin Mary, at the first instant of her conception was preserved immaculate from all stain of original sin, by the singular grace and privilege of the Omnipotent God, in virtue of the merits of Jesus Christ, the Saviour of mankind, and that this doctrine was revealed by God, and therefore must be believed firmly and constantly by all the faithful' (From the papal bull, Ineffabilus Deus, quoted in the Tablet,

December 12, 1953)"[6] The Roman Catholic Church teaches that Mary remained a perpetual virgin all her life. This, of course, is contrary to the plain declarations of Scripture. See Matthew 13:54-56; Psalms 69:8; Matthew 1:24-25; etc. Listen to Boettner again: "... on November 1, 1950, with the ex cathedral pronouncement by pope Pius XII from St. Peter's chair that Mary's body was raised from the grave shortly after she died, that her body and soul were reunited, and that she was taken up and enthroned as Queen of Heaven. And to this pronouncement there was added the usual warning that anyone who may henceforth doubt or deny this doctrine is utterly fallen away from the divine and Catholic faith.' That means that it is a mortal sin for any Roman Catholic to refuse to believe this doctrine."[7] In 1965, pope Paul VI proclaimed Mary the Mother of the Church. Who knows what shall come next. Mary was a highly favoured woman but she was just a woman. She had to believe on Christ to be saved like anyone else. This is what Baptists believe and always have. In ages past this belief was treason against the State-Church.

Purgatory

The Roman Catholic doctrine of Purgatory was established by Gregory I in 593 A. D. Boettner describes Purgatory as follows: "The Roman Catholic Church has developed a doctrine in which it is held that all who die at peace with the church, but who are not perfect must undergo penal and purifying suffering in an intermediate realm known as purgatory. Only those believers who have attained a state of Christian perfection go immediately to heaven. All unbaptized adults and those who after baptism have committed mortal sin go immediately to hell. The great mass of partially sanctified Christians dying in fellowship with the church, but who nevertheless are encumbered with some degree of sin go to purgatory where, for a longer or shorter time, they suffer until all sin is purged away, after they are translated to heaven."[8] Boettner again: "The sufferings in purgatory are said to vary greatly in intensity and duration, being proportioned to the guilt and impurity or impenitence of the sufferer. They are described as being in some cases comparatively light and mild, lasting perhaps only a few hours, while in others for thousands of years. They differ from the pains of hell at least to this extent, that there is eventually an end to the sufferings of purgatory, but not to those in hell. They are in any event to end with the last judgment. Hence purgatory eventually is to be emptied of all its victims." "As regards the intensity of the suffering, Bellarmine, a noted Roman Catholic theologian says: "The pains of purgatory are very severe, surpassing anything endured in this life." The manual of the Purgatory Society, with the imprimatur of Cardinal Hays, says: "According to the Holy Fathers of the Church, the fire of purgatory does not differ from the fire of hell, except in point of duration. 'It is the same fire' says St. Thomas Aquinas, 'that torments the reprobate in hell, and the just in purgatory. The least pain in purgatory surpasses the greatest suffering in this life.' Nothing but the eternal duration makes the fire of hell more terrible than that of purgatory."[9]

Origin of Purgatory

How could such a damnable doctrine as purgatory come into being? Who could have dreamed up such a teaching? No one, except he be instructed of the devil. Folks, credit for this heresy goes to Augustine. And, to spite this, we often hear Augustine bragged on by Baptist preachers in Baptist churches. Surely they are uninformed who would exalt Augustine in one degree. Listen to Dowling: "He (Gregory I) seriously inculcated a belief in the pagan doctrine concerning the purification of departed souls by a certain kind of fire, which he called Purgatory, and which doctrine, as Gieseler asserts, was first suggested by Augustine, the bishop of Hippo, towards the close of the fourth century."[10] Fisher: "The introduction of the doctrine of purgatory was due to the influence of Augustine, who suggested that imperfect Christians may be purified in the intermediate state, by purgatorial fire, from their remaining sin. His conjecture was converted into a fixed belief."[11] Boettner says, in his book on page 229, "In the writings of Augustine (died, 430 A.D.) the doctrine of purgatory was first given definite form...." It goes without saying that the true churches opposed such a teaching. Doing this incurred the wrath of the Church-State or State-Church!

NOTES ON CHAPTER 10

1 The New Schaff-Herzog Religious Encyclopedia, Volume 3, page 309.
2 Roman Catholicism, page 286.
3 Sermons on the Trail of Blood, page 308.
4 The History of Romanism, page 121.
5 Roman Catholicism by Boettner, page 136-137.
6 Roman Catholicism, page 158.
7 Roman Catholicism, page 162.
8 Roman Catholicism, page 218.
9 Roman Catholicism, page 220.
10 History of Romanism, page 108.
11 History of the Christian Church, page 142.

Chapter 11

MORE DEVELOPMENTS IN THE HIERARCHY

In the last chapter we noticed a few dogmas that were added to the Roman Catholic Church. It might be good if, in this chapter, we look at a whole list of them with comment upon only a few. The student should search out and study all of them. Opposition to them by our Baptist ancestors brought them much persecution.

List of Heresies

Several of the Histories list the developments of the Hierarchy. Here we will look at the one contained in Loraine Boettner's book:

SOME ROMAN CATHOLIC HERESIES AND INVENTIONS

and the dates of their adoption over a period of 1650 years.[1]

1. Prayers for the dead, began about A. D. - 300.
2. Making the Sign of the Cross - 300.
3. Wax candles, about - 320.
4. Veneration of angels and dead saints, and use of images - 375.
5. The Mass, as a daily celebration - 394.

6. Beginning of the exaltation of Mary, the term "Mother of God" first applied to her by the Council of Ephesus - 431.
7. Priests began to dress differently from laymen - 500.
8. Extreme Unction - 526.
9. The doctrine of Purgatory, established by Gregory I - 593.
10. Latin Language, used in prayer and worship, imposed by Gregory I - 600.
11. Prayers directed to Mary, dead saints and angels, about - 600.
12. Title of pope, or universal bishop, given to Boniface III by Emperor Phocus - 607.
13. Kissing the pope's foot, began with pope Constantine - 709.
14. Temporal power of the popes, conferred by Pepin, king of the Franks - 750.
15. Worship of the cross, images and relics, authorized in - 786.
16. Holy water, mixed with a pinch of salt and blessed by a priest - 850.
17. Worship of St. Joseph - 890.
18. College of Cardinals established - 927.
19. Baptism of Bells, instituted by pope John XIII - 965.
20. Canonization of dead saints, first by pope John XV - 995.
21. Fasting on Fridays and during Lent - 998.
22. The Mass, developed gradually as a sacrifice, attendance made obligatory in the 11th century - 998.
23. Celibacy of the priesthood, decreed by pope Gregory VII (Hildebrand) - 1079.
24. The Rosary, mechanical praying with beads, invented by Peter the Hermit - 1090.
25. The Inquisition, instituted by the Council of Verona - 1184.
26. Sale of Indulgence - 1190.
27. Transubstantiation, proclaimed by pope Innocent III - 1215.
28. Auricular Confession of sins to a priest instead of to God, instituted by pope Innocent III, in Lateran council - 1215.
29. Adoration of the Wafer (Host), decreed by pope Honorius III - 1220.

30. Bible forbidden to laymen, placed on the Index of
    Forbidden Books by the Council of Valencia - 1229.
31. The Scapular, invented by Simon Stock,
    an English monk - 1251.
32. Cup forbidden to the people at Communion
    by Council of Constance - 1414.
33. Purgatory proclaimed as a dogma by
    the Council of Florence - 1439.
34. The doctrine of Seven Sacraments affirmed - 1439.
35. The Ave Maria (part of the last half was completed
    50 years later and approved by pope Sixtus V
    at the end of the 16th century - 1508.
36. Jesuit order founded by Loyola - 1534.
37. Tradition declared of equal authority with
    the Bible by the Council of Trent - 1545.
38. Apocryphal books added to the Bible
    by the Council of Trent - 1546.
39. Creed by pope Pius IV imposed as the official creed - 1560.
40. Immaculate Conception of the Virgin Mary,
    proclaimed by pope Pius IX - 1854.
41. Syllabus of Errors, proclaimed by pope Pius IX, and ratified
    by the Vatican Council, condemned freedom of religion,
    conscience, speech, press, and scientific discoveries which
    are disapproved by the Roman Church, asserted the
    pope's temporal authority over all civil rulers - 1864.
42. Infallibility of the pope in matters of faith and
    morals, proclaimed by the Vatican council. - 1870.
43. Public Schools condemned by pope Pius XI - 1930.
44. Assumption of the Virgin Mary (bodily
    ascension into heaven shortly after her death),
    proclaimed by pope Pius XII - 1950.
45. Mary proclaimed Mother of the Church,
    by pope Paul VI - 1965.

Add to these many others: monks, nuns, monasteries, convents, forty days Lent, holy week, Palm Sunday, Ash Wednesday, All Saints day, Candlemas day, fish day, meat day, incense, holy oil, holy palms, Christopher medals, charms, novenas, and still others.

Extreme Unction

We will examine only a few of the above, beginning with Extreme Unction. This is one of the seven sacraments of the Roman Catholic Church (Sacrament: A means of Grace). This sacrament (?) consists of a priest anointing a person, near the point of death, with sacred oil. The Unction (holy oil) is placed upon the eyes, ears, nostrils, mouth, and hands (the five senses). At each anointing the priest says "By this holy unction, and through his great mercy, may God indulge thee whatsoever sins thou hast committed by sight." And this he does for each of the five senses.

The Catholic Church confirms that this practice was started by the apostle James. They affirm that the priest has the power to absolve the dying person from his sins. At this point let us look at two canons of the Catholic Church as recorded by Dowling.

(1) "Whoever shall affirm that extreme unction is not truly and properly a sacrament, instituted by our Christ our blessed Lord, and published by the blessed Apostle James, but only a ceremony received from the fathers or a human invention: Let Him Be Accursed."

(2) "Whoever shall affirm, that the sacred unction of the sick does not confer grace, nor forgive sin, nor relieve the sick: but that its power has ceased, as if the gift of healing existed only in past ages: Let Him Be Accursed."[2] See also Boettner's book, pages 191-192

Our ancestors, opposing this heresy, found themselves opposed by the power of the State-Church. Truly, the Mother of Harlots, riding upon the scarlet beast is drunk with the blood of the saints (Revelation 17).

Baptism of Bells

This custom was first introduced by pope John XIII, who died in 972. He named the great bell of the Lateran Church at Rome, John the Baptist. Each bell that is sprinkled (baptized), consecrated, is given the name of some saint. This is so the people might believe they are being called to divine service by the saint whose name has been given to the bell. Inscribed upon the consecrated bell is: "I adore the true God; I call the people; I collect the priests, I worship the saints; I teach the festivals; I deplore the dead; I drive away pestilence and devils."[3]

Can you believe this? Neither did our ancestors and they suffered for it.

Transubstantiation

The Roman Catholic Church teaches that when the priests consecrate the wine and wafer it becomes the actual blood and the actual body of the Lord Jesus Christ. The bread and wine are turned into flesh and blood when the priest says the words in Latin: "Hoc est corpus meus." (This is my body). This is where the expression "Hocus-Pocus" originated. See *Babylon: Mystery Religion* by Ralph Woodrow, page 129.

The Lord's Supper is a symbolic ordinance. The unleavened bread is only a symbol of the Lord's body which was broken for His people. The wine is only a symbol of His blood that was shed for the remission of the sins of many. The following poem shows how silly the Roman Catholic doctrine of transubstantiation is:

A Roman Miracle (?)

A pretty maid, a Protestant, was to a Catholic wed;
To love all the Bible truths and tales, quite early she'd been bred.
It sorely grieved her husband's heart that she would not comply
And join the Mother Church of Rome and heretics deny.

So day by day he flattered her, but still she saw no good
Would ever come from bowing down to idols made of wood;
The mass, the host, the miracles, were made but to deceive;
And transubstantiation, too, she'd never dare believe.

He went to see his clergyman and told him his sad tale
"My wife's an unbeliever, sir, you can perhaps, prevail;
For all your Romish miracles my wife has strong aversion,
To really work a miracle may lead to her conversion."

The priest went with the gentleman - he thought to gain a prize.
He said, "I will convert her, sire, and open both her eyes."
So when they came into the house, the husband loudly cried,
"The priest has come to dine with us!" "He's welcome," she replied.

And when, at last, the meal was o'er, the priest at once began
To teach his hostess all about the awful state of man;
The greatness of our Saviour's love, which Christians can't deny
To give Himself a sacrifice and for our sins to die.

"I will return tomorrow, lass, prepare some bread and wine;
The sacramental miracle will stop your soul's decline."
"I'll bake the bread," the lady said. "You may," he did reply.
"And when you've seen this miracle, convinced you'll be, say I."

The priest did come accordingly, the bread and wine did bless.
The lady asked, "Sir, is it changed?" The priest answered, "Yes,
It's changed from common bread and wine to truly flesh and blood;
Begorra, lass, this power of mine has changed it into God!"

So having blessed the bread and wine, to eat they did prepare;
The lady said unto the priest, "I warn you to take care.
For half an ounce of arsenic was mixed right in the batter,
But since you have its nature changed, it cannot really matter."

The priest was struck real dumb - he looked as pale as death.
The bread and wine fell from his hands and he did gasp for breath.
"Bring me my horse!" the priest cried. "This is a cursed home!"
The lady replied, "Begone; tis you who shares the curse of Rome."

The husband, too, he sat surprised, and not a word did say.
At length he spoke, "My dear," said he, "The priest has run away;
To gulp such mummery and tripe, I'm not, for sure, quite able;
I'll go with you and renounce this Roman Catholic Fable."
- Author Unknown

Catholic Church Councils

We cannot take the time to comment upon each of these developments. The student should examine each one. Our Baptist ancestors opposed them all. True Baptists oppose them today.

In the development of the Roman Catholic Hierarchy, many church councils were called. One of the main purposes of these councils was to examine how the Hierarchy could stamp out what they called heresy. This "heresy" was usually what we believe to be truth. A list of these councils is found in many of the Church Histories. Here we list only those up to the dividing of the Roman Catholic Hierarchy into the Roman and Greek Orthodox churches.

The First: This one was called by Constantine the Great. It was held at Nicea. There were three hundred eighty-one bishops present. Points to be discussed were the Arian question, the celebration of Easter, the Meletian schism, the baptism of heretics and the status of the lapsed in the persecution under Licinius. It was here that the Nicene Creed was promulgated. Constantine the Great and Eusebius were very prominent in this council.

The Second: This Council was called by Theodosius the Great. It was held at Constantinople in 381 A.D. It was to confirm the Nicene faith and deal with the Arian controversy. There were one hundred fifty bishops present.

The Third: This Council was called by Theodosius II and Valentian III. It was held at Ephesus in 431 A.D. There were two hundred fifty bishops present. This Council aimed at the Nestorian Controversy. He preached against Mary being called "the Mother of God." He said, "Mary did not give birth to divinity, but to man, the instrument of divinity." He recommended that Mary be called "mother of Christ" instead of "Mother of God." On the very first day of this council Nestorius was condemned and declared deposed from all clerical office.

The Fourth: This Council was held at Chalcedon in 451 A.D. It was called by the emperor Marian. There were 600 Metropolitans (city bishop) present. Eutychianism was condemned. This was a confounding of the human and divine natures. This council decreed the same rights and honors to the bishop of Constantinople as to the bishop of Rome. It was here that the creed of Chalcedon was adopted. That creed promotes Mary worship. In regard to the person of Christ that creed states: "Born of the Virgin Mary, the Mother of God according to manhood."

The Fifth: This council was called by Justinian. It was held at Constantinople in 553 A.D. There were 165 bishops present. They met to condemn and suppress certain writings. This is known as the Three Chapters Controversy. It was mainly political (as were many of the councils).

The Sixth: It was called by Constantine Pogonatus and met at Constantinople, November 7, 680 A.D. to September 16, 681 A.D. This dealt with the controversy concerning the two wills in Christ (Monothelitism). It also anathematized pope Honorius for heresy.

The Seventh: This Council was called by the infamous Empress Irene. It was held at Nicea in 787 A.D. It was here that both image and saint worship was established. This council determined that "As the sacred and life-giving cross is everywhere set up as a symbol, so also should the images of Jesus Christ, the Virgin Mary, the holy angels, as well as those saints and other pious and holy men be embodied in the manufacture of sacred vessels, tapestries, vestments, etc., and exhibited on the walls of churches, in the homes, and in all conspicuous places, by the roadside and everywhere," to be revered by all who might see them.[4]

The Eighth: This last Eastern Council was called by Basilius Maredo and was held at Constantinople in 869 A.D. There was much trouble in the air. Photius the Greek was Partriarch of Constantinople. Nicholas I was pope at Rome. In 863 A.D. these two men had excommunicated each other. Catholicism was without a head. This council was called to settle this difficulty. The difficulty was not repaired and has not been as yet.

Roman Catholic and Greek Orthodox

In closing this chapter we give word or two about this 869 division in the hierarchy. When Constantinople repudiated the Roman Religion for what is called "Christianity," he angered the Roman Senate. He removed the seat of the empire to Byzantium, an old city rebuilt and renamed Constantinople. This set about a rival between the bishop of Rome and the bishop of Constantinople as to which was the most powerful. This led to the split.

There are some differences between the two churches. The Greek church rejects sprinkling or pouring for baptism while Rome uses nothing else. The Greek church practices infant communion. Rome used to, but quit. The Greek church gives the wine and bread to both clergy and laity. Rome gives wine only to the priest. The Greek church does not practice celibacy while Rome does. Greeks reject papal infallibility while Rome holds to it. The Greek leader is called Patriarch while the Roman leader is called pope.

NOTES ON CHAPTER 11

1 *Roman Catholicism, pages 7-9.*
2 *History of Romanism, pages 524-525.*
3 *History of Romanism, page 207.*
4 *The New Schaff-Herzog Religious Encyclopedia, Volume 8, page 198.*

Chapter 12

THE PETROBRUSIANS

People of the past, holding to Baptist principles, have been known by many names. In one country they would be called after the place; in another they would take their name after an able spokesman or writer among them. Such is the case of this group of our ancestors that we are about to study. Always remember: True Baptist ancestors are identified by their doctrine and not by their name.

Peter de Bruys

This group of our ancestors was located in the south of France in the provinces of Languedoc and Provence, mainly. About the year 1110, Peter de Bruys appeared preaching the gospel of our Lord Jesus Christ. Who was Peter de Bruys?

He was, for a time, a Roman Catholic priest. History does not preserve for how his conviction for truth came about. We know that God used some providence in bringing this man to the truth.

Some men within the corrupt churches still preached the truth. Some feel the influence of Claudius of Turin (died about 832) had been felt in southern France. This man taught that whoever sought salvation anywhere except in Christ, was an idolater. He condemned image worship. He taught that prayers to dead saints could render service to no man. He taught we should worship every virgin and every manger as well as the virgin Mary or the manger at Bethlehem. Crucifixes were an abomination. He denied Peter had received any personal power to bind or loose. He denied that works of an external nature earned favor with God.[1] Maybe Peter de Bruys was influenced by this man's teachings or someone like him.

More probably, he was influenced by the true churches that were located, very early, in the south of France. Persecutions of our Baptist ancestors in Italy and other areas drove them into the hill country of France as well as into the Alps. It could be that Peter de Bruys met with these folks and came to know the truth through them.

William Cathcart has the following to say about Peter de Bruys: "Peter de Bruys commenced his ministry about 1125, and such was his success that in a few years in the places about the mouth of the Rhone, in the plain country about Thoulouse, and particularly in that city itself, and in many parts of the province of Gascoigne he led great throngs of men and women to Jesus, and overthrew the entire authority of popes, bishops, and priests."[2]

Their Doctrine

Following is a quote from the Presbyterian historian, James Wharey: "The whole system of doctrines, inculcated by this Peter upon his followers, who from his were called Petrobrusians, is not known; yet there are five of his opinions that have reached us: 1. That persons ought not to be baptized till they come to the use of reason. 2. That it is not proper to build churches, and that such as are built should be pulled down. 3. That the holy crosses should be destroyed. 4. That the body and blood of Christ are not distributed in the sacred supper, but only the sign of them. 5. That the oblations, prayers, and good works of the living do not profit the dead."[3]

From this we see they rejected infant baptism and believed only in believer's baptism. They believed money was wasted in the construction of great buildings and people would be likely to idolize the building. Crosses and crucifixes to them were of no avail. They held the Lord's Supper to be a symbolic church ordinance. Purgatory was an institution of the devil. We see, in this ancient people, folks not unlike ourselves.

Augustus Neander

This historian makes several conjectures against Peter de Bruys which he concedes cannot be proved. He does make several statements that we want to share here:

"It is certain that he rejected the authority of the church and of the great teachers, to whom it was customary to appeal, and would recognize nothing as obligatory on faith but what could be proved from the Bible... He was an opponent of infant baptism, since he regarded personal faith as a necessary condition for true baptism, and denied the benefit in this case of another's faith. As he could not allow, according to this, any validity whatever to infant baptism, he must consequently rebaptize, or bestow true baptism for the first time, on those who joined his party. The followers of Peter de Bruys refused to be called Anabaptists, a name given to them for the reason just mentioned: because the only baptism, they said, which they could regard as the true one, was a baptism united with knowledge and faith, by which man is cleansed from his sins. The mass, the pretension of the priests that they could produce Christ's body and repeat the sacrifice, Peter of Bruis looked upon as the grand means for upholding and promoting the dominion of the priesthood: this doctrine, therefore, he vehemently attacked... His zeal against the veneration paid to the cross, led him to say that the instrument with which Christ was so cruelly put to death, was so far from deserving reverence that it should rather be abused and destroyed in every way to avenge his sufferings and death... On one Good-Friday, the Petrobrusians got together a great multitude of people, collected all the crosses which they could lay hold of, and made a large bonfire of them, at which, in contempt of the church laws, they cooked meat, which was distributed to all present... He rejected prayer, offerings, alms for the departed, maintaining "that all depends on a man's conduct during his life on earth; this decides his destiny. Nothing that is done for him after he is dead can be of any use to him. "For twenty years, Peter of Bruis, had labored as a preacher in South France, when seized by an infuriated mob at St. Gilles, in Languedoc, he was hurried away to the stake. But... his doctrines still continued after his death to have an influence in many districts, particularly around Gascoigne."[4]

Peter de Bruys Was a Baptist

Armitage writes: "In the Petrobusians we find a sect of Baptists for which no apology is needed. Peter of Bruis seized the entire Biblical presentation of baptism, and forced its teaching home upon the conscience and the life, by rejecting the immersion of babes and insisting on the immersion of all believers in Christ, without any admixture of Catharistic nonsense."[5]

Peter the Venerable, Abbot of Clugny wrote a book against what he called the heresy of the Petrobrusians. Vedder, after reviewing what he wrote, comes to the following conclusion: "It is evident that the 'errors' of the Petrobrusians were what Baptists have always maintained to be the fundamental truths of the Scriptures. Any body of Christians that holds to the supremacy of the Scriptures, a church of the regenerate only, and believer's baptism, is fundamentally one with the Baptist churches of today, whatever else it may add to or omit from its statement of beliefs."[6]

Cathcart writes: "Peter and his followers were decided Baptists, and like ourselves they gave a fresh baptism to all converts. They reckoned that they were not believers when first immersed in the Catholic church, and that as Scripture baptism required faith in its candidates, and for the same reason they repudiated the idea that they rebaptized them, confidently asserting that because of the lack of faith they had never been baptized."[7]

Information Source

Peter the Venerable, abbot of Clugny was born in 1093, and died in 1157. He is considered by all the historians that I have read, to be a scholar. It is said that he would rebuke the pope or anyone who needed it. He wrote against the Jews and the Saracens and others. Because of the great success of the preaching of Peter de Bruys (Peter of Bruis) he felt compelled to write against the Petrobrusians. History is indebted to him for the account of what the Petrobrusians believed. The histories quoted in this chapter used him as their source. It would be a blessing to every student of Bible history to read pages 912-916 in William Cathcart's Baptist Encyclopedia. In this section he quotes from Peter the Venerable to prove the doctrines held by Peter de Bruys and the Petrobrusians. Vedder and others do this too. There can be no doubt that Peter de Bruys was a Baptist.

Persecution

Holding to the doctrines they preached and believed brought them into conflict with the Catholics and thus with those in control of the state. They suffered for their beliefs. "All who live godly in Christ Jesus shall suffer persecution." Hassell writes: "In the first years of the twelfth century Peter of Bruis (Petrobrusians) went forth like another John the Baptist, full of the Spirit and of power, and lived for twenty years as an evangelist in the south of France, which he seems to have filled completely with his doctrine, till he was overtaken by the wrath of the priesthood he had challenged, and was burned alive by a mob of monastics somewhere about 1120. Thus the seed was planted of what widened afterward into the famous and greatly dreaded 'heresy' of the Waldenses and Albigenses. Peter de Bruys was a strong Baptist."[8] Jones and other historians date his being burned about 1130.

NOTES ON CHAPTER 12

1 A Manual of Church History, Volume 1, pages 558-559.
2 Baptist Encyclopedia, page 912.
3 Sketches of Church History, page 174.
4 General History of the Christian Religion and Church, Volume 4, pages 595-597.
5 The History of the Baptists, Volume 1, page 294.
6 A Short History of the Baptists, page 15.
7 Baptist Encyclopedia, page 912.
8 History of the Church of God, page 438.

Chapter 13

THE HENRICIANS

This group of our ancestors takes their name from Henry of Lausanne. He had been a monk in the Roman Church. The Monastery of Clugny in Burgundy was the most famous cloister of these times. It had been founded early in the tenth century. It was famous for the piety and scholarship of its abbots and monks. It had become, by the twelfth century, an immoral scandalous place. During its worst times Henry became an inmate of Clugny.

Historians are not sure where he was born. Some say in Switzerland, others say Italy. The historians say he was probably born at the close of the eleventh century. He was a man of great piety and high morals. He became disgusted with the immorality of the monks at Clugny so he renounced his vows. He began to preach the gospel from one place to another.

Description of Henry

Thomas Armitage quotes from Neander's Life of Bernard of Henry: "He had all the attributes to deeply impress the people, great dignity in personal appearance, a fiery eye, a thundering voice, a lively step, a speech that rushed forth impetuously as it flowed from his heart, and Bible passages were always at hand to support his addresses. Soon was spread abroad the report of his holy life and his learning. Young and old, men and women, hastened to him to confess their sins and said they had never seen a man of such severity and friendliness whose words could move a heart of iron to repentance, whose life should be a model for all monks and priests."1

Henry seems to have started out as a reformer of the Catholic Church. "He appeared in the garb of a penitent, his long beard hanging upon his breast, his feet bare even in winter, a staff in his hand; a very young John the Baptist, in a living voice. In drawing his picture, an enemy speaks of 'his face through the quickness of his eyes,' as 'like a perilous sea; tall of body, quick of gait, gliding in his walk, quick of speech, of a terrible voice, a youth in age, none more splendid than he in dress.'"2

Henry in Mans

In 1116 this lithe, young Baptist apostle of the Alps drew near to the thriving city of Mans, and sent to obtain permission of Hildebert the bishop to preach in his diocese. This prelate was a disciple of Berengarius, and so looked with favor on Henry's efforts to purify the Church. He was about to depart from Rome, but instructed his archdeacon to treat Henry kindly and allow him to preach. The fame of his piety had reached the city before him, and the people believed that he possessed a prophetic gift. He entered Mans, and while the bishop was visiting Rome the people received him with delight; the priests of the lower order sat at his feet, almost bathing them with tears, while most of the higher clergy protested against him and stood aloof. A platform or pulpit was specially erected for him, from which he might address the people. He made marriage a chief matter in his sermons. He would free it from unnatural restrictions, would celebrate it in early life and make it indissoluble. He would not accept the repentance of an unchaste woman until she had burned her hair and her garments in public. He condemned extravagant attire and marriage for money. 'Indeed,' says his enemy, 'he was marvelously eloquent,' a remark which couches his matter as well as his manner. While the priests wept over his exposure of their corruptions, the people were enraged at the priests. They refused to sell any thing to them, threatened their servants with violence, and their safety was secured only by the shield of public authority. The clergy came to dispute with Henry, but the people handled them roughly and they fled for safety. Chagrined at their defeat, they united in a letter forbidding him to preach, but the people protected him and he went on boldly.

When the bishop returned the people treated his religious acts with contempt and said: 'We do not want your benedictions. You may bless the dirt. We have a father and a priest who surpasses you in dignity, holy living and understanding. Your clergy avoid him as if he were a blasphemer, because of the spirit of a prophet he is uncovering their vices, and out of the Holy Scriptures is condemning their errors and excesses.' The bishop had an interview with Henry, but dared not tolerate the stanch reformer any longer. Henry, therefore, retired to Poitiers and other southern provinces of France, where he continued to labor with great success, in some cases whole congregations leaving the Catholics and joining his standard. The people gave him a ready hearing, for the Catharists and Peter had prepared his way. He had met Peter in the Diocese of Narbonne and received from him the direction of the rising sect.[3]

It is probable that Henry, through association with Peter de Bruys, ceased to be a reformer and became known by the Roman Church as a heretic. Newman says he seems "to have associated himself with Peter de Bruys and for ten years these zealous preachers carried on conjointly their evangelistic work."[4]

St. Bernard's Account of Henry's Influence

Henry C. Vedder quotes from one of St. Bernard's letters to the Count of Toulouse, to warn him against Henry:

"The churches are without congregations, congregations without priests, priests without their due reverence, and, worst of all, Christians without Christ. Churches are regarded as synagogues, the sanctuary of God is said to have no sanctity, the sacraments are not thought to be sacred, and feast days are deprived of their wonted solemnities. Men are dying in their sins, souls are being dragged everywhere before the dread Tribunal, neither being reconciled by repentance nor fortified by Holy Communion. The way of Christ is shut to the children of Christians, and they are not allowed to enter the way of salvation, although the Saviour lovingly calls on their behalf, 'Suffer little children to come into me.' Does God, then, who, as he has multiplied his mercy, has saved both man and beast, debar innocent little children from this his so great mercy? Why, I ask, why does he begrudge to little ones their Infant Saviour, who was born for them? This envy is of the devil. By this envy death entered into the whole world. Or does he suppose that little children have no need of a Saviour, because they are children?"[5]

It seems very obvious from these words of St. Bernard that Henry refused baptism to infants and baptized only believing adults.

Henry Was a Baptist

I would like to give a brief account of Henry by S. H. Ford:

"In the beautiful city of Lausanne, surrounded by the towering Alps, the sheltering homes of God's hidden ones, an Italian hermit learned the simple truths of the gospel. The idleness of the hermit was at once exchanged for the armor and the toil of an ambassador of Christ. To the dwellers in those valleys he broke the bread of life; and over those mountain peaks he passed, bringing glad tidings to beautiful, yet darkened France. From Mans, from Poictiers, from Bordeaux, he was successively banished, after what victories or defeats we know not. Of martial valor, of deeds of chivalry preformed on those same spots, we have many flowing record. What would we not give to know the words and acts of this simple gospel preacher, as he passed through those proud old cities, with their grim castles and splendid cathedrals, and glorious recollections of heraldry and conquest looming up in the Gothic twilight of that age. But like the apostolic record, which notes the entrance of Paul into Philippi, where the beauties of Grecian art, column, and statue, and temple, robed in the autumnal charms of a vicious loveliness, surrounded him on every side, one fact only has importance sufficient for enduring record: 'There they preached the Gospel.' So of Henry. More than this we know not.

"He passed through these cities, exercising his ministerial function with the utmost applause of the people, and disclaiming with vehemence and fervor against the superstitions they had introduced into the Christian Church."

"We have no satisfactory account," adds Mosheim, "of the doctrines of this man; we merely know that he censured the baptism of infants, and the corrupt manners of the clergy."

But we have a satisfactory account of his doctrines, given by Mosheim himself, and more especially by Wall. Henry was a Baptist, believing in the spirituality of Christ's kingdom, the supreme authority of Christ as King, and the immersion of true believers.

In the old and melancholy city of Toulouse, where four thousand heretics were burned during a century, the hero hermit, Henry, lifted his voice, "cried aloud, and spared not." Toulouse, from whose cathedral summits are seen the mingling steams of the Cervennes and the Tarn, sweeping on through the beautiful vale of the Garonne; and in the obscure distance of the Pyrenees, rearing their silvered heads to heaven, as though inviting to their mountain fastnesses the shorn lambs of Christ's fold; Toulouse, in the darkness and stillness of its death-sleep, was suddenly convulsed by the embodied power and wisdom of God - the Gospel.

The clergy woke to the danger of their craft. His opposition to their human dogmas, their splendid buildings, their vestments, instrumental music - the whole train of priestly wrappages, brought down their vengeance on the daring innovator. The great Saint Bernard, we have seen, thundered out his maledictions, and poor Henry, driven from Toulouse, fled to the mountains, was pursued, and brought before a council at Rheins. This was in 1158. He held that the church was a spiritual body composed of regenerated persons. He also held that no person should be baptized until he knew he was saved. He rejected infant baptism. He denied that children, before they reach the years of understanding, can be saved by receiving baptism. So great was this man's influence that the whole congregations left the Romish churches and joined with him."[6]

Let me here give the quote from Wall that Ford probably referred to. Please remember that William Wall is the supposed champion (?) of infant baptism among the Pedobaptists (baby baptizers). Wall writes: "Now because I take this Peter Bruis (or Bruce perhaps his name was) and Henry to be the first antipaedobaptist preachers that ever set up a church or society of men holding that opinion against infant-Baptism, and rebaptizing such as had been baptized in infancy...."[7] This takes them a long way toward Baptists.

Historians Say the Henricians Were Baptists

"It does not seem open to reasonable doubt, therefore, that Henry of Lausanne, like Peter of Bruys and the Waldenses, taught that only believers should be baptized, and that the baptism of unconscious babes is a travesty upon the baptism of the New Testament."[8]

John T. Christian, Sir William Jones, David Benedict, G. H. Orchard, J. M. Cramp, Richard Cook and almost all of the historians outside Baptist ranks, identify the Henricians and the Petrobrusians together. Please see our chapter on the Petrobrusians for more of their doctrinal belief.

Persecution

It has been our thesis in this Notebook that those holding Baptist beliefs have always been persecuted by those of the Catholic faith. The Henricians are no exception. William Jones tells of Henry's death. "At Toulouse, he was warmly opposed by the great St. Bernard, that luminary of the Catholic Church, who though he wrote against them with great bitterness, is nevertheless constrained to admit that Henry was a learned man, and greatly respected by his numerous followers. The latter, however, to avoid his fury, was compelled to save himself by flight. He was nevertheless seized in his retreat, and carried before Pope Eugenius III, who assembled a council at Rheins, in which he presided in person, and having received a number of accusations against Henry, committed him in the year 1158 to a close prison, in which he soon ended his days."[9]

Dear reader, this might be our end had not our Baptist forefathers brought religious liberty to this great country in which we live.

NOTES ON CHAPTER 13

1 *The History of the Baptists, Volume 1, page 288.*
2 *The History of the Baptists, Volume 1, page 289.*
3 *The History of the Baptists, Volume 1, page 289.*
4 *A Manual of Church History, Volume 1, page 561.*
5 *A Short History of the Baptists, pages 117-118.*
6 *The Origin of the Baptists, pages 53-55.*
7 *History of Infant Baptism, Volume 2, page 273.*
8 *A Short History of the Baptists, by Henry Vedder, page 118.*
9 *History of the Christian Church, page 277.*

Chapter 14

THE ARNOLDISTS

The name "Arnoldists" comes from a man named Arnold. He was born in Brescia (of Italy) but the date is unknown. He was executed by the Roman church in Rome, in 1155 A.D. After his death his followers were called "Arnoldists." Some of the historians believe he never separated from the Roman church and therefore was a reformer. Others believe he did and therefore was a Baptist. I cannot tell but do believe that many of his followers did separate from Rome and became Baptists. You judge the matter righteously.

Many traits belong to the Baptists. True Baptists, by whatever name they may be called, have always had as a trait, a love for religious liberty. We and our ancestors have always believed that the government should not control the churches. We have also held that the government should not be a church government, as such. More than any one man in the twelfth century, Arnold of Brescia loved religious freedom. It would be easy to see that many Baptists would espouse this cause. It seems probable that they also were responsible for the views he held.

Orchard's Sketch of Arnold of Brescia

All of the church historians give nearly the same account of Arnold, quoting the same sources. At this point let us look at Orchard's account:

"A reformer now appeared in Italy, and one who proved himself a powerful opponent to the church of Rome, and who in fortitude and zeal was inferior to no one bearing that name, while in learning and talents he excelled most. This was ARNOLD OF BRESCIA; a man allowed to have been possessed of extensive erudition, and remarkable for his austerity of manners; he traveled into France in early life, and became a pupil of the renowned Peter Aberlard. On leaving this school, he returned into Italy, and assumed the habit of a monk, began to propagate his opinions in the streets of Brescia, where he soon gained attention. He pointed his zeal at the wealth and luxury of the Roman clergy. The eloquence of Arnold aroused the inhabitants of Brescia. They revered him as the apostle of religious liberty, and rose in rebellion against the bishops. The church took an alarm at his bold attacks; and in a council (1139,) he was condemned to perpetual silence. Arnold left Italy, and found an asylum in the Swiss canton of Zurich. Here he began his system of reform, and succeeded for a time, but the influence of Bernard made it necessary for him to leave the canton. This bold man now hazarded the desperate experiment of visiting Rome, and fixing the standard of rebellion in the very heart of the capitol. In this measure, he succeeded so far as to occasion a change of the government, and the clergy experienced for ten years a reverse of fortune, and succession of insults from the people. The pontiff struggled hard, but in vain, to maintain his ascendancy. He at length sunk under the pressure of the calamity. Successive pontiffs were unable to check his popularity. Eugenius III withdrew from Rome, and Arnold, taking advantage of his absence, impressed on the minds of the people the necessity of setting bounds to clerical authority; but the people, not being prepared for such liberty, carried their measures to the extreme, abused the clergy, burnt their property, and required all ecclesiastics to swear to the new constitution. "Arnold," says Gibbon, "presumed to quote the declaration of Christ, that his kingdom was not of this world. The abbots, the bishops, and the pope himself, must renounce their state, or their salvation." The people were brave, but ignorant of the nature, extent, and advantages of a reformation. The people imbibed, and long retained the color of his opinions. His sentiments also were influential on some of the clergy in the Catholic church. He was not devoid of discretion, he was protected by the nobles and the people, and his services to the cause of freedom; his eloquence thundered over the seven hills. He showed how strangely the clergy in vice had degenerated from the primitive times of the church. He confined the shepherd to the spiritual government of his flock. It is from the year 1144, that the establishment of the senate is dated, as the glorious era, in the acts of the city. Arnold maintained his station above ten years, while two popes, either trembled in the Vatican, or wandered as exiles in adjacent cities. "The wound appeared unto death," but the pope having mustered his troops, and placing himself at their head, soon became possessed of his official dignity. Arnold's friends were numerous, but a sword was no weapon in the articles of his faith.

In 1155, this noble champion was seized, crucified, and burnt. His ashes were thrown into the river. "The clergy triumphed in his death; with his ashes, his sect was dispersed; his memory still lives in the minds of the Romans." Thus, the deadly wound was healed. Though no corporeal relic could be preserved to animate his followers, the efforts of Arnold in civil and religious liberty were cherished in the breasts of the future reforming spirits, and inspired those mighty attempts, in WICKLIFFE, HUSS, and others."

His memory was long and fondly cherished by his countrymen, and his tragical end occasioned deep and loud murmurs; it was regarded as an act of injustice and cruelty, the guilt of which lay upon the pope and his clergy, who had been the occasion of it. The disciples of Arnold; who were numerous, obtained the name of ARNOLDISTS; these separated from the communion of the church of Rome, and long continued to bear their testimony against its numerous abuses."[1]

With his love for liberty all Baptists will agree. That the corruption of the Roman popes and clergy was great we also agree. That this man was a great man and an able man we all agree.

Was Arnold a Baptist?

William Wall writes: "Also the Lateran council under Innocent II, 1139, did condemn Peter Bruis, and Arnold of Brescia, who seems to have been a follower of Bruis, for rejecting infants' baptism."[2]

William Jones quotes Dr. Allix: "But there was a still more heinous thing laid to his charge, which was this: He was unsound in his judgment about the sacrament of the altar and infant baptism - (in other words, he rejected the popish doctrine of transubstantiation and the baptism of infants)."[3]

Comments here seem appropriate. If Wall is correct in saying Arnold was a disciple of Peter de Bruys, then certainly he was a Baptist, or held many of their views for Peter was a Baptist. The fact that Arnold rejected the popish fable of transubstantiation and the evil doctrine of infant baptism would move him deeply into the Baptist camp.

Orchard quotes St. Bernard, the Catholic, against Arnold: "The sentiments of Arnold on the ordinance is thus established, Bernard, whose influence occasioned Arnold's leaving Zurich, accuses his followers of mocking at infant baptism. He also received a like accusation from Evervimus, in Germany, who said the Arnoldists condemn the (catholic) sacraments, particularly baptism, which they administer only to the adult. They do not believe infant baptism, alleging that place of the gospel, whoever shall believe and be baptized shall be saved."[4] (Sounds Baptistic to me)!

S. H. Ford comments about Arnold: "He was a Baptist. For holding just what Baptists now hold, and for no other charge, he was arrested, condemned, crucified, and then burned, and his ashes thrown into the Tiber. The Arnoldists, the Henricians, and Petrobrusians we have found, and by their enemies, showed them to be Baptists."[5]

John T. Christian writes of the Arnoldists: "By the year 1184 the Arnoldists were termed Albigenses, a little later they were classed as Waldenses. Derckhoff, one of the German writers on the Waldenses affirms: There was a connection between the Waldenses and the followers of Peter de Bruys, Henry of Lausanne and Arnold of Brescia, and they finally united in one body about 1130 as they held common views."[6]

Persecuted

We conclude our study of the Arnoldists with a quote from Thieleman J. van Braght that deals with the doctrine of the Arnoldists and Arnold's martyrdom:

ARNOLD, A LECTOR AT BRESCIA, AFTER MUCH
PERSECUTION, BURNT AT ROME, FOR HIS VIEWS AGAINST
INFANT BAPTISM, THE MASS, ETC., A. D. 1145

"In our account of those who opposed infant baptism, the twelfth century, we made mention, for the year 1139, of one Arnold, a lector at Brescia, in Italy, and stated, that, having been instructed by Peter Abelard, he, besides the doctrine he maintained against the mass and transubstantiation, also taught against infant baptism; on account of which Pope Innocent II commanded him to be silent. Thereupon he fled into Germany or Switzerland, where for a time he continued to teach. Thence, after the death of the aforesaid pope, he came to Rome. But obtaining there an incredible number of followers, and being severely persecuted by the Popes Eugenius and Adrian, he fled to the Emperor Frederick Barbarossa, who delivered him into the hands of the pope; and thus he finally, at Rome, placed to the stake, burnt to ashes, and the ashes thrown into the Tiber, lest the people should show him honor. It is recorded that this occurred A. D. 1145, after he had, as is reckoned, strenuously maintained the above doctrine for about six years.

Abraham Mellinus, writing of the belief of Arnold, says: "He also taught quite differently concerning the sacrament of the altar, and (notice), of infant baptism, from that which was taught in the Roman church at that time. He doubtless, in this respect, held the views of Peter de Bruis and Henry of Toulouse (of whom we shall speak afterwards), rejecting transubstantiation, and denying that the mass is a sacrifice for the living and the dead, and that (notice again) either baptism or the faith of others saves infants."

NOTE: Abraham Mellinus, who states this concerning the belief of Arnold, was a preacher of the Calvinistic church, in St. Anthony's Polder, and, consequently, himself an advocate of infant baptism. Nevertheless, he distinctly says of Arnold, whom he recognized as a pious martyr, that he taught quite differently concerning infant baptism, and also that this baptism and the faith of others do not save children, etc., the opposite of which the Romanists maintained."[7]

Notes on Chapter 14

1 A Concise History of Baptists, pages 148-152.
2 The History of Infant Baptism, Volume 2, page 261.
3 History of the Christian Church, page 280.
4 A Concise History of the Baptists, pages 152-153.
5 The Origin of the Baptists, pages 57-58.
6 A History of the Baptists, Volume 1, page 67.
7 Martyrs Mirror, page 292.

Chapter 15

THE WALDENSES

Here is a group of our ancestors about which we have much information. We possess some of their writings and their confessions of faith. Their story is one of great blessings and great persecutions.

Most of our historians write about the Waldenses and the Albigenses together. William Nevin writes: "We shall consider these two sects together because they are inseparable, both as to their origin, and their doctrines."[1] We will treat them separately in this Notebook, though I believe them to be the same in origin and doctrine.

Their Name

Mosheim and others think they took their name from Peter Waldus, a rich merchant of the city of Lyons. He did become one of them but they did not take their name from him. Robert Robinson gives the following account of the name Waldenses: "From the Latin vallis came the English valley, the French and Spanish valle, the Italian valdesi, the low Dutch valleye, the provencal vaux, vaudois, the ecclesiastical vallenses, valdenses, ualdenses, and waldenses. The words simply signify vallies, inhabitants of vallies and no more."[2]

The Novatians, Donatists, Paulicians and many others had suffered severe persecution from the Roman Empire and the developing

Roman Catholic Church in previous centuries. Of those persecuted, it would be natural that they flee for refuge to the mountains and vallies of the Pyrenees and the Alps. Here they would join together for they believed the same doctrines and were persecuted by the same Dragon. They took the name Waldenses after the valleys in which they dwelt. Sometimes the Waldenses were called by other names which we shall presently see.

Their Antiquity

Their antiquity proves they did not take their name from Peter Waldus (Waldo). In their own writings they claimed linage all the way back to Christ and His apostles. At this time I would like to quote from one of their historians, Samuel Morland. His book was first published in 1658 A. D. Its republication is a blessing for Baptist historical studies today. It is written in the old English and therefore most will not put forth the effort to read it. Our quotes here will be in modern English.

"Again it is as manifest, and necessarily follows, that the Waldenses who escaped the Massacres in France, in the year 1165, and came from thence into the valleys of Piemont (Piedmont), were not the first Founders of that Religion, but rather that they joined themselves to those their faithful Brethren, for the better fortifying and mutual edification of each other's faith, just as those other Waldenses did, who having recourse to Bohemia, closed with the faithful Professors of the Greek Church there, who retained the ancient and true Religion; (note the Papal). Neither is it at all probable, that it could be otherwise; for the Waldenses knew right well, that the seat of their chief Adversary was in Italy; and therefore they would not have been so void of all sense and common prudence, as to have undertaken so long and tedious a Journey over the Alps, had they not been well assured that the Natives of those Valleys who professed the same Religion with them, would receive them and embrace them as their Brethren. D'Aubigne, a very judicious Historian seems to be clearly of this opinion. And Mr. Perrin, among his other Manuscripts, makes mention of a certain Epistle of the Waldenses, inscribed, an Epistle to the most severe King Lancelau, the Dukes, Barons, and most ancient Nobility of the Realm. The little troop of Christians falsely called by the name of poor people of Lions or Waldenses. By which it is most evident, that they had not their original from the said Waldo, but that this was a mere nick-name or reproachful term put upon them by their Adversaries, to make the world believe, that their Religion was but a Novelty, or a thing of yesterday."[3]

The underlining in this quote is by me. The Waldenses existed hundreds of years before Waldo. They were made up of brethren and sisters who fled into the wilderness to escape the Dragon's persecution. There the mountains protected them and they flourished. They believed their own origin was with Christ and the Apostles. Hear Morland again: "The professors of the Reformed Religion may clap their hands forever against all the Disciples of the Church of Rome, and say, that they are now able manifestly and undeniably to probe and make good the continual Succession of their Religion from the days of Christ and His Apostles down to this present age."[4]

Historical Testimony

A. W. Mitchell, Presbyterian, gives the following about the origin of the Waldenses: "Romish historians as far back as the year A. D. 1250, represented them as the oldest sect of heretics, though unable to tell when or how their heresy began. Their own account of the matter uniformly has been that their religion has descended with them from father to son by uninterrupted succession from the time of the apostles. There certainly is no improbability in the conjecture that the gospel was preached by some of those early missionaries who carried Christianity into Gaul. The common passage from Rome to Gaul at that time lay directly through the Cottian Alps, and Gaul we know received the gospel early in the second century at the latest, probably before the close of the first century. If the apostle Paul ever made that 'journey into Spain' (Romans 15:28) which he speaks of in his epistle to the Romans, and in which he proposed to go by way of Rome, his natural route would have been in the same direction, and it is not impossible that his voice was actually heard among those retired valleys. The most common opinion among Protestant writers is, that the conversion of the Waldenses was begun by some of the very early Christian missionaries, perhaps by some of the Apostles themselves, on their way to Gaul, and that it was completed and the churches more fully organized by a large influx of Christians from Rome, after the first general persecution under Nero. The Christians of Rome, scattered by this terrible event, would naturally flee from the plain country to the mountains, carrying with them the gospel and its institutions."[5]

The same author quotes from the book Glorious Recovery by the Waldenses of Their Valleys by Henry Arnaud, one of the most intelligent of the Waldensian pastors. 'Neither has their church ever been reformed, whence arises its title of evangelistic. The Waldenses are in fact descended from those refugees from Italy, who, after St. Paul had there preached the gospel, abandoned their beautiful country, and fled, like the woman mentioned in the Apocalypse, to these wild mountains, where they have to this day, handed down the gospel from father to son, in the same purity and simplicity as it was preached by St. Paul.' This is not following fables, for there is nothing in the relation either improbable or absurd. When the Christians at Rome were bound to stakes, covered with pitch, and burnt in the evenings to illuminate the city, it is wonderful, if the glare of such fires should induce those yet at liberty, to betake themselves for shelter, to the almost inaccessible valleys of the Alps, and to the clefts of the rocks, trusting to that God in whose hands are the deep places of the earth, and considering that the strength of hills is his?"[6]

Waldenses by Various Names

These Mountain and Valley dwellers are called by various names in the history books but they were all Waldenses or ancient Baptists. Let us here look at another extract from Samuel Morland: "Thus those who escaped the Massacres in France, were by the popish party surnamed either according to the places where they inhabited, or the chief of their Leaders; for example, from Waldo, a Citizen of Lyons, they were named Waldenses, and from the Country of Albie, Albigenses. And because those who did adhere to the doctrine of Waldo came out of Lyons, naked and stript of all their Goods and Estates, they were in derision, styled, The Poor of Lyons. In Dauphine they were nicknamed in mockery Chaignards. And for as much as part of them went over the Alps, they were called Tramontani. In England they were known by the name of Lollards, from one Lollard, who was one of their Chief Instructors in that Isle. In Provence they were usually termed Siccars, from a vulgar word then in use, which signified Cutpurses. In Italy they had been given the title of Fraticelli, or Men of the Brotherhood, because they lived together like Brethren. In Germany, they were named Gazares, a word which signifies execrable, and wicked in the highest degree. In Flanders they went under the name Turlepins, that is to say, Men inhabiting with, or companions of Wolves, because those poor people were oft times constrained in the heat of persecution, to inhabit the Woods and Deserts, amongst wild and savage beasts. Sometimes to render them more execrable, their Adversaries borrowed the names of several Heretics to brand them with. Thus for as much as they made profession of purity in their Life and Doctrine; they were called Cathares, that is, Puritans. And because they denied the Host which the Priest holds up at Mass, to be God, they were called Arrians, as those who denied the Divinity of the eternal Son of God. And because they maintained that the Authority of Kings and Emperors of the World did not depend upon the Jurisdiction of the Pope, they were called Manichai, as men asserting two first Principles. And for such like causes as these they were surnamed Gnostics, Calaphrygians, Adamites, and Apostolicks. Yea sometimes their Adversaries were outrageous, Matthew Paris calls them Ribaux, that is, Rogues, Rascals, Scoundrels, Varlets, or base Fellows. The author of the Thresor des Histories, calls them Bougres, that is Buggerers or Sodomites. Rubis reports, that the word Sorcerer was in those days expressed by the term Waldenses."[7]

Another Word on Origin

One of the most touching books in my library is called Bright Lights in Dark Times. The author of the book is not listed. It is a brief book telling of the Waldenses. It tells of their origin, their valleys, their life and testimony in those valleys and of their persecutions. I should like to quote here from that book on the origin of the Waldenses.

"The origin of the Waldenses, like those of all distant objects, remains in some obscurity. Various opinions have been advanced by their historians, some contending for, and others against, a great antiquity. The former endeavor to prove that a separate church has existed in the Alpine valleys from the earliest ages of Christianity, while the latter will not admit an earlier origin than the eleventh of twelfth century."

"History and tradition alike, however, support the opinion that an almost uninterrupted testimony has been maintained, and handed down from primitive times. 'With the dawn of history,' observes an English historian, 'we of the Alps, where they still exist under the ancient name of the Vaudois, who by the light of the New Testament, saw the extraordinary contract between the purity of primitive times and the vices of the gorgeous hierarchy which surrounded them.' As throwing some light on their early conversion to Christianity, another writer says: 'Traces still exist of the Roman road which crossed the Cottian Alps, and extended from Milan to Boulogne, being the usual thoroughfare through which the Roman legions traveled from Italy to Gaul and Britain. While noticing their progress, in reading history, let it be remembered that the same road was probably the means of conveying many who brought glad tidings, and published the gospel of peace to the dwellers in the mountains and elsewhere. The famous city of Lyons, in the South of France, contained a community of Christians, as early as the second or third century; their bishop was Ireneaus, the pupil of Polycarp, himself the pastor of the church at Smyrna, and the disciple of St. John. It is not improbable that he was the instrument of converting the simple mountaineers from Paganism

- Tradition also speaks of St. Paul as having traveled in this direction towards Spain, preaching to the inhabitants.'"

"The Vaudois themselves have always maintained that the religion they followed had been preserved from father to son, and from generation to generation, from all time immemorial. Their own historians too, are of the same opinion. 'The Vaudois of the Alps,' writes one of the latest, 'are according to our belief the primitive church preserved in theses valleys.'"

"Thus we have abundant testimony in favor of a very early origin: let us now look for a moment at what is stated by those who hold a contrary opinion. These are for the most part, Romish writers who appear anxious to prove that the Waldenses were merely a sect, which sprang up about the close of the twelfth century. Peter Waldo - the merchant Reformer of Lyons, as he was called - being their founder. There appears but little more reason for connecting Peter Waldo with the origin of the Waldenses than the similarity of names, which, however, is no more than a coincidence. 'The appellation,' says Dr. Gilly in his Waldensan Researchers 'of Valdesi in Italian, Vaudois in French, and Waldensian in English church history, means neither more nor less than men of the valleys.'"

"We may easily understand why the Roman Church should attempt to cast doubt on the antiquity of the Waldensian Church. To admit it was to acknowledge that a distinct church, separate from 'the one, only, apostolic church' (as she proudly boasted) had existed and flourished from all time, thus yielding what she most of all desired, complete and universal supremacy."[8]

Concluding Remarks

It can be seen by this, why the Protestant writers desire to find a founder for Baptist churches during the Reformation. If true churches existed (and they did) at the time of the Protestant Reformation, then the Reformers did not go far enough. They should have 'come out of the

Roman church' and sought membership in the true churches. Since they did not do that they must find a late date for the origin of the Baptists.

Since the Waldenses were Baptists (for the most part) we date our origin with them. Since we have dealt at length with the origin of the Waldenses, it remains in the pages ahead, to examine their doctrines and their persecutions to determine if they were our Baptist ancestors. They really were as we shall see.

NOTES ON CHAPTER 15

1 *Alien Baptism and the Baptists, page 55.*
2 *Ecclesiastical Researches, pages 302.*
3 *The History of the Evangelical Churches of the Valleys of Piedmont, page 12.*
4 *The History of the Evangelical Churches of the Valleys of Piedmont, page 14.*
5 *The Waldenses, pages 27-28.*
6 *The Waldenses, pages 28-29.*
7 *The History of the Evangelical Churches of the Valleys of Piedmont, pages 12-13.*
8 *Bright Lights in Dark Times, pages 11-14.*

Chapter 16

THE WALDENSES CONTINUED

In the preceding chapter we saw something of the Waldenses as to their origin, place and what they believed about their ancestry back to Christ and the apostles. They definitely believed themselves to have been of apostolic origin.

In this chapter we would like to consider their beliefs. It is belief or doctrine by which we identify our Baptist ancestors. We again issue caution. Not all the Waldenses believed alike just as not all Baptists believe alike. We only claim that among the ancient Waldenses we find the true churches of our Lord Jesus Christ.

Another caution must be kept in mind. Their enemies wrote much against them. That writing is often unfavorable. As Edward Overbey writes, "The information concerning them is small and often written by their enemies. Their enemies didn't understand their beliefs and usually wrote from a prejudiced viewpoint."[1] Let us proceed to see some of their doctrine.

Waldenses Not Protestants

One of the leading doctrines of Baptists is their claim not to be Protestants. This is the claim of Historical Baptists. Today many Southern Baptists speak of their being the largest Protestant denomination in America. Historical Baptists believe no such thing. In this, the Waldenses are in accord.

Let us quote two Presbyterian writers. First, A.W. Mitchell writes: "The Waldenses disclaim the name 'Protestant.' They say they never came out from Rome, inasmuch as they were never in Rome."[2] His writing is about the Waldenses after the Reformation had begun.

The next quote comes from James Wharey and tells of the origin of the name 'Protestant' as a group. "In a diet of the German states assembled at Spire in 1526, it was decided that a petition should be presented to the emperor, to call a general council without delay; and, in the mean time, that each one should be left to manage the religious concerns of his own territory, in his own way. In a diet at the same place, in 1529, this decree was revoked, and all changes in the public religion were declared to be unlawful, until the decision of a general council should take place. Against this proceeding, the elector of Saxony, the landgrave of Hesse, and other patrons of the Reformation, entered their protest, and appealed to the emperor, and to a future council. Hence originated the name of Protestants, borne from this time onward by those who forsook the communion of the church of Rome."[3] Since the Waldenses existed long, long before this they could not be Protestants.

The Antichrist

"A Treatise concerning Antichrist, Purgatory, the Invocation of the Saints, and the Sacraments" is a writing of the Waldenses that has been preserved for us. John Paul Perrin, one of the Waldensian historians, dates this work at 1120 A. D., about fifty years before Peter Waldo. Many historians attribute this writing to Peter de Bruys. What it says about Antichrist sounds very Baptistic to me. Let us lift an extract from it out of the history by William Jones.

"Antichrist is a falsehood, or deceit varnished over with the semblance of truth, and of the righteousness of Christ and His spouse, yet in opposition to the way of truth, righteousness, faith, hope, charity, as well as to moral life. It is not any particular person ordained to any degree, or office, or ministry, covering and adorning itself with a show of beauty and piety, yet very unsuitable to the church of Christ, as by the names, and offices, the scriptures, and the sacraments, and various other things, may appear. The system of iniquity thus completed with its ministries, great and small, supported by those who are induced to follow it with an evil heart and blind-fold – this is the congregation, which taken together, comprises what is called Antichrist or Babylon, the fourth beast, the whore, the man of sin, the son of perdition. His ministers are called false prophets, lying teachers, the ministers of darkness, the spirit of error, the apocalyptic whore, the mother of harlots, clouds without water, trees without leaves, twice dead, plucked up by the roots, wandering stars, Balaamites and Egyptians."

"He is termed Antichrist because, being disguised under the names of Christ and of His church and faithful members, he oppugns the salvation which Christ wrought out, and which is truly administered in His church –and of which salvation believers participate by faith, hope, and charity. Thus he opposes the truth by the wisdom of this world, by false religion, by counterfeit holiness, by ecclesiastical power, by secular tyranny, and by the riches, honours, dignities with the pleasures and delicacies of the world. It should therefore be carefully observed, that Antichrist could not come, without a concurrence of all these things, making up a system of hypocrisy and falsehood –there must be, the wise of this world, the religious orders, the Pharisees, ministers, and doctors: the secular power, with the people of the world, all mingled together. For although Antichrist was conceived in the times of the apostles, he was then in his infancy, imperfect and unformed, rude, unshapen, and wanting utterance. He then wanted those hypocritical ministers and human ordinances, and the outward show of religious orders which he afterwards obtained. As he was destitute of riches and other endowments necessary to allure to himself ministers for his service, and to enable him to multiply, defend, and protect his adherents, so he also wanted the secular power to force others to forsake the truth and embrace falsehood. But growing up in his members, that is, in his blind and dissembling ministries, and in worldly subjects, he at length arrived at full maturity, when men, whose hearts were set upon this world, blind in the faith, multiplied in the church, and by the union of church and state, got the power of both in their hands."[4]

This is a very Baptistic teaching, among most, before the influence of Plymouth Brethren interpretation of prophecy came on the scene. This Antichrist treatise is one of the most interesting documents I've ever read.

Confession of Faith

Samuel Morland gives an ancient Confession of Faith of the Waldenses which he dates at 1120 A. D. He also points out that this was 400 years before Luther or Calvin. I would like to give that Confession here with omissions that we will speak about. Only the names of the Books of the Bible are omitted.

Article 1

"We believe and firmly hold all that which is contained in the twelve Articles of the symbol, which is called the Apostle's Creed, accounting for Heresy whatsoever is disagreeing, and not consonant to the said 12 Articles."

Article 2

"We do believe that there is one God, Father, Son, and Holy Spirit."

Article 3

"We acknowledge for the Holy Canonical Scriptures, the Books of the holy Bible, viz..." (At this point in the article are listed the same books that are found in our Bible today. The article also lists the Apocryphal books and remarks the following about them): "Here follow the Books Apocryphal, which are not received of the Hebrews. But we read them…for the instruction of the People, not to confirm the Authority of the Doctrine of the Church."

Article 4

"The Books above said teach this, that there is one God, Almighty, all wise, and all good, who has made all things by His goodness, For He formed Adam in His own image and likeness, but that by the envy of the Devil, and the disobedience of the said Adam, Sin has entered into the World, and that we are sinners in Adam and by Adam."

Article 5

"That Christ was promised to our Fathers who received the Law, that so knowing by the Law their sin, unrighteousness and insufficiency, they might desire the coming Christ to satisfy for their sins, and accomplish the Law by Himself."

Article 6

"That Christ was born in the time appointed by God the Father. That is to say, in the time all iniquity abounded, and not for the cause of good works, for all were sinners: but that He might show us grace and mercy, as being faithful."

Article 7

"That Christ is our life, truth, peace, and righteousness, as also our Pastor, Advocate, Sacrifice, and Priest, Who died for the salvation of all those that believe, and is risen for our justification."

Article 8

"In like manner, we firmly hold, that there is no other Mediator and Advocate with God the Father, save only Jesus Christ. And as for the Virgin Mary, that she was holy, humble, and full of grace: and in like manner do we believe concerning all the other Saints, viz. that being in Heaven, they wait for the Resurrection of their Bodies at the Day of Judgment."

Article 9

"We believe that after this life, there are only two places, the one for the saved, and the other for the damned, the which two places we call Paradise and Hell, absolutely denying that Purgatory invented by Antichrist, and forged contrary to the truth."

Article 10

"We have always accounted as an unspeakable abomination before God, all those Inventions of men, namely, the Feasts and the Vigils of Saints, the Water which they call holy. As likewise to abstain from Flesh upon certain days, and the like; but especially the Masses."

Article 11

"We esteem for an abomination and as Anti-Christian, all those human Inventions which are a trouble or prejudice to the liberty of the Spirit."

Article 12

"We do believe that the Sacraments are signs of the holy thing, or visible forms of the invisible grace, accounting it good that the faithful sometimes use the said signs or visible forms, if it may be done. However, we believe and hold, that the abovesaid faithful may be saved without receiving the signs aforesaid, in case they have no place nor any means to use them."

Article 13

"We acknowledge no other Sacraments but Baptism and the Lord's Supper."

Article 14

"We ought to honor the secular powers, by subjection, ready obedience, and paying of Tributes."[5]

As Baptists of today most of us are able to accept this Confession of Faith. We may not totally agree with the wording of the Apostles'

Creed as to the Church and Christ going into Hell but even those phrases could be interpreted to our satisfaction. We would use the word "ordinance" instead of "sacrament." The word "sacrament" today has the idea of a means of grace. The Waldenses used it in the same meaning as we use "ordinance." So, all in all, this is a Baptist confession.

What Say the Historians

Edward Overbey: "The historical evidence shows that they hold to the Bible as their final authority for faith and practice and that the salvation was wholly of grace through faith in Christ as Saviour. They also believed that the ordinances were only baptism and the Lord's Supper and they were only symbolic, that only believers should be baptized, that baptism was by immersion, and that salvation and baptism were the requirements for church membership."[6]

Henry Vedder: He is quoting from Roman Catholic writers who accuse the Waldenses with error: "They (the Waldenses) assert that the doctrine of Christ and the apostles, without the decrees of the church, suffices for salvation... They say holy Scripture has the same effect in the vulgar tongue as in the Latin. Everything preached which is not to be proved by the text of the Bible they hold to be fable... They say that a man is then truly for the first time baptized when he is brought into their heresy. But some say that baptism does not profit little children, because they are never able actually to believe."[7]

We could go on multiplying from historians. Almost all of the church histories identify the Waldenses with the Novatians, Donatists, Paulicians, Petrobrussians, Henricians, and Ana-Baptists. Our Baptist ancestors were among the ancient Waldenses.

NOTES ON CHAPTER 16

1 *A Brief History of the Baptists, page 43.*
2 *The Waldenses, page 273.*
3 *Sketches of Church History, pages 234-235.*
4 *History of the Christian Church, pages 327-328.*
5 *History of the Evangelical Churches of the Valleys of the Piedmont, pages 30-34.*
6 *A Brief History of the Baptists, page 46.*
7 *A Short History of the Baptists, page 123.*

Chapter 17

THE WALDENSES CONCLUDED

Having received the history and doctrine of the ancient Waldenses, it remains now to study their persecution. Holding to the truth of God's Word is sure to bring persecution. No people, as a group, suffered more than the Waldenses. The Mother of Harlots made herself drunk with the blood of this noble people. Hunted and killed by the old Whore of Revelation, the ancient Waldenses gained a martyr's crown. Great will be their reward in heaven.

Milton's Poem

To pay tribute to the slain Waldenses, the blind Baptist poet, John Milton wrote the following poem:

> *"Avenge, O Lord, Thy slaughtered saints, whose bones*
> *Lie scattered on the Alpine mountains cold;*
> *E'en them, who kept Thy truth so pure of old,*
> *When all our fathers worshipped stocks and stones,*
> *Forget not: in Thy book record their groans,*
> *Who were Thy sheep, and in their ancient fold*
> *Slain by the bloody Piedmontese, that roll'd*
> *Mother with infant down the rocks. Their moans*
> *The values redoubled to the hills, and they*

To heaven. Their martyred blood and ashes sow
O'er all the Italian fields, where still doth sway
The triple tyrant; that from these may grow
An hundred-fold, who, having learnt Thy way,
Early may fly the Babylonian woe!"

How well did this ancestor describe our fore-fathers and their suffering at the hands of the Roman Catholic Church during those dark days. For many of you, reading this Notebook, it will be hard to believe what Satan, through his church, has done to the Baptists of old. It will be even harder for you to believe that they would do the same again should Providence allow it!

Loss of Houses and Goods

Thieleman J. van Braght has the following to say about the Catholics and their destroying the homes of the Waldenses and the confiscating of their goods. "Of the demolition of the houses of the Waldenses - the fifth chapter of the Council of Toulouse contains the following brief ecclesiastical ordinance respecting the demolition of the houses of the heretics, namely, of the Waldenses and Albigenses: 'We ordain that the houses in which a heretic is discovered, shall be razed to the ground, and the land or farm upon which a heretic is found, shall be confiscated.' Of the forfeiture of all their goods - In the 35th chapter of the Council of Beziers we read: 'Also the houses in which any heretic shall be found, living or dead, accused or condemned, being there with the knowledge or consent of the proprietors of said houses, provided such proprietors have attained their legal age, you shall cause to be demolished, and shall confiscate all the goods of those who live in them, unless they can legally prove or show their innocence or ignorance.'"[1]

For the Waldenses to legally prove anything was extremely difficult or impossible seeing the legal system was the tool of the Apostate Church of Satan.

Everywhere Persecuted

At this point I would like to give a few headlines from Martyrs Mirror by van Braght. These are found in the book on pages 330-333. Under each headline the writer describes what he has headlined. Every student of Baptist history should purchase this book and read it. "Many Persons Called Waldenses Martyred At Steyer, In Austria, And Great Numbers Of Them Burnt For Their Faith, At Zuidenity, In Poland, A. D. 1315." "Four Persons Called Brethren Of The Poor Life, Or Waldenses, Burnt For The Faith, At Marseilles, In France, A. D. 1317." "Persecution Of The Believers Called Waldenses, By Pope John XXII, A. D. 1319." "Persecution Unto Death Against The Believing Waldenses, In Bohemia And Poland; In Which Also One Echard Was Burnt For The Same Faith, A. D. 1330." "Persecution Of The Waldensian Brethren, In France, By Pope Urban VI, A. D. 1365." "Severe Persecution In Flanders, Artois, And Hainault, In Which Peronne Of Aubeton, A Pious Woman, Is Publicly Burnt For The Faith, About A. D. 1373." "Thirty-six Persons Called Waldenses, Burnt For The Faith, At Bingen, A. D. 1390." "Great Persecution Of The Believing Waldenses On The Baltic Sea; Four Hundred And Forty-three Of Them Severely Tortured And Put To Death, In The Mark And Pomerania, About A. D. 1390."

Many, many other such notations are found in the book, Martyrs Mirror. These are listed to show how severe and wide spread the persecutions were.

Persecution by Crusades

There are so many sources of information and descriptions of the persecutions that it is difficult to know what to include in our study. Rather than many quotes from different authors I wish to list a lengthy one from one book, Bright Lights in Dark Times.

"There were, however, during the thirteenth and fourteenth centuries, some detached instances of persecution, and one notably of a more general character, which happened at the close of the year 1400. We may notice this, as it will form a link between the great Albigensian crusade, and the first general Papal invasion of the valleys, of which we shall give a more particular account. "The scene of this catastrophe was the Valley of the Pragelas. It was the Christmas of 1400, and the inhabitants dreaded no attack, believing themselves sufficiently protected by the snows which then lay deep on their mountains. They were destined to experience that bitter fact that the rigors of the season had not quenched the fire of their persecutors' malice. An inquisitor named Borelli, at the head of an armed troop, broke suddenly into Pragelas, meditating the entire extinction of its population. The miserable inhabitants fled in haste to the mountains, carrying on their shoulders their old men, their sick and their infants, knowing what fate awaited them should they leave them behind. In their flight a great many were overtaken and slain. Nightfall brought them deliverance from the pursuit, but no deliverance from horrors not less dreadful. Without shelter, without food, the frozen snow around them, the winter's sky overhead, their sufferings were inexpressibly great. When morning broke, what a heart-rending spectacle did day disclose! Of the miserable group the hands and feet of many were frozen; while others were stretched on the snow, stiffened corpses. Fifty young children, some say eighty, were found dead with cold, some lying on the bare ice, others locked in the frozen arms of their mothers, who had perished on that dreadful night along with their babes. In the Valley of Pragelas, to this day, sire recites to son the tale of that Christmas tragedy."

We now pass on to the year 1487, the date of the first general crusade against the Waldenses. At length that lamp, which had burned uninterruptedly since primitive times, was to be extinguished. The mailed hand of the enemy was now about to fall and scatter, for a time at least, the testimony in the mountains. Since the sudden and barbarous attack related above the process of extermination had rather languished, and in consequence the Waldensian opinions were both taking deeper root, and at the same time spreading far and wide beyond the limits of the valleys. Alarmed at these rapid advances, Pope Innocent VIII, who then filled the Papal chair, determined by a combined and decisive effort, once and for ever, to root out the heretics and the vigor of his great namesake, Innocent III, and remembering no doubt how effectually that famous pontiff had swept away the heretics, from the plains of Dauphine and Provence, he resolved upon the same course.

Once more a crusade was to be preached; once more was Europe to witness the sad and humiliating spectacle of a host of ruffians let loose upon their fellow creatures, to pillage and ravage, and torture and slaughter at their will, and this, too, at the dictate of him who presumed to be Christ's vicar upon earth! The same infamous tactics were resorted to, the same horrible inducements again held out that had characterized the former crusade. Plenary pardon for all their sins, and unrestrained license upon the persons and promised to those who faithfully performed their part in this holy war. Once more thousands flocked to the banner of the Pope's legate, rejoiced to avail themselves of heaven on such easy means. What "dark times," indeed, were these, when men were induced to believe that their crimes could be expiated by the commission of more, and still darker ones!

And now all Europe rang with the din of preparation; bands of men from every country, in obedience to the Papal bull, marched towards the centre from which operations were to commence: "the only people," it is said, "left ignorant of the commotion it had excited, and the bustle of the preparation it had called forth, were those poor men on whom the terrible tempest was about to fall."

The joint army numbered about 18,000 regular soldiers, besides the thousands of ruffians already mentioned. This host was divided into two divisions, the one directing an attack from the French, the other on the Italian, side of the Alps; and so advancing, the one from the south-east, and the other from the north-west, to meet in the Valley of Angrogna, the centre of the territory, and there strike the final blow. We will follow first the progress of the

French division of this host, that which advanced against the Alps of Dauphine.

"This portion of the crusade," it is related, "was led by a daring and cruel man, skilled in such adventures, the Lord of La Palu. He ascended the mountains with his fanatics, and entered the Vale of Loyse, a deep gorge overhung by towering mountains. The inhabitants, seeing an armed force twenty times their number enter their valley, despaired of being able to resist them, and prepared for flight. They placed their old people and children in rustic carts, together with their domestic utensils, and such store of victuals as the urgency of the occasion permitted them to collect, and driving their herds before them, they began to climb the rugged sloped of Mount Pelvoux, which raises some six thousand feet over the level of the valley. They sang canticles as they climbed the steeps, which served at once to smooth their rugged path, and to dispel their terrors.

"About half-way up there is an immense cavern called Aigue-Froid, from the cold springs that rush out from its rocky walls. In front of the cavern is a platform of rock, where the spectator sees beneath him, only fearful precipices, which must be clambered over before one can reach the entrance of the grotto. Into this grotto, as into an impregnable castle, the Vaudois enter. Their women, infants, and old men they placed in the inner hall; their cattle and sheep they distributed along the internal cavities of the grotto. The able-bodied men posted themselves at the entrance. Having barricaded with huge stones both the doorway of the cave and the path that led to it, they deemed themselves secure. But a device of their pursuer rendered all these precautions vain. La Palu ascended the mountain on the other side, and approaching the cave from above, let down his soldiers by ropes from the precipice that overhangs the grotto. The platform in front then was secured by his soldiers. The Vaudois might have cut their ropes and defeated their foes as they were being lowered one by one, but the boldness of this maneuver would seem to have paralyzed them. They retreated into the cavern to find it their grave. La Palu saw the danger of permitting his men to follow them into the depths of their hiding place. He adopted the easier and safer method of piling up at the entrance all the wood he could collect, and setting fire to it. A huge volume of black smoke began to roll into the cave, leaving to the unhappy inmates the miserable alternative of rushing out and falling by the sword that waited for them, or of remaining in the interior to be stifled by the murky vapor. Some rushed out, and were massacred; but the greater part remained till death slowly approached them by suffocation. 'When the cave was afterwards examined,' says Muston, 'there were found in it 400 infants, suffocated in their cradles, or in the arms of their dead mothers. Altogether there perished in this cavern more than 3,000 Vaudois, including the entire population of Val Loyse.'"

Having distributed the property of these poor sufferers amongst the bands of ruffians and assassins that accompanied him, La Palu next advanced upon the neighboring valleys of Argentiere and Fraissiniere. But the inhabitants, learning the fate of their brethren, determined upon resistance, as therein only lay their chance of safety. Accordingly they barricaded the passes of the valleys, and showed such a front to the foe when he advanced that he relinquished the attempt there, and left them in peace.

But this wonderful deliverance was not vouchsafed to the dwellers in the Valley of Pragelas, the scene of the terrible tragedy of Christmas 1400. "Again," says the historian, "terror, mourning, and death were carried into it. The peaceful inhabitants, who were expecting no such invasion, were busy reaping their harvests, when this horde of assassins burst upon them. In the first panic they abandoned their dwellings and fled. Many were overtaken and slain; hamlets and whole villages were given to the flames; the caves in which multitudes sought refuge could not afford them any protection. The horrible barbarity of the Val Loyse was repeated in the Valley of Pragelas. Combustible materials were piled up, and fires kindled at the mouths of their hiding-places, and when extinguished all was silent within. Folding together in one motionless heap lay mother and babe, patriarch and stripling; while the fatal smoke, which had cast them into that deep sleep, was eddying along the roof, and slowly making its exit into the clear sunlit summer sky."[2]

NOTES ON CHAPTER 17

1 Martyrs Mirror, page 316.
2 Bright Lights in Dark Times, pages 49-56.

Chapter 18

THE ALBIGENSES

As has been stated elsewhere in this Notebook, the Albigenses and the Waldenses were the same people in doctrine and in origin. In this chapter we will note several historians' comments about them.

Origin

William Nevins writes: "On the French side of the Pyrenees was the little village of Abby in the province of Albigeois. Here came the Novatians and Donatists, and later the Paulicians, and later still, the Waldenses. But as they all held identical views, in opposition to the Roman Church, they mingled and blended into one harmonious whole, and became known as the Albigenses, from the town near which they lived, and then the name was given to others with like views that inhabited the surrounding provinces."[1]

Thomas Armitage writes: "They arose in Southern France early in the eleventh century and were first known as Publicani; but at last took their name from the city of Abbi, the center of the Albigeois district. They were first called Albigenses by Stephen Borbone, 1225."[2] That this is the origin of the name Albigenses is the testimony of all the historians.

Their Doctrine

Our Baptist historians are almost all agreed that the Albigenses were, in doctrine, much like the Baptists of today. Rather than quote them all, I will give here a section from W. A. Jarrel. He quotes from many of them.

"To the charge that the Albigenses held to Manichaeism, I reply: (1) By reminding the reader of Vedder's words beginning this article. (2) That, as they are identical with the Paulicians, the refutation of this charge in Chapter XI., is the refutation of this charge against the Albigenses. (3) To this I add the following: Robinson, one of the most careful and reliable historians, did not sufficiently credit that charge to affirm it. His cautious words are: "The Albigenses were Manichaeans, or nearly so," "Nearly so" is not "so." There are certain modified forms of Manichaeism which, while erroneous, would not unchurch any party. Mosheim says that those who held to Manichaeism held it "differently interpreted and modified by different doctors." Prof. Carl Schmidt says: "The representations which Roman Catholic writers, their bitter enemies, have given them, are highly exaggerated." Even admitting them slightly tainted with Manichaeism, since they lived in an age of little thought and learning, it would no more affect their claims to be churches of Christ than slight errors of the head, especially of the unlearned, now unchurch. (4) But there is no proof conclusive that the Albigenses were so much as tainted with Manichaeism. Wadington, speaking of the great Romish controversialists attempt to blacken their characters, (Bishop Bossuett) observes: "He has failed to prove their Manichaean doctrine."

.... He calls them indeed "new" Manichaeans and admits that 'they had softened some of their errors.' But they had parted with the characteristic error, or in fact they never held it." On p. 291 Wadington observes: "Manichaeism was the frightful term employed to express their delinquency; but it is more probable that their real offence was the adoption of certain mystical notions, proceeding, indeed, from the feelings of the most earnest piety, but too spiritual to be tolerated in that age in that church."

Though the charge that the Albigenses rejected marriage, baptism and the supper has been refuted in page 119, refuting the same charge against them under the name Paulicians, the readers will notice that these charges are, incidentally, further refuted in the following: The Encyclopedia Britannica says of them: "The statement that they rejected marriage, often made by the Roman Catholics, has probably no other foundation in fact than that they denied marriage as a sacrament; and many other statements of their doctrines must be received at least with suspicion, as coming from prejudiced and implacable opponents."

Alanus, speaking of the Albigenses, says: "They rejected infant baptism. It does not appear that they rejected either of the sacraments." Collier says: "They refused to own infant baptism." Brockett says: "Nothing is said of Hoveden of their rejection of the sacraments of baptism and the eucharist, which would certainly have been mentioned by so careful a writer as Hoveden, had it existed. Indeed, his strongest objection to them was their refusal to take an oath." Favin, a historian, is quoted as saying: "The Albigenses do esteem the baptizing of infants superstitious." Izam, the Troubadour, a Dominican persecutor of these heretics, says: "They admitted another baptism." Chassanion is quoted as saying: "I cannot deny that the Albigenses, for the greater part, were opposed to infant baptism; the truth is, they did not reject the sacraments as useless, but only as unnecessary to infants."

They had no Campbellism in them. As Armitage observes: "They rejected the Roman church traditions and ceremonies. They did not take oaths, nor believe in baptismal regeneration; but they were ascetic and pure in their lives; they also exalted celibacy." Their encouraging celibacy, as they believed in marriage, was probably for the reason Paul encouraged it temporarily, because of persecution being harder to endure in families than when single.

As refusing to take oaths was a practice of many of these ancient Baptists, I here stop to say: While that matter with Baptists is a matter of little importance, yet I believe they were, probably, nearer right than we are; for, while by "swear not at all" our Savior alluded to only profanity, yet, as Archbishop Whately observes, I believe that men who will tell a lie will swear one as readily, once the penalty is out of the way; hence, instead of taking an oath annex the penalty of swearing a lie to telling it in court.

In church government the Albigenses were Baptists. A historian says: "Their bards or pastors were every one of them heads of their churches, but they acted on nothing without the consent of the people and the clergy," i.e. the ministers who had charge of no church. "Deacons expounded the gospels, distributed the Lord's Supper, baptized, and sometimes had the oversight of churches, visited the sick and took care of the temporalities of the church." Chr. Schmidt says: "Their ritual and ecclesiastical organization were exceedingly simple."

This was so much the case that the Romish church, not seeing any church in so simple an organization, thought they had no churches, and Prof. Schmidt has, thereby, been misled into the same conclusion. In Chapter XI - noticing them as Paulicians - they were clearly proved to have been, in church government, Baptist.

The Albigenses were pure in their lives and a zealous people in good works. Carl Schmidt says of them: "Their severe moral demands made impression because the example of their preachers corresponded with their words. In a short time the Albigenses had congregations with schools and charitable institutions of their own... The Roman Catholic Church, so far as it still could be said to exist in the country, had become an object of contempt and derision. This state of affairs, of course, caused great alarm in Rome."

Thus, "the Albigensian heresy," as the Lord Macaulay observes, "brought about civilization, the literature, the national existence of the most opulent and enlightened part of the great European family."[3]

Their Persecution

The story of the crusades of the Catholic Church against the Albigenses is one of the darkest ever recorded in history. Adolf Hitler, in his personal hatred of the Jews was mild in his persecution of them compared to what the Roman Church did to the Albigenses and the Waldenses.

At this point we give the words of Thomas Armitage:

"One crusade succeeded another. Innocent III, offered the prelates and nobles all the blessings of the Church for the use of their sword and the possessions of the heretics as an additional reward. Their own prince, Count Raymond VI, was compelled to slaughter his subjects, and the pope summoned the King of Northern France with all his nobles to the same bloody work. Half a million men were gathered, four Archbishops joined the invaders with twelve bishops and countless nobles. Towns were sacked, seven castles surrendered to the pope, and five hundred villages, cities and fortresses fell."

Barons, knights, counts and soldiery flocked like eagles to the prey from all directions. Their superstition was fed by the promise of two years' remission of penance, and all the indulgences granted to the invaders of the Holy Sepulcher; and their cupidity was fired by the tender of the goods and lands of the heretics, as well as the right to reduce them to Mohammedan slavery. They followed the lead of Arnaud, the legate of the Holy See, bearing the cross and pilgrims' staves, from the adjacent countries, French, German, Flemish, Norman. They first attacked Beziers, which was strongly fortified and garrisoned; but it was taken by storm and thirty thousand were slain. Seven thousand had taken refuge in the Church of St. Magdalene, and the monk Peter tells us with the most ferocious coldness that they 'killed women and children, old men, young men, priests, all without distinction.' There were many Catholics in the town, and the 'Holy Legate' was asked how these should be spared, when he commanded: 'Kill them all, God will know his own!' Lest a heretic should escape they piled all in an indiscriminate heap, and the Chronicle of St. Denis gives the whole number as six thousand. After Beziers had fallen, July 22, 1209, Carcassone was invested. There Count Roger, the nephew of Raymond, was inveigled under the pretense of safe-conduct and a treating for peace out of the city into the enemies' camp and by treachery was made a prisoner as a heretic. When his men found their captain gone they retreated by a private passage, the great city fell, and its captain died in a dungeon, as the pope expresses it, 'miserably slain at the last.' The French barons agreed that any fortress which refused to surrender on demand, but resisted, should when captured find every man put to the sword in cold blood by the cross-bearers, that horror might appall every heart in the land. Their own historian says: 'They could not have dealt worse with them than they did; they massacred them all, even those who had taken refuge in the cathedral; nothing could save them, nor cross, nor crucifix, nor alters. The scoundrels killed the priests, the women, the infants, not one, I believe, escaped.' Eight hundred nobles were either hanged or hewn to pieces, and four hundred heretics were burnt in one pile.

The story of this murdered people for about half a century is heart-sickening in the extreme. They held many errors of the head, but no prince ever ruled over grander subjects. They were far advanced in refinement, and were high-toned in morality. Their record is the brightest, briefest and bloodiest in the annals of pious, persecuting deviltry. In begins in the middle of the twelfth century, and was blotted out before the middle of the thirteenth. It is a short, swift stream of gore mingling with their mountain torrents, but more romantic than their Alps. If the eternal snow and ice had not turned these eternally pale, the frozen steel of St. Dominic had chilled them forever, when the pravity of his infernal machine made them witnesses of a rushing destruction, without parallel in human villainy."[4]

Bright Lights in Dark Times

Thank you for your patience concerning the persecution of the Albigenses. I feel I must give one more example found in that great little book, Bright Lights in Dark Times.

"This was the famous crusade against the Albigenses, a people identical with the Waldenses in regard to the purity of their faith, but who dwelt on the French as the Waldenses on the Italian side of the Alps. History intimately connects them with the latter.

We shall now give some account of the progress of this crusade before entering upon the persecutions of the Waldenses of Piedmont, which began at a later date.

The mighty host thus gathered together was formed into three great armies, over each of which an archbishop, a bishop, and mitred abbot. But the soul of the movement was the notorious Simon de Montfort, one of the darkest names in the annals of persecution. The abbot Arnold (well called the dragon abbot) was the spiritual, as De Montfort was the military leader, of the hosts. And now they poured over the rich provinces of the Albigenses, 'Forward' was the cry of the holy abbot. You shall ravage every field, you shall slay every human being; strike and spare not. The measure of their iniquity is full, and the blessing of the Church is on your head." Thus commanded of the priest, the vast army marched through the land of vineyards, and of olive-yards, burning, slaying, ravaging as they went, the peasantry being ridden down and slaughtered in cold blood.

Little or no resistance could be offered in the open country, against such an overwhelming and infuriated host. But the great cities did not as readily submit to be butchered in cold blood. The inhabitants closed their gates on the approach of the crusaders and, when summoned, refused to surrender. The terrible fate of Beziers and Carcassonne, two of the principal cities of the Albigenses, is thus recorded: "The soldiers of the cross, the priests of the Lord," as they called themselves appeared before Beziers: which had been

198 BAPTIST HISTORY NOTEBOOK ~ BERLIN HISEL

well provisioned and garrisoned. The bishop of the place was in the army; he was allowed by Arnold to offer his advice to the people and recommend a surrender; "Renounce your opinions and save your lives: was the bishop's advice; but the Albigenses firmly replied that they would not renounce a faith which gave them the Kingdom of God and His righteousness. "Then," said Arnold, "there shall not be left one stone upon another; fire and sword shall devour men, women, and children." The town fell into the hands of the besiegers, and fearfully was the injunction obeyed. The knights, pausing at the gates, asked abbot how the soldiers were to distinguish Catholics from heretics; "Slay them all," he replied, "the Lord knoweth them that are His." The slaughter began: men, women and children, and clergy were massacred indiscriminately, while the bells of the cathedral were rung till the slaughter was complete. Trembling multitudes fled to the churches, in hope of finding a sanctuary within the hallowed walls; but not one human being was left alive. The vast population of Beziers, who so lately had thronged the streets and marts, now lay in slaughtered heaps. The numbers, thus slain are estimated variously from twenty to one hundred thousand. The city was given up to plunder, then set on fire."

Having thus completed their bloody work at Beziers, the crusade moved on to Carcassonne to inflict a similar vengeance on that devoted city. It is thus graphically described: "The terrible fate which had overtaken Beziers - in one day converted into a mound of ruins, dreary and silent as any on the plains of Chaldea - told the other towns and villages the destiny that awaited them. The inhabitants, terror stricken, fled to the woods and caves. Even the strong castles were left tenantless, deeming it vain to think of opposing so furious and overwhelming a host. Pillaging, burning, massacring, the crusaders advanced to Carcassonne. The city stood on the right bank of the Ande, its fortifications were strong, its garrison numerous and brave, and the young count Raymond Roger, was at their head. The assailants advanced to the walls, but met a stout resistance. The attack was again renewed, but was as often repulsed. Meanwhile, the forty days' service was at an end, and bands of crusaders, having fulfilled their term, and earned heaven, were departing to their homes. The Papal legate, seeing the host melting away, judged it perfectly right to call wiles to the aid of his arms. Holding out to Raymond Roger the hope of an honorable capitulation, the swearing to respect his liberty, Arnold induced the viscount to present himself at his tent. "The latter," says Sismondi, "profoundly penetrated with the maxim of Innocent III that to keep faith with those that have it not is an offence against the faith, caused the young viscount to be arrested, and all the knights who had followed him.

"When the garrison saw that their leader had been imprisoned, they resolved along with the inhabitants, to make their escape overnight by a secret passage known only to themselves. The crusaders were astonished on the morrow, when not a man could be seen upon the walls; and still more mortified was the Papal legate to find that his prey had escaped him, for his purpose was to make a bonfire of the city, with every man, woman and child within. But if this greater revenge was now out of his reach, he did not disdain a smaller one still in his power. He collected a body of some 450 persons, partly fugitives from Carcassonne whom he had captured, and partly the 300 knights who had accompanied the viscount; and of these he burned 400 alive, and the remaining 50 he hanged."

Such were the principal scenes enacted in this terrible crusade against the Albigenses, an inhuman wickedness without a parallel even in the history of crimes. While we blush to think the human heart capable of such enormities, we cannot forget that a just retribution surely awaits the guilty souls of those who committed them. How unspeakably solemn is that woe pronounced by our Lord, "Whoso shall offend one of these little ones which believe in me, it were better for him that a millstone were hanged about his neck, and that he were drowned in the depths of the sea" (Matthew XVIII. 6).[5]

NOTES ON CHAPTER 18

1 Alien Baptism and the Baptists, page 55.
2 History of the Baptists, Volume 1, page 278.
3 Baptist Church Perpetuity or History, pages 125-128.
4 History of the Baptists, Volume 1, pages 279-280.
5 Bright Lights in Dark Times, pages 41-45.

Chapter 19

THE ANABAPTISTS

The word Anabaptist signifies to re-baptize or baptize again. Those who baptized those who were sprinkled in infancy or those who baptized those from irregular churches were called, by their enemies, Anabaptists. They rejected this title of "Rebaptizers," saying that such persons as they baptized had never been baptized before. What they had received was not baptism, whatever else it was.

No doubt there were many who were called Anabaptists who were of a radical sort. With them we claim no kin as I am sure they would claim no kin with us. In a later chapter we will have something to say about the Anabaptists of Munster, etc., with which most of the Anabaptists of those days had no connection or sympathy. Yet within those called Anabaptists by their enemies, we find the true churches of our Lord Jesus Christ. They were our ancestors. In the process of time the "ana" was dropped and we became known as the Baptists.

Mosheim

There are a few quotes from John Lawrence Mosheim that have become quite famous among Baptists. He was a Lutheran historian and these quotes are important for that very reason.

"The true origin of that sect which acquired the denomination of Anabaptists by their administering anew the rite of baptism to those who came over to their communion, and derived that of Mennonites from the famous man to whom they owe the greatest part of their present felicity, is hidden in the depths of antiquity, and is, of consequence, extremely difficult to be ascertained."[1]

Several things appear evident from this quotation. The Anabaptists movement did not begin with the Reformation. Those who credit John Smythe (Smith) or others with the founding of the Anabaptists do not have the support of Mosheim. If their origin is hidden in the depths of antiquity this goes a long way toward the doctrine of perpetuity which true Baptists hold.

AGAIN

Mosheim, after stating that they were not entirely in error when they boasted of their decent from the Waldenses, Petrobrusians and other ancient sects, who are usually considered as witnesses of the truth in periods of darkness and superstition writes: "Before the rise of Luther and Calvin, there lay concealed, in almost all the countries of Europe, particularly in Bohemia, Maravia, Switzerland, and Germany, many persons, who adhered tenaciously to the following doctrine, which the Waldenses, Wickliffites, and Hussites, had maintained, some in a more disguised and others in a more open and public manner; viz. 'That the kingdom of Christ, or the visible church which He established upon earth, was an assembly of true and real saints, and ought therefore to be inaccessible to the wicked and unrighteous, and also exempt from all those institutions which human prudence suggests, to oppose the progress of iniquity, or to correct and reform transgressors.'"[2]

We are truly indebted to Mosheim for this statement. Before ever Luther or Calvin led in the Reformation, the Anabaptists were worshipping in the caves and dens of the earth, hiding from the Roman Catholic persecution. When the Reformation began, Anabaptist churches sprang up all over Europe overnight. Mosheim here explains how. They already existed, worshiping in secret. They just came out in the open when the Reformation took form. They claimed their origin with the Waldenses, Petrobrusians and others who claimed their origin with Christ and the apostles.

AGAIN

One more quote from Mosheim concerning the Anabaptist faith: "Notwithstanding all this, it is manifest, beyond all possibility of contradiction that the religious opinions which still distinguish the Mennonites from all other Christian communities, flow directly from the ancient doctrine of the Anabaptists concerning the nature of the church. It is in consequence of this doctrine, that they admit none to the sacrament of baptism, but persons who are come to the full use of their reason; because infants are incapable of binding themselves by a solemn vow to a holy life and it is altogether uncertain whether, in mature years they will be saints or sinners."[3]

The nature of the church has been the most distinguished mark of difference between all of our ancestors and the Roman Catholic Church. The Montanists, Novatianists, Donatists, Paulicians, Petrobrusians, Henricians, Arnoldists, Albigenses, Waldenses and all of our Baptist ancestors have contended for the purity of the church. To them, a church was a group of saved people, baptized upon a profession of faith. Since infants can make no profession of faith, infant baptism was rejected. True Baptists today believe the same thing. The truth of the Lord's church is a great truth with far reaching effects.

Depths of Antiquity

Dr. John. T. Christian, in his excellent history of the Baptists, gives several quotes from different authors concerning the ancient origin of the Anabaptists. We begin with his quote from Alexander Campbell, the father of the Campbellites: "Alexander Campbell, in his debate with Mr. Macalla says: 'I would engage to show that baptism as viewed and practiced by the Baptists, had its advocates in every century up to the Christian era ...and independent of whose existence (the German Anabaptists), clouds of witnesses attest the fact, that before the Reformation from popery, and from the apostolic age, to the present time, the sentiments of Baptists, and the practice of baptism have had a continued chain of advocates, and public monuments of their existence in every century can be produced.'"

"Again in his book on Christian Baptism (p. 409, Bethany, 1851), he says, 'There is nothing more congenial to civil liberty than to enjoy an unrestrained, unembargoed, liberty of exercising the conscience freely upon all subjects respecting religion. Hence it is that the Baptist denomination, in all ages and in all countries, has been, as a body, the constant asserters of the rights of man and of liberty of conscience. They have often been persecuted by Pedobaptists; but they never politically persecuted, though they have had it in their power.'"[4]

Alexander Campbell knew the Baptists were descendants of the Anabaptists and the Anabaptists descended from the apostles. Baptists have existed in all ages, from the time of Christ and His apostles.

John T. Christian also quotes from Robert Barclay, a Quaker, upon this subject: "We shall afterwards show the rise of the Anabaptists took place prior to the Reformation of the Church of England, and there are also reasons for believing that on the Continent of Europe small hidden Christian societies, who have held many of the opinions of the Anabaptists, have existed from the times of the apostles. In the sense of the direct transmission of Divine Truth, and the true nature of spiritual religion, it seems probable that these churches have a lineage or succession more ancient than that of the Roman Church (Barclay, The Inner Life of the Societies of the Commonwealth, 11, 12, London, 1876)."[5]

A great many of the historians of other denominations are a lot fairer with the Baptists than the liberal historians of our own denomination. Certainly, Barclay, the Quaker historian, gives a fair statement of the Anabaptists.

Anabaptists Ancestors

Actually, all of our ancestors were termed Anabaptists for that is exactly what they were. Listen to Vedder: "Like the Novatians, the Donatists were Anabaptists, but their rebaptizing seems to have been based on a false idea (that is Vedder's false idea), namely, that in baptism the chief thing is not the qualifications of the baptized, but those of the baptizer. The Donatists and Novatians both rebaptized those who came to them from the Catholic Church, not because they did not believe these persons regenerate when baptized, but because they denied the "orders" of the Catholic clergy. These ministers had been ordained by traditores, by bishops who were corrupt; they were members of a church that had apostatized from the pure faith, and therefore had no valid ministry or sacraments; and for this reason their baptism could not be accepted."[6]

While disagreeing with Vedder about the Novatians and Donatists being wrong on their reasons for anabaptism, it is more-the-less a good statement. It shows that our earliest ancestors were Anabaptists. The idea that many modern Baptist have, is somewhat like Vedder's on alien baptism. Some Reformed Baptists, and others not so reformed, will say the whole alien baptism movement began with Dr. James Robinson Graves. This is a silly charge for the question of alien baptism has always been the dividing issue. Being correct on the nature of the Lord's church means a rejecting of alien baptism.

Waldenses Were Anabaptists

Vedder gives the following connection between the Anabaptists and the Waldenses: "The utmost that can be said in the present state of historical research is that a moral certainly exists of a connection between the Swiss Anabaptists and their Waldensian and Petrobrusian predecessors, sustained by many significant facts, but not absolutely proved by historical evidence. Those who maintain that the Anabaptists originated with the Reformation have some difficult problems to solve, among others the rapidity with which the new leaven spread, and the wide territory that the Anabaptists so soon covered. It is common to regard them as an insignificant handful of fanatics, but abundant documentary proofs exist to show that they were not inferior in learning and eloquence to any of the reformers; that their teachings were scriptural, consistent and moderate, except where persecution produced the usual result of enthusiasm and vagary."

"Another problem demanding solution is furnished by the fact that these Anabaptist churches were not gradually developed, but appear fully formed from the first - complete in polity, sound in doctrine, strict in discipline. It will be found impossible to account for these phenomena without an assumption of a long-existing cause. Though the Anabaptist churches appear suddenly in the records of time, contemporaneously with the Zwinglian Reformation, their roots are to be sought farther back."[7]

It seems, without doubt, then, that the Anabaptists and the Waldenses before them were the same people. All of the honest historians see the historical problem of dating the Anabaptists as beginning with the Reformation.

Anabaptist Beliefs

Later in this Notebook we will examine the Anabaptist movement as it related to Luther, Calvin, Zwingh and the Reformation. To close out this chapter with some of their beliefs we give a quote from W. A. Jarrel.

"In the time of the Reformation, the genuine Anabaptists were the great and evangelical movement. Out of their principles and spirit grew all that was good in Luther's Reformation. Historians credit the Anabaptists with being the originators of the separation of church and State, of modern liberty and of the doctrine of a regenerate church membership."

In faith the Anabaptists of the Reformation were one with the Baptists of to-day.

In a paper read by Rev. Henry S. Burrage, D. D., one of the highest authorities on this subject, before the "American Society of Church History," in 1890, on "The Anabaptists of the Sixteenth Century," he says: "What were some of the ideas that characterized the Anabaptists movement of the sixteenth century? The following are especially worthy of attention: (1) That the Scriptures are the only authority in matters of faith and practice. (2) That personal faith in Jesus Christ only secures salvation; therefore infant baptism is to be rejected. (3) That a church is composed of believers who have been baptized upon a personal confession of their faith in Jesus Christ. (4) That each church has entire control of its affairs, without interference on the part of any external power. (5) That the outward life must be in accordance with such a confession of faith, and to the end it is essential that church discipline should be maintained. (6) That while the State may properly demand obedience in all things not contrary to the law of God, it has no right to set aside the dictates of conscience, and compel the humblest individual to set aside his views, or to inflict punishment in case such surrender is refused. Every human soul is directly responsible to God.'"[8]

NOTES ON CHAPTER 19

1 Church History, pages 490-491.
2 Church History, page 491.
3 Church History, page 498.
4 A History of the Baptists, Volume 1, pages 84-85.
5 A History of the Baptists, Volume 1, page 85.
6 A Brief History of the Baptists, page 66.
7 A Brief History of the Baptists, page 130.
8 Baptist Church Perpetuity or Baptist History, pages 182-183.

Chapter 20

THE BOGOMILS

We have studied the major groups of our Baptist ancestors thus far. Our "roots" are easy to see in the Montanists, Novatians, Donatists, Cathari, Paterines, Paulicians, Petrobrusians, Henricians, Arnoldists, Waldenses, Albigenses and Anabaptists. There are, however, many smaller and not so well known groups among whom we also find some of our ancestors. Beginning with this chapter we wish to look at a few of these groups.

The Bogomils will call forth our attention at this time. According to the non-Baptist historians, most of the Bogomils were Dualistic. These historians get most of their source information from a monk named Euthymius, who wrote against them and other heretics (as he supposed). He died in 1118 A. D. He was their enemy.

Location

They were located primarily in Thrace and Bulgaria. First we have a quote from John T. Christian: "The Bogomils were a branch of the Cathari, or Paulicians, who dwelt in Thrace. Their name appears to have been derived from one of their leaders in the midst of the tenth century, though others declare that their name comes from a Slavic word which is defined, 'Beloved of God.' The Bogomils were repeatedly condemned, and often persecuted, but they continued to exist through the Middle Ages, and still existed in the sixteenth century."[1]

Trace is the area now between Greece and Turkey. If the Bogomils were a branch of the Cathari or Paulicians, they were some of our ancestors. It seems to me that they were in our line of ancestry, at least part of them were.

Henry Vedder has the following concerning them: "The Bogomils are a typical form of this party (Paulicians), more Christian and less Manishaean than some others, and especially interesting because they survived all persecutions down to the Reformation period. Various explanations have been given of the name; some say it means 'friends of God'; other trace the party to a Bulgarian bishop named Bogomil, who lived about the middle of the tenth century. What is certain is that the thing is older than the name; that the party or denomination called Bogomils existed long before this title was given to them. They represented through the medieval period, as compared with Rome, the purer apostolic faith and practice, though mixed with some grotesque notions and few serious errors."[2]

The "grotesque notions and serious errors" should not bother us too much. Such things exist today among some who call themselves Baptists. Vedder testifies here to the antiquity of their belief, existing long before their name. He also represents them as distinct from, and more pure in doctrine and practice than, the Roman Catholic Church. Also his linking them with the Paulicians says much about the Baptistic tendencies.

Agreed with the Cathari

J. C. L. Gieseler, in his Compendium of Ecclesiastical History, connects the Bogomils with the Cathari. "From the Euchetae rose the Bogomili, who first made their appearance in the year 1116, when the Emperor Alexius unmaskt their leader Basilius by treachery, and had him burnt to death. In their peculiar doctrine and customs, they agree so marvelously with the Cathari of the western world, that the connection of the two parties, for which also there is historical testimony, cannot fail to be recognized. Even after their master's death the Bogomili maintained their ground in the Greek empire, especially in the region of Philippopolis."[3]

Geiseler links them to the Cathari and gives in his footnotes the historians he used as support. He also tells of the burning of one of their leaders. Persecution, we have seen, is linked to those who held to truth in opposition to the error of the Roman Catholic Church.

Thomas Armitage also calls them Cathari and tells something about them.

"The Bogomiles were a branch of the Cathari. Herzog thinks that they took their name from a Bulgarian Bishop of the tenth century, that they were an offshoot from the Paulicians, and says that they abounded in the Bulgarian city of Philippopolis. They were condemned as heretics and suffered great persecution. Basil, one of their leaders, was burnt in Constantinople in 1118, before the gates of St. Sophia. The Paulicians of Bulgaria furnished the Cathari of Southern France. Gibbon thinks that they found their way there either by passing up the Danube into Germany or through Venice in the channels of commerce, or through the imperial garrisons sent by the Greek Emperor into Italy. But come as they might, we find them at Orleans A. D. 1025, in the Netherlands 1035 and in Turin 1051. About half a century later banishment from their own country drove them in great numbers to the west, and they appeared plentifully at Treves and Soissons, in Champagne and Flanders. Their teachings soon attracted the attention of the priests, the peasantry, and even the nobles. Their followers became so numerous as to demand condemnation by the Council of Toulouse, 1119, and that of Tours, 1163. But despite excommunications and curses, they so grew that in 1167 they held a council of their own and openly formulated their faith and ecclesiastical order, which they stoutly held, against both the Roman hierarchy and the secular power for almost a century."[4]

Antiquity of the Bogomils

Dr. John T. Christian quotes from Dr. L. P. Brockett who wrote a history of them: The Bogomils of Bulgaria and Bosnia: "Their historians claimed for them the greatest antiquity. Dr. L. P. Brockett, who wrote a history of them says: 'Among these (historians of the Bulgarians) I have found, often in unexpected quarters, the most conclusive evidence that these sects were all, during their early history, Baptists, not only in their views on the subjects of baptism and the Lord's Supper, but in their opposition to Pedobaptism, to a church hierarchy, and to the worship of the Virgin Mary and the saints, and in their adherence to church independency and freedom of conscience in religious worship. In short, the conclusion has forced itself upon me that in these Christians of Bosnia, Bulgaria, and America we have an apostolic succession of Christian churches, New Testament churches, and that as early as the twelfth century these churches numbered a converted, believing membership, as large as that of the Baptist churches throughout the world today.'"[5]

All these things said of the Bogomils by their historian, Brockett, surely make our ancestors to be among them.

Charges Against Them

Just as Baptists of today who do not believe that baptism saves are charged by some Campbellites with not believing in baptism, the Bogomils were falsely accused by their enemies. Here let us look at a lengthy quote from Vedder:

"It ought always to be borne in mind, however, that for the larger part of our information regarding those stigmatized as heretics we are indebted, not to their own writings, but to the works of their opponents. Only the titles remain of the bulk of heretical writings, and of the rest we have, for the most part, only such quotations as prejudiced opponents have chosen to make. That these quotations fairly represent the originals would be too much to assume. With respect to the Bogomils, our knowledge is exclusively gained from their bitter enemies and persecutors. All such testimony is to be received with suspicion, and should be scrupulously weighed and sifted before we accept it. Where these prejudiced opponents did not knowingly misstate the beliefs of 'heretics,' they often quite misunderstood them, viewing these beliefs as they did through the distorting lenses of Roman or Greek Catholicism."

We get our chief information about Bogomil doctrine from the writings of one Euthymius, a Byzantine monk who died in 1118, who wrote a learned refutation of these and other "heresies" of his time. His account is generally accepted by historians as substantially correct - a most uncritical conclusion. The Bogomil theology as set forth by Euthymius was a fantastic travesty of the gospel, with marked Manishaean elements. God had two sons, the elder of whom, called Satanael, was chief among the hosts of heaven and created the material universe. In consequence of his ambition and rebellion he was driven from heaven with his supporters among the angelic hosts. Then God bestowed power on His younger Son, Jesus, who breathed the breath of life into man and he became a living soul. Thenceforth there was a constant conflict between Satanael and Jesus, but the former met with signal defeat in the resurrection of Jesus, and is destined ultimately to complete overthrow. These are also traces of the docetic heresy in the theology of the Bogomils; they were said to deny that Jesus took real flesh upon himself, but believed his body to be spiritual.

Euthymius charges the Bogomils with rejecting pretty much everything believed by other Christians. They did not accept the Mosaic writing as part of the word of God, though they did accept the Psalms and New Testament; they rejected water-baptism, like the modern Quakers; they declared the Lord's Supper to be the sacrifice of demons, and would have none of it; they thought churches the dwelling places of demons, and the worship of the images in them to be mere idolatry; the fathers of the church they declared to be the false prophets against whom Jesus gave warning; they forbade marriage and the eating of flesh, and fasted thrice a week.

Some of these charges clearly appear to be misapprehensions. Trine-immersion, the doctrine of baptismal regeneration and infant baptism, were taught by the Catholic Church. Denial of these may have been taken by prejudiced prelates to be denial of baptism itself. There is evidence that the Bogomils practiced the single immersion of adult believers. No doubt they did call the mass "the sacrifice of demons," or something to that effect; but only to a bigoted and ignorant Catholic would that imply rejection of the Lord's Supper, scripturally celebrated."[6]

It is this man Euthymius that Neander and other historians (Mosheim, etc.) follow in their histories. I fully agree with Vedder that "all such testimony is to be received with suspicion, and should be scrupulously weighed and sifted before we accept it." We have said over and over in this Notebook that our enemies are the wrong ones to tell the world what we believe.

John T. Christian

The following quote from Dr. Christian is appropriate here. "Some Roman Catholic writers have affirmed that the Bogomils did not practice baptism, or observe the Lord's Supper; and, that further, they denied the Old Testament Scriptures. This probably means no more than that they rejected infant baptism, and quoted the New Testament as supreme and authoritative in the matter."[7]

Their Persecution

All of the historians, almost, are agreed that the Bogomils suffered much under and from persecution. I conclude this chapter with another quote from Dr. John T. Christian's most excellent history: "The persecutions of the Bogomils, as of other Paulicians, were continuous and severe. Every effort was made to destroy them. "Yet it was not stamped out," says Conybeare, "but only driven underground. It still lurked all over Europe, but especially in the Balkans, and along the Rhine. In these hiding places it seemed to have gathered its forces together in secret, in order to emerge once more into daylight when an opportunity presented itself. The opportunity was the European Reformation, in which, especially, under the form of Anabaptism and Unitarian opinion, this leaven of the early apostolic church is found freely mingling with and modifying other forms of faith. In engendering this great religious movement, we feel sure that the Bogomils of the Balkan States played a most important part" (The Key of Truth, CXCVI)."[8]

NOTES ON CHAPTER 20

1 A History of the Baptists, Volume 1, page 58.
2 A Short History of the Baptists, pages 75-76.
3 Ecclesiastical History, Volume 3, pages 495-499.
4 The History of the Baptists, Volume 1, page 278.
5 A History of the Baptists, Volume 1, page 58.
6 A Short History of the Baptists, pages 76-77.
7 A History of the Baptists, Volume 1, page 58.
8 A History of the Baptists, Volume 1, pages 58-59.

Chapter 21

THE LOLLARDS

There was a great deal of people called Lollards. Many of them were just reformers. Some of them, no doubt were Baptists. It is difficult to sort them out. John Wycliffe came on the scene and his followers were called Lollards. Quite naturally, his translation of the Scriptures would find much acceptance among the Baptists. He held many interesting views, yet, in my opinion, he was a reformer and not a Baptist.

Thomas Armitage has an interesting statement: "Froude finds a resemblance between some of Wycliffe's views and those of the Baptists, and others have claimed him as a Baptist. But it were more accurate to say that many who carried his principles to their legitimate results became Baptists. His foundation principles were: 'That all truth is contained in the Scriptures, and that Christ's law sufficeth by itself to rule Christ's church; that we must receive nothing but what is in the Scripture; that whatever is added to it or taken from it is blasphemous; that no rite or ceremony ought to be received into the church but that which is plainly confirmed by God's word; that wise men leave that as impertinent which is not plainly expressed; that we admit to conclusion that is not proven by Scripture testimony; and that whoever holds the contrary opinions is not a Christian, but flatly the devil's champion.'"[1]

As Baptists, we heartily agree with these principles. We also feel that one who believes these principles and follows them to their logical end will become a Baptist. This statement by Armitage is a very good one.

Origin of the Lollards

At this point we will notice what a few different ones have to say upon this subject. The Religious Encyclopedia has this article:

"The name Lollards is applied both to a semi-monastic charitable society originating in Brabant in the fourteenth century and to the English followers of John Wycliffe. The Brabantine Lollards are mentioned by J. Hocsem, a canon of Liege c. 1350, in a notice of the year 1309, and from his account it is obvious that they received their name from the Middle Dutch loellen ("to sing softly, hum"). They first appeared prominently on the outbreak of the plague in Antwerp c. 1350, devoting themselves to the care of the sick and the burial of the dead, and received their name Alexians (q.v.) from their patron saint. Suspected of heresy from the very start, they were tolerated conditionally after 1347, and their dubious reputation transferred their name to the adherents of Wycliffe when he began in 1380 to assail the accepted teachings of the Church in regard to the Eucharist. The term was so used for the first time by Thomas Walden and the Cistercian Crompe in 1382, who applied it to Wycliffe's friends Hereford and Repington. Five years later five itinerant preachers are described as Lollards, and the name henceforth appears frequently in English documents, finally losing all trace of its Dutch origin and becoming the national term of derision for Wycliffe's followers from the fourteenth to the sixteenth century."[2]

Walter Lollard

Many historians feel the name "Lollards" came from an able preacher whose name was Walter Lollard. G. H. Orchard writes: "A bold and intrepid teacher was raised up among the Beghards, or Picards, in 1315, in the person of Walter Lollard, who became an eminent bard or pastor among them, and from whom the Waldenses were called Lollards. Clark says, Lollard stirred up the Albigenses by his powerful preaching, converting many to the truth, and defending the faith of these people. Moreland asserts he was in great reputation with the Waldenses, for having conveyed their doctrines into England, where they prevailed all over the kingdom. Mosheim remarks, that Walter was a Dutchman, and was a chief among the Beghards, or Brethren of the free spirit."

"He was a man of learning and of remarkable eloquence, and famous for his writings. Walter was in unity of views in doctrine and practice with the Waldenses. He was a laborious and successful preacher who resided on the Rhine; but his converts are said to have covered all England. The Lollards rejected infant baptism as a needless ceremony. In 1320, Walter Lollard was apprehended and burnt. In him the Beghards on the Rhine lost their chief, leader and champion. His death was highly detrimental to their affairs, but did not, however, ruin their cause; for it appears they were supported by men of rank and great learning, and continued their societies in many provinces of Germany."[3]

It seems most probable, to me, that they did take their name from Walter Lollard (around 1315 A.D.) and later on were considered to be followers of John Wycliffe (around 1371 A.D.). It really appears to me that all the reformers were influenced greatly, in the areas of truth that they held, by Baptist people, by whatever name they were called. Who knows what great influence Walter Lollard and men like him had on Wycliffe. Certainly the Baptists of those days wanted folks to have a translation of the Bible. Certainly they believed the Bible to have all the answers for men's rule of faith and practice. It could very well be that Wycliffe received those principles from them. He certainly did not receive them from the Catholic Church with which he was, at first, affiliated.

John T. Christian writes of Walter Lollard: "Walter Lollard, a Dutchman, of remarkable eloquence, came, according to Fuller, into England, in the reign of Edward III, 'from among the Waldenses, among whom he was a great bard or pastor.' His followers rapidly increased so that Abelard declared 'our age is imperiled by heretics, that there seems to be no footing left for the true faith.' Knighton, the English chronicler, says: 'More than one-half of the people of

England, in a few years became Lollards.'"⁴ It seems there were Lollards in England before Wycliffe became a great leader there. Yes - I think Walter had a great influence on John!

Spurgeon in Connection with the Lollards

Richard Cook gives the following extract from the writings of Charles Haddon Spurgeon:

"Mr. Spurgeon has expressed himself upon English Baptist history. He says, "It would not be impossible to show that the first Christians who dwelt in this land were of the same faith and order as the churches now called Baptist. All along our history from Henry II to Henry VIII there are traces of the Anabaptists, who are usually mentioned either in connection with the Lollards or as coming from Holland. All along there must have been a great hive on the Continent of these 'Reformers before the Reformation; for despite their being doomed to die, almost as soon as they landed, they continued to invade this country to the annoyance of the priesthood and hierarchy.'" Spurgeon quotes the following statement from W. J. E. Bennett, of Frome, a ritualist, whose hatred of the Anabaptists rendered him least likely to manufacture ancient history for them. Mr. Bennett says; "The historian Lingard tells us, that there was a sect of fanatics, who infested the north of Germany, called Puritans. Usher called them Waldenses; Spelman, Paulicians, (the same as Waldenses). They gained ground and spread all over England; they refused all Romish ceremonies, denied the authority of the Pope, and more particularly, refused to baptize infants. Thirty of them were put to death for their heretical doctrines, near Oxford; but the remainder still held to their opinions in private, until the time of Henry II 1158; and the historian Collier tells us that wherever the heresy prevailed, the churches were either scandalously neglected, or pulled down, and infants left unbaptized." "We are obliged to Mr. Bennett for this history, which is in all respects authentic, and we take liberty to remark upon it, that the reign of Henry II is a period far more worthy of being called remote, than the reign of Henry VIII, (the founder of the Episcopal Church,) and if Baptists could trace their pedigree no farther, the church of Thomas Crammer, (the Episcopal,) could not afford to sneer at them as a modern sect. Concerning the poor, persecuted people that are referred to in this extract, it seems that under Henry II they were treated with those tender mercies of the wicked, which are so notoriously cruel. 'They were apprehended and brought before a council of the clergy, at Oxford. Being interrogated about their religion, their teacher named Gerard, a man of learning, answered in their name, that they were Christians and believed the doctrines of the apostles. Upon a more particular inquiry, it was found that they denied several of the received doctrines of the church, such as purgatory, prayers for the dead, and the invocation of saints; and refusing to abandon these damnable heresies, as they were called, they were condemned as incorrigible heretics, and delivered to the secular arm to be punished. The King, (Henry II) at the instigation of the clergy, commanded them to be branded with a red hot iron on the forehead, to be whipped through the streets of Oxford, and having their clothes cut short by their girdle, to be turned into the open fields, all persons forbidden to afford them any shelter or relief, under the severest penalties. This cruel sentence was executed with its utmost rigor, and it being the depth of winter, all these unhappy persons perished with cold and hunger.'"5

Their Doctrines

David Benedict, in his History of the Baptists (page 308) says that Walter Lollard "was in sentiment the same as Peter de Bruis." We refer our readers to the chapter on the Petrobrusians for Peter's doctrinal beliefs. To say Walter and Peter believed alike is to say Walter Lollard was a Baptist.

John T. Christian writes: "It is certain that the Lollards, who had preceded Wycliffe and had widely diffused their opinions, repudiated infant baptism. The testimony of Neal is interesting. He says: 'That the denial of the rights of infants to baptism was a principle generally maintained among Lollards, is abundantly confirmed by the historians of those times, (Neal, History of the Puritans, II, 354).'"

"The followers of Wycliffe and Lollard united and in a short time England was full of the 'Bible Men.' ' 'Tis, therefore, most reasonable to conclude,' said Crosby, 'that those persons were Baptists, and on that account baptized those that came over to their sect, and professed the true faith, and desired to be baptized into it.'"

"Lollards practiced believers' baptism and denied infant baptism. Fox says one of the articles of faith among them was that faith ought to precede baptism.' This at least was the contention of a large portion of those people."

"The Lollard movement was later merged into the Anabaptist, and this was hastened by the fact that their political principles were identical. The Lollards continued to the day of the Reformation."[6]

J. M. Cramp writes: "Some of them, perhaps the majority, opposed infant baptism. Indeed, it is expressly affirmed by several historians that they refused to baptize their new-born children, and that they were charged before the ecclesiastical authorities with maintaining that infants who died unbaptized would be saved. This was an unpardonable sin in the eyes of the Pedobaptists, and the Lollards suffered grievously for it."[7]

This should be ample examples that their ancient doctrine was the 'faith once delivered to the saints' and the doctrine of true Baptists today.

Their Persecutions

We have seen again that holding to the truth, during ages past, meant severe persecution. With the Lollards this also holds true. Much of their persecution is found in Martyrs Mirror. Both the Church of England and the Roman Catholic Church persecuted the saints of God.

Here we will look at a lengthy quote from Thomas Armitage:

"Fuller says that Henry was more cruel to the Lollards 'than his predecessors,' and Fox states that he was the first English monarch who burnt heretics. But Camden alludes to a case, it is thought the one recorded in the Chronicle of London, of one of the Albigenses who was burnt in 1210; and Collier tells of a deacon who became a Jew, was degraded by a council at Oxford, 1222, and burnt under Henry III. This inhuman torture had long existed on the Continent, and Burnet attributed its late introduction into England to the high temper of the people, who would not submit to such severity. But this consideration is not satisfactory, while the fact stands that Parliament deliberately enacted the law for the burning of heretics, making a nation responsible for their murder, while in other lands the will of the prince was sufficient to burn heretics without statute law. The English sheriffs were forced to take an oath to persecute the Lollards, and the justices must deliver a relapsed heretic to be burned within ten days of his accusation. The fact is, that the pope dictated English law at the shrine, and Archbishop Chicheley says openly, in his constitution, 1416, that the taking of heretics 'ought to be our principal care.'"

John Badly, a Lollard and a poor mechanic, was brought before Archbishop Arundel, March 1, 1409, on the charge of heresy touching 'The Sacrament.' He said that he believed in the omnipotent God in Trinity, but if every wafer used in the sacrament were Christ's veritable body, soul and divinity, there would be 20,000 gods in England. Being condemned to death March 16, he was bound with chains, put into an empty barrel and burnt in Smithfield, in the presence of the Prince of Wales, afterward Henry V, who at the stake offered him a yearly stipend from the treasury if he would recant. Even where the accused recanted the punishment was barbarous. John Florence, accused of heresy, renounced his views but was sentenced to be whipped for three Sundays before the congregation in the Norwich Cathedral, and for three Sundays more in his own parish church Shelton, bearing a taper and clothed only in canvas undergarments. The English had become mere serfs to a religious despotism, which brought them to the climax of wickedness that murdered its best subjects for claiming the sacred immunity to worship God as they would. England made certain shades of opinion in the Church 'high treason to the crown,' simply constructive treason at the most; for so-called heresy was made disloyalty under the pretense that the 'King of Glory was contemned under the cover of bread.' In other words, the denial of the 'Real Presence in the sacrament of the altar' was made an overt act against the monarch of the realm. And so, the chief aim of king and Parliament was legally to grill to ashes the most patriotic people of England. The secular method of punishing treason was by hanging or beheading, but Bale says that at the Parliament at Leicester it was enacted (Henry V) that the Lollards should be hanged for treason against the king and burnt for heresy against God.

It was in keeping with this double-handed tyranny that Lord Cobham (Sir John Oldcastle) was put to death. He was a Welshman of great ability and consecration to Christ who had been imprisoned in the Tower, but had escaped and was recaptured after being hunted for four years, with a price on his head. Bishop Bale says that: 'Upon the day appointed, he was brought out of the Tower with his arms bound behind him, having a very cheerful countenance. Then he was laid upon a hurdle, as though he had been a most heinous traitor to the crown, and so drawn forth into St. Gile's field, where they had set up a new pair of gallows. As he was come to the place of execution, and was taken from the hurdle, he fell down devoutly upon his knees, desiring Almighty God to forgive his enemies. Then was he hanged up there in the middle in chains of iron, and so consumed alive in the fire.' That is, he was hanged over the fire as a traitor, and then burnt as a heretic, 1418. This state of things did not cease down to the time of Henry VIII, when tyranny changed hands only from the pope to the monarch. When the head of Anne Boleyn fell upon the scaffold, no man dared to proclaim her innocent, even on religious grounds, and the king used the power which the law left in his hands to persecute either Catholic or Protestant as he would. Indeed, for three hundred years no great soul arose in England who was able to arrest the despotism of pope and sovereign. Religious freedom or bondage ebbed or flowed through the will of the monarch, and, in that matter, the nation counted for little as against imbecile pope or royal despot.

When a heretic was condemned, the church bells tolled, the priest thundered, and the sentence of excommunication was pronounced. The priest seized a lighted candle from the altar and cried: 'Just as this candle is deprived of its light, so let him be deprived of his soul in hell.' All the people were obliged to say 'So be it;' then came the fine, imprisonment and death. Under Henry VIII it was proposed to consolidate all the penal laws against religion, when he said: 'Leave that to me.' He and his bishops then framed the 'Six Article Act,' which decreed that if a man denied that the bread and wine in the Supper were the very Christ, he should suffer death by burning and forfeit all his possessions to the king, as in high treason. No mercy was shown under any circumstances."[8]

Thus we conclude that our ancestors were to be formed among the Lollards. Their doctrines match ours. They suffered for those doctrines.

NOTES ON CHAPTER 21

1 The History of the Baptists, Volume 1, pages 315-316.
2 The New Schaff-Herzog Encyclopedia of Religious Knowledge, Volume 7, page 15.
3 A Concise History of the Baptists, pages 332-333.
4 A History of the Baptists, Volume 1, pages 183-184.
5 The Story of the Baptists, pages 74-75.
6 A History of the Baptists, Volume 1, page 187.
7 Baptist History, pages 143-144.
8 The History of the Baptists, Volume 1, pages 323-325.

Chapter 22

THE BOHEMIAN AND MORAVIAN BRETHREN

Among these groups we find our Baptist ancestors. All of the Brethren were not Baptists but many were. Bohemia is the region now western Czechoslovakia while Moravia is the Central part of the same country. Baptists have always been missionary, therefore we find them, by different names, in every place they were able to go. Not a country in Europe or Asia successfully kept them out.

Description of the Land

Robert Robinson, writing in 1792, gives the following description of the land: "Bohemia is derived from Bohmen, which signifies the country of the Boii, a tribe of Celts, who many years ago retired into what was then called the Hercynian forest to avoid the Roman kingdom of Bohemia properly so called, the dutchy of Silesia, and the marquistate of Moravia. It has Austria and Bavaria on the south, Brandenburgh and Lusatia on the north, Poland and Hungary on the east, and Bavaria and Saxony on the west. This country is about three hundred miles long, and two hundred and fifty broad, and almost surrounded with impenetrable forests and lofty mountains."[1]

228 BAPTIST HISTORY NOTEBOOK ~ BERLIN HISEL

One can easily see why this country would attract the Baptist people. They were always hiding in mountains, valleys and caves to escape the persecution of the Roman Catholic Church. The Bible words it like this: "And to the woman were given two wings of a great eagle, that she might fly into the wilderness, into her place, where she is nourished for a time, and times, and half a time, from the face of the serpents" (Revelation 12:14). One of the great blessings in the study of Baptist history, for me, is to see our historians apply this passage (correctly so) to our Baptist ancestors. Alas - modern dispensationalism has missed the meaning again altogether!

The Gospel in Bohemia

Early, the Gospel of our Lord Jesus Christ went into this region. Orchard writes: "We have authentic evidence in the writings of the apostle Paul that he preached the gospel of the Christ in Illyricum, and that Titus visited Dalmatia; hence the Bohemians infer that the gospel was preached in all the countries of Sclavonia in the first ages of Christianity. They also say that Jerome, who was a native of Stridom, translated the Scriptures into his native tongue, and that all the nations of Sclavonian extraction, the Poles, the Hungarians, the Russians, the Wallachians, the Bohemians, and Vaudois, use this translation to this day."[2]

The mountainous country also drew early those suffering persecution from the Beastly Rome. Orchard, writing of the persecution of the Paulicians writes: "The severest persecution experienced by them was encouraged by the empress Theodora, A. D. 845. Her decrees were severe, but the cruelty with which they were put in execution by her was horrible beyond expression. Mountains and hills were covered with inhabitants. Her sanguinary inquisitors explored cities and mountains in lesser Asia. After confiscating the goods and property of one hundred thousand of these people, the owners to that number were put to death in the most barbarous manner, and made to expire slowly under a variety of the most exquisite tortures. The flatterers of the empress boast of having extirpated in nine years that number of Paulicians. Many of them were scattered abroad, particularly in Bulgaria."[3] Thus we have the Paulician influence in Bohemia.

Peter Waldo

Peter Waldo fell among and became a Baptist - a Waldensian. They did not get their name from him but existed many years before he came on the scene. He went about everywhere preaching the Gospel. His influence was also felt in Bohemia, and strongly so.

J. M. Cramp writes: "In the year 1170, Peter Waldo, a merchant of Lyons, renounced his secular engagements, and devoted himself to the revival of religion. He procured a translation of the New Testament into the French language, and spent his life in toilsome journeys among the people, during which he circulated portions of the Scriptures, preached, and by other methods sought to promote true godliness. Being joined by a number of like-minded men, their united efforts produced an extensive reformation. The "Poor Men of Lyons," as they were called, because they sacrificed worldly prospects and lived in poverty, became a numerous and formidable body. But persecution scattered them. Waldo himself escaped to Bohemia, and died there. Many of his followers settled in the same country."[4]

The Paulicians came there about 845 A. D. and now, in the twelfth century, we see them joined by the followers of Peter Waldo. It is easy to see how Bohemia and Moravia became strongholds for Baptists truth.

Called Waldensians

An article in the Religious Encyclopedia links these "Brethren" with the Waldenses. "Thy members of this newly constituted community called themselves 'Brethren,' and were known in many different portions of the country by the names of their chief centers such as Kunwalders, Bunylaw Brethren, and the like. As a whole they termed themselves

Jednota Bratrska, which they later rendered into Latin as Unitas Fratrum. Their characteristic designation was Brethren, which had already been current in various older Bohemian communities. The name Fratres legis Christi first arose in the second half of the sixteenth century, but never became general. Their opponents usually termed them Waldensians or Pickards (a corruption of Beghards), and this designation, found even in royal decrees, became so general that they themselves employed it in the titles of many of their writings, terming themselves "the Brethren who for envy and hatred are called Waldensians or Pickards."[5]

John Huss

Huss had great influence on the people of Bohemia. The followers of Huss were called "Bohemian Brethren" and "Hussites." Though he was not a Baptist, he held many of their views and promoted much truth. Robert Robinson writes: "John Huss, who was professor of divinity in the university of Prague, and preacher in one of the largest churches in the city, was a man of eminent abilities and more eminent zeal. He taught much of the doctrine of Wycliffe. His talents were popular, his life irreproachable, and his manners the most affable and engaging. He was the idol of the people: but execrated by the priests. He was not a Baptist: but, as his sermons were full of what are called anabaptistical errors, Wicklivites, Waldenses, and all sorts of heretics became his admirers and followers, and as he in the spirit of a true Bohemian endeavored to curb the tyranny of the churchmen, who the nobles knew were uniting with the house of Austria to enslave the state, he was patronized by the great, and all Bohemia was filled with his doctrine and praise."

Again: "We said just now that these two eminent men, Huss and Jerome taught what are called anabaptistical errors. The following are a few of this sort. 'The law of Jesus Christ is sufficient of itself for the government of the church militant.' 'The church is the mystical body of Christ, of which He is the head.' 'They are not of the world, as Christ was not of this world.' 'The world hates them because it hates Christ, that is, the virtue and the truth of God.' 'Christians ought not to believe in the church (the Roman Church).' 'All human traditions savour of folly.' 'A multitude of human doctrines and statues is useless, and on many accounts pernicious.' 'No other law beside the rule of Scripture ought to be prescribed to good men.' 'The devil was the author of multiplying traditions in the church.' 'Deacons or elders by the instinct of God, by the Gospel of Jesus Christ, without any license from a pope or a bishop, may preach and convert spiritual children.' We do not say, that these reformers followed their principles whither they led: but we do contend that some of their hearers reasoned consequently from them, and so became Baptists."[6]

No study of the Bohemian Brethren would be complete without a study of Huss and Jerome. The above truths they taught, followed logically, would lead one to the Baptist camp.

Robert Robinson Again

All Bohemian historians say Picards or Waldenses settled in Bohemia in the twelfth century at Staz and Laun on the river Eger. Many affirm there was a sect or Arian vagrants there long before, who had fled from Mesopotamia from the athanasian persecution in successive ages from all parts of Europe. On this account, most Bohemian catholic historians call their country "a sink of heresy, and Prague the metropolis, a common and safe asylum for all sorts of heretics."[7]

It seems like the persecuted fled there for freedom of worship and freedom from persecution like our American ancestors came to this country for the same reasons.

Two Classes

Robinson writes: "The Bohemian and Moravian Baptists were then divided into two classes; the one constituted of calvinist Picards, and resided at different places all over the kingdom. Some of their ministers kept school: others practiced physick. The other class lived all together in Moravia, and is called in edict by the new German name Anabaptists."[8]

They conducted schools for young women which were above reproach. Many of the nobles sent their daughters there. This, in turn, led to the conversion of their husbands when they later married. The result was that a great many of the nobility of Bohemia and Moravia were Baptists. Baptists have always been evangelistic in every way.

Their Persecution

These brethren, like the faithful truth bearers before them suffered much at the hands of Rome. Of the Bohemian Brethren, Armitage writes: "Endless numbers evaded the inquisitors, but in 1387 one hundred of them were burnt.... About A. D. 1500 the Brethren of all sects in Bohemia were so numerous in city and country, that Pope Alexander VI sent Dominican monks to preach amongst them and hold colloquies, to win them back to his fold. But this failing, King Ladislaus II was persuaded, in 1503, to issue bloody edicts banishing their laymen, who refused to recant, and committing their preachers to the flames.... This persecution continued long, its tortures, imprisonments, and burnings ending only with the king's death...."[9] Sir William Jones tells much of their persecution in his history.

We conclude this chapter with the martyrdom of John Huss, taken from Henry Vedder's history.

"One of the things to which the council of Constance speedily devoted its attention was the agitation in Bohemia, which had now become a matter of European notoriety. Huss had never denied, but rather affirmed, the authority of an ecumenical council. King Sigismund, of Hungary (who was also the emperor), summoned Huss to appear before the council and gave the reformer a safe conduct. In June, 1415, he had his first public hearing, and two other hearings followed; in all of them he stood manfully by his teachings and defended them as in accord with Scripture. During the rest of the month, frequent attempts were made to induce him to retract, but he stood firmly by his faith. On July 6th condemnation was finally pronounced, and it is said that, on this occasion, the emperor had the grace actually to blush when reminded of the safe conduct he had given. Huss was then publickly degraded from the priesthood with every mark of ignominy, and delivered, with Rome's customary hypocrisy, to the civil power for execution. Thus the church could say that she never put heretics to death! When being tied to the stake he preached and exhorted until the fire was kindled, when he began singing with a loud voice, "Jesus, Son of the living God, have mercy on me." This he continued until his voice was stifled by smoke and flame, but his lips were seen to move for a long time, as in prayer. When his body was consumed, the ashes were cast into the Rhine, that the earth might no more be polluted by him."[10]

NOTES ON CHAPTER 22

1 Ecclesiastical Researches, page 477.
2 A Concise History of Baptists, page 230.
3 A Concise History of Baptists, page 137.
4 Baptist History, page 98.
5 The New Schaff-Herzog Religious Encyclopedia, Volume 2, page 214.
6 Ecclesiastical Researches, pages 481-482.
7 Ecclesiastical Researches, pages 508-509.
8 Ecclesiastical Researches, pages 523-524.
9 History of the Baptists, Volume 1, pages 318-320.
10 A Short History of the Baptists, pages 92-93.

Chapter 23

THE PICARDS AND BEGHARDS

Terms of reproach often became the designation of some of our ancestors. It is true that some who were not our Baptist ancestors were sometimes called by the same name. Thus, the Waldenses (people of the valleys) were known also by names of reproach. Sometimes these people would be called after the name of a prominent leader among them. In this way the same people would be called by a variety of names. People, in different countries believing the same doctrines, would have different names to describe them in their native land.

The chapter before us will deal with two of those names of reproach: Picards and Beghards. The spelling of these names varies with the historians. Among these people, so designated, we will find our ancestors.

Picards or Pickards

It is the opinion of Orchard that the names originated from the country of Picardy (I think). Writing of Peter Waldo and his followers he says, "On being forced from France, particularly Dauphine and Picardy, in which places Waldo had been very successful he first retired into Germany, with many of his followers, who were called Picards, carrying along with him, wherever he went, the glad tidings of salvation: at last settled in Bohemia...."[1]

The Religious Encyclopedia says of Picards (Pickards): "A corruption of 'Beghards,' applied as a term of reproach to the Bohemian Brethren."[2]

William Wall thinks the term comes from a man. He writes: "The third sect is of those whom they call Pyghards: they have their name from a certain refugee of the same nation, who came hither ninety-seven years ago, when that wicked and sacrilegious John Zizka declared a defiance of the churchmen and all the clergy. (This was 1420)."[3]

Possibly all three views have truth in them. At any rate, the term was one of reproach given them by their enemies. It has always been so of the ancient people now called Baptists.

Bohemia

It seems that Picards was a term that really stuck with the Bohemian Brethren. Orchard writes: "We do not discover in history the exact source from which these pious people at this time arose, though it is not improbable they were followers of Peter de Bruys, Henry, or Arnold of Brescia which circumstance is supported by the era of events, though at a later period they were named Picards These Baptists obtained this influence...."[4] The term "Picard" is applied over and over to the Waldenses in Bohemia by the historians.

Maximilian II

When Maximilian II became emperor of Bohemia he brought s season of liberty of conscience to his people. Here I insert a quote from Robert Robinson: "Maximilian after he became emperor openly declared to Henry III of France, as he passed through Vienna, that such princes as tyrannize over the conscience of men, attacked the supreme being in the noblest part of his empire, and frequently lose the earth by concerning themselves too much with celestial matters. He used to say of Huss, they very much injured that good man. His physician, Crato, was one day riding with him in his carriage, when his imperial majesty, after much lamenting the contentions of mankind about religion, asked the doctor which sect he thought came nearest the simplicity of the apostles? Crato replied, 'I verily think the people called Picards.' The emperor added, 'I think so too.'"5

This is a lovely statement. God's people should be such to hold the respect of their leaders if their leaders have any conscience in matters of religion. The above statement compliments what we believe about perpetuity.

Doctrine of the Picards

William Wall, in his work on Infant Baptism, quotes from a letter written by one Joannes Slechter Costelecius of Bohemia, written to Erasmus. It amounts to a declaration of faith from the Pyghards. Here is the quote: "These men have no other opinion of the pope, cardinals, bishops, and other clergy, than as of manifest Antichrist: they call the pope sometimes the beast, and sometimes the whore, mentioned in Revelation. Their own bishops and priests they themselves do choose for themselves, ignorant and unlearned laymen that have wives and children. They mutually salute one another by the name of brother and sister."

"They own no other authority than the Scriptures of the Old and New Testament. They slight all doctors both ancient and modern, and give no regard to their doctrine."

"Their priests, when they celebrate the offices of the mass (or communion) do it without any priestly garments: nor do they use any prayer or collects on this occasion, but only the Lord's Prayer: by which they consecrate bread that has been leavened."

"They believe or own little or nothing of the sacraments of the church. Such as come over to their sect must everyone be baptized anew in mere water. They make no blessing of salt nor of the water; nor make any use of consecrated oil."

"They believe nothing of divinity in the sacrament of the Eucharist; only that the consecrated bread and wine do by some occult sign represent the death of Christ: and accordingly, that all that do kneel down to it or worship it are guilty of idolatry. That that sacrament was instituted by Christ to no other purpose but to anew the memory of his passion, and not to be carried about or held up by the priest to be gazed on. For that Christ Himself, who is to be adored and worshipped with the honour is to be adored and worshipped with the honour of latria, sits at the right hand of God, as the Christian church confesses in the Creed."

"Prayers of the saints and for the dead they count a vain and ridiculous thing: as likewise auricular confession, and penance enjoined by the priest for sins. Eves and fast days are, they say, a mockery, and the disguise of hypocrites."

"They say the holidays of the Virgin Mary, and apostles and other saints, are the invention of idle people. But yet they keep the Lord's day, and Christmas, and Easter, and Whitsuntide, etc. He says there were great numbers of this sect then in Bohemia."[6]

This was all written by a Catholic to a Catholic about the Picards. It pretty well declares them to be Baptists. Probably, when the writer accuses them of using bread that has been leavened, he means no more than it had not been blessed by a priest. Wall tries to argue that when they baptized anew those who came over to their sect, that it is not certain that they judged baptism in infancy valid. He thinks they just judged all baptism received in the corrupt way of the church of Rome to be so. Since Wall seeks to vindicate infant baptism, he would seek to justify it here.

The Beghards

Gieseler writes: "The rest of the sects dissenting from the dominant Church were designated by the common name of the Beghards. Amongst whom the Fratricelli, and brothers and sisters of the free spirit formed two principle variations. Among the Beghards of southern France, Italy and Sicily, the inclination for the Fratricelli prevailed. The German Beghards frequently called Lollards, were, on the contrary, for the most part professors of the free spirit...."[7]

He classes them with Lollards whom we have seen to be Baptists. Notice the company in which Hassell quotes Keller as putting them: "As established by Ludwig Keller, the present royal archivest at Munster, in his thorough and authoritative work on "The Reformation and the Older Reforming Parties Exhibited in their Connection," published at Leipzig in 1885, the evangelical Anti-catholic Christians from the eleventh to the sixteenth centuries, known as Petrobrusians, Henricians, Waldenses, Pikards, Beghards, Buguins, Spirituales, Sabbati, Insabbati, Apostolic Brethren, Poor men in Christ, Friends of God, Mystics and Bohemians, were, in the darkness of the Dark Ages, Arminians...."[8] Hassell, being a primitive Baptist, sees most Calvinists as Arminians. He is quoted here to show he considered Beghards among those we call our Baptist ancestors.

The Name "Beghards"

G. H. Orchard writes: "It is allowed by Mosheim, that many dissenters of the Paulician character, in this century, led a wandering life in Germany, where they were called Gezari, i.e., Puritans. These good men grounded their plea for religious freedom on Scripture, and were called brethren and sisters of the free Spirit, while their animated devotion gained them the name of Beghards. When this term first sprang up in Germany, it was used to designate a person devout in prayer: at after periods it was used to point out all those communities which were distinct from Rome...."[9]

Neander agrees with this origin of the name Beghard. He writes of the Friends of God: "Accordingly they were nick-named after the common fashion in that age of applying some opprobrious epithet to those who, for one reason or another, were looked upon as enthusiasts or priests; they were called Beghards - people who prayed much."[10]

Benedict: "Picards, Pighards and Beghards - all these names appear to have the same origin, but were pronounced differently in different countries, in conformity to the language of each. Such is the testimony of Dr. Wall, who furthermore says, that such as come over to their church must be baptized anew, in mere water - of course they were Anabaptists."[11]

George P. Fisher: "At the end of the twelfth century there were formed, in the Netherlands, societies of praying women, calling themselves Beguines, and afterward similar societies of men, called Beghards. Many of them, to secure protection, connected themselves with the Tertiaries. Many, following the rule of poverty,

became mendicants along the Rhine, and, adopting heretical opinions, made of the names of Beguine and Beghard, elsewhere than in the Netherlands, synonymous with heretics."[12]

Conclusion

It seems that all the Waldenses were called by different names. These names were ones of reproach. The so-called "heretics" by the Roman Catholic Church believed the doctrines we hold today. They all suffered much for their faith. The Picards and Beghards suffered along with the rest. Their persecution is the same as that of the Bohemian Brethren and Lollards and Bogomils, etc. The New Schaff-Herzog Encyclopedia of Religious Knowledge gives a section on the persecution of the Beghards. It is found in Volume 2, pages 29-30.

NOTES ON CHAPTER 23

1 A Concise History of Baptists, page 104.
2 The New Schaff-Herzog Religious Encyclopedia, Volume 9, page 50.
3 History of Infant Baptism, Volume 2, pages 295-296.
4 A Concise History of Baptists, page 231.
5 Ecclesiastical Researches, page 521.
6 History of the Infant Baptism, Volume 2, pages 296-297.
7 A Compendum of Ecclesiastical History, Volume 4, pages 219-221.
8 History of the Church of God, page 335.
9 A Concise History of Baptists, page 324.
10 General History of the Christian Religion and Church, Volume 5, page 388.
11 History of the Baptists, page 53.
12 History of the Christian Church, page 207.

Chapter 24

ANABAPTISTS AND
THE REFORMATION

Let us first remark that the Baptists rejected the name "Anabaptist." It was their contention that they never practiced anabaptism. They argued that they simply baptized and never made any attempts to rebaptize. They practiced baptism while rejecting infant baptism. They preferred the name "Catabaptist" (a submersion, an immersion). Gieseler writes in a footnote: "They naturally disowned the name of Anabaptists, - as they declared infant-baptism invalid, they rather called theirs Catabaptism."[1] Therefore in writing of the Anabaptists and the Reformation the reader will understand the former term.

The "Anabaptists" did not originate with the Reformation. They had had a continued existence from Christ and His apostles and were never a part of Roman Catholicism. When the Reformers came on the scene, they undertook a work God never called them to do. How does one reform Antichrist? It cannot be done! The Reformers overlooked the prophetic declarations of the Scripture concerning the fate of mystic Babylon. "And he cried mightily with a strong voice saying, Babylon the great is fallen, is fallen, and is become the habitation of devils, and the hold of every foul spirit, and a cage of every unclean and hateful bird" (Revelation 18:2). "Rejoice over her thou heaven, and ye holy apostles and prophets; for God hath avenged you on her. And a mighty angel took up a stone like a great millstone, and cast it into the sea, saying, Thus with violence shall the great city Babylon be thrown down, and shall be found no more at all" (Revelation 18: 20-21). The doom of Roman Catholicism is as sure as the prophecies of God.

The Church of Rome, as an organization has never been, is not now, and never shall be a church of Christ. She did not originate with the church of Jesus Christ. She is of an entirely different parentage.

This is not to say that there are not some saved people in Catholicism. No doubt there are some. But God's call to them is not to reform her but to come out of her. "And I heard another voice from heaven, saying, come out of her, My people, that ye be not partakers of her sins, and that ye receive not of her plagues" (Revelation 18:4).

God's Overruling Providence

In spite of the wrong undertakings of the Reformers, God overruled to use it for his own glory. In some ways it was a blessing to the Anabaptists (Baptists). In some ways it was not.

Try to imagine yourself living in those days. Like your ancestors, you must hide to worship God. The Roman Catholic Church with her inquisitors would be searching for you every day. Discovery would expose you to mock trial by those appointed by the Devil's first-born son, the Pope. Condemned for heresy, you would be turned over to the secular power to be drowned in rivers, burnt at the stake and that usually after much torture. All this, you know, had been going on for centuries.

Then you begin to hear about Martin Luther. His is speaking out against the Romish Whore. He is being protected by the German princes. He is translating the Bible into the language of the people. He believes in immersion. He is befriending the Anabaptists. (All this was true at first though he later changes his mind). He talks about freedom of conscience. Would not your heart be stirred to excitement? Yes! The Anabaptists were, at first, thrilled by the Reformation. In enabled them to come out of hiding and worship in the open (see our chapter on the Anabaptists). So much good came from the Reformers.

The Good Doesn't Last

As the Reformation proceeded there came a great falling-out between the Baptists and the Reformers. Here I quote from Leonard Verduin: "Before the Reformation was ten years along it had become evident that not all who were rebelling against the medieval order were of one mind and heart. It had become apparent that within the camp of the dissenters there were deep-seated differences, tensions of such dimensions that a parting of the ways was in the making. It had become plain that the Reformers would as a result be obliged to deploy some of their forces to a second front; they would have to divide their energies between two opponents, Rome and the Radicals."[2]

By Radicals, he means the Anabaptists. The Anabaptists supported the Reformation as long as it followed the Scriptures. When it became apparent that none of the Reformers were going far enough and were unwilling to stand completely with the Scriptures, the Anabaptists withdrew pointing out the inconsistencies of the Reformers. This meant the Reformers must take on the Anabaptists. This they did, persecuting them wherever and whenever they had the power.

An Illustration

At this point let us look at one point in which the Reformers fell short and the Anabaptists spoke out on. Later we will look at several more points of doctrine. Here I will be quoting from The Reformers and Their Stepchildren by Leonard Verduin. It is the most helpful book I've read or ever heard of on this time period.

"Let us take, for example, that very central doctrine of the Reformation, the doctrine of justification by faith and its bearing on the place of good works in the scheme of salvation. In his haste to establish the doctrine of justification by faith rather than by works, Luther down-graded good works; the only place he had left for good works was at the very end, as a sort of postscript or appendage, something that needed attention after salvation was an accomplished fact. We meet in Luther, to put it theologically, a very heavy emphasis on the forensic aspect of salvation and a correspondingly light emphasis on the moral aspect. Luther was primarily interested in pardon, rather than in renewal. His theology was a theology that addresses itself to the problem of guilt, rather than to the problem of pollution. There is an imbalance that caused Luther to collide with the Epistle of James.

The people of the Second Front showed from the very first a critical attitude toward Luther's disparagement of good works. They did not go along with his one-sided forensic theology. They complained that "Luther throws works without faith so far to one side that all he had left is a faith without works." They suggested that Luther's sola fide was heresy - if taken, as it was taken by some, to mean faith unaccompanied. In this matter, which takes us to the very heart of the Lutheran vision, the men of the Second Front stood to the right of Luther, so much so that their enemies accused them of being "heaven-stormers" and "work-saints," people who think to earn salvation by their good works."[3]

The Anabaptist Doctrine Very Old

The names by which the Reformers called the Anabaptists reveal that their origin was very old. Another quote from Verduin (he calls the Anabaptists Stepchildren):

"The Stepchildren wanted to be known as 'evangelicals,' as 'brethren,' or simply as 'Christians' or 'believers.' On their part they called the Reformers 'Scribes' or 'the learned ones'; those who followed these were called 'name-Christians' or 'heathen.'

"Not one of the ugly names used by contemporaries to designate the Stepchildren was new; not one of them was coined in the sixteenth century. All were old terms of opprobrium, most of them very old. Nor were the ideas that are characteristic of the Stepchildren's vision new; these too were old, very old. Not one of them was invented in Reformation times. When we examine the thinking of the Stepchildren in its several items, whether it be rejection of the "christening" or the refusal to swear an oath, or certain convictions in the matter of economics, or an apparent toning down of the sacrament, etc., we find that it was not in any sense new when the Second Front rallied to it. This explains why no new names were invented. Men have need of new names only if and when they encounter new commodities; there were no new commodities; hence there was no need for the coming of any new names.

"It must also be pointed out in this connection that the record does not credit the vision that prevailed at the Second Front to any person alive in those times. Who it was that broached the idea, so central in the vision of the Stepchildren, that the Church of Christ must consist of believing people and of them exclusively, the sources say not a word. Nor do the sources say who it may have been that first challenged the propriety of "christening." The same situation confronts us when we examine the rest of the vision of the Stepchildren. This is passing strange, if it is assumed, as has become the vogue, that the Stepchildren were simply the fruitage of the Reformation. Imagine the story of the rise of Communism without the mention of its Karl Marx!

"How is all this to be explained? The answer can be quite simple. We do not read of any new commodities or new names, or of any father of it all, for the simple reason that what erupted at the Second Front was a resurgence, a reiteration, a restatement, precipitated in a way by what began with the posting of the now famous Theses, but essentially older than 1517. What erupted at the Second Front was a resurgence of those tendencies and opinions that had for centuries already existed over against the medieval order; it was connected with ancient circles in which, in spite of the persecutions, a body of ancient opinions and convictions was still alive. It was not a thing arising without deeper root out of the events that began in 1517. To ignore this fact is to fall into error, an error the more serious since even the experts have strayed into it."[4]

It is amazing to me how Verduin, a scholar in the Reformed Church, sees truth so clearly and remains where he is. His grasp of the Anabaptists of the Reformation is head and shoulders above the rest of the historians. Just as the doctrines of these Anabaptists had no originator for them during the Reformation, so their churches had no modern originator. Both their church and their doctrines go back to Christ and His apostles.

Church Truth

We have seen that our ancestors believed in a pure church. They practiced church discipline. This truth caused division early as seen in the Montanists, Novatians and Donatists. To them, the church was composed of saved, baptized and holy people. When Constantine wed the government to the false churches, he re-organized the government. The church (false church) was to have included in it all the citizens of the Empire. Infant baptism helped to accomplish this. They thought the church and the society was the same thing. Our Baptist ancestors said the church was but an organization within the society for the betterment of society.

The Reformers made the same mistake as the Catholics. They, too, thought of the church and society as the same thing. Luther wanted both - a church based on personal faith and a regional church composed of everyone in a given locality. These two views can never be combined. Those who restrict the church to believers will conflict with those who view the church as embracing everyone in a certain locality. Luther started out trying to combine the two but later had to give up the former and accept the latter. This brought him and the other Reformers into conflict with the Anabaptists. They left him. He persecuted them.

Luther and the other Reformers spent much of their time trying to prove or justify such an exclusive church. Thus, they were in the same boat with the Catholics. They were just using different oars. Since they couldn't prove the inclusive church position but would not abandon it, they mounted hatred for the Anabaptists who left them. Persecution, just as bitter as that of Rome, was practiced by them on the Anabaptists.

Conclusion

The Reformers were not reformed enough. They were unwilling to be radical enough. They swung away from Rome but not far enough. They were courageous but lacked courage. We will continue to deal with this subject in the next chapter. Let me close this one with Leonard Verdiun's observation:

"We have spoken of an exodus. That word is warranted. The people of the Second Front had indeed been at one time a part of the flock that had rallied to the cause of the Reform; in this sense the Stepchildren were the children of 1517. But they abandoned the Reformers because of an earlier conditioning; in this respect they were not the children of 1517. The Second Front resulted from an exodus of people who had come to the Reformation already conditioned, and this conditioning made it predictable that they would not feel at home there permanently and would, for that reason, depart again.

"That this is what happened, we have from the mouth of Luther himself. He wrote: 'In our times the doctrine of the Gospel, reestablished and cleansed, has drawn to it and gained many who in earlier times had been suppressed by the tyranny of Antichrist, the Pope; however there have forthwith gone out from us Wiedertaufer, Sacramentschearmer und andere Rottengeister... for they were not of us even though for a while they walked with us.'

"In this word from the hand of Luther we read the following three things: (1) that people who in earlier times had been suppressed by papal tyranny had joined his movement (they were therefore already estranged from the medieval order); (2) that these did not stay with him, seeing that they were really not homogeneous with him and his ideas; (3) that they thereupon came to be known as Wiedertaufer, etc. The present volume is in a large way an exegesis of this terse statement made by Luther. The uncomplimentary names he used are nothing but synonyms for 'Stepchildren of the Reformation.'

"Now that we have stated the nature of the Reformers' dilemma, we may well ask how they happen to be torn between these two alternatives, these two irreducible views concerning the delineation of the Church? Why was it so painfully difficult to choose between these two possibilities? Whence came this problem that drained away a sizable part of the Reformers' following?

"The dilemma resulted from the fact that the Reformers were torn between two loyalties. On the one hand was a loyalty to the New Testament Scriptures, which know no Church other than the believer's Church, a Church based on personal faith. On the other hand was a loyalty to what the Dutch call "het historisch gewordene" (that which has come about with the passing of time), in which the Church was construed so as to include all in a given locality. Only by repudiating history, twelve whole centuries of it, could one escape from the dilemma - unless he were prepared to repudiate the New Testament. This latter escape neither the Reformers nor the Stepchildren were willing to use. So there was the other escape, the repudiation of het historisch gewordene. To reject it was a radical step, too radical except for radicals, who took this way out and so came to stand alone, as Stepchildren.

"As we have already said, in the dealings with the Stepchildren a great many terms of reproach were bandied about. Although these names were used in spite, they do, each in its turn, put in focus a phase of the master struggle, the struggle regarding the delineation of the Church. Each of these smear-words points up an aspect of the battle that raged at the Second Front. We shall in this study pick up some of the most commonly used terms of reproach, examine them somewhat carefully, one in each chapter. Together these studies will sketch, so it is hoped, the essential outlines of the battle of the Second Front.

"Before we delve into our subjects we wish to point out that this neither was nor is a mere academic matter. The Stepchildren were not speculative theologians, eager to win an argument; they were deeply religious men, and the matter had a definitely existential dimension for them. We shall discover that for us also the matter is far from a mere monk's quarrel."[5]

NOTES ON CHAPTER 24

1 *A Compendium of Ecclesiastical History, Volume 5, pages 355-356.*
2 *The Reformers and Their Stepchildren, page 11.*
3 *The Reformers and Their Stepchildren, page 12.*
4 *The Reformers and Their Stepchildren, pages 13-14.*
5 *The Reformers and Their Stepchildren, page 18-20.*

Chapter 25

ANABAPTISTS AND THE REFORMATION CONTINUED

The problem between the Reformers and the Anabaptists was not a new one. As we stated in the last chapter the main problem was on the question of the nature of the church. Christianity is a totally different concept than all other religions. The Baptist concept is a totally different concept to the Reformer's concept of a church.

Before Christ, all societies were bound together by a common religious loyalty. For instance, in Daniel 3, all the Babylonians and those under their jurisdiction were to bow down to the same image. In Acts 19, all the Ephesians were to worship Diana. Even the religion of Israel was common to the society in the Old Testament. This is why the Jews asked Jesus if it were lawful to pay tribute to Caesar. How could they pay tax to Caesar and still be loyal to the religious community? Separation of church and state was a new concept to them and one they could not understand.

The Roman Government prescribed the object of worship for all its citizens. The early churches only sought to worship God, not to remove the State's object of worship. They wanted to be citizens but worship their own God. Rome could not bear this so they persecuted the church as did the Jews before them.

In the New Testament, Christ's teachings conceive of the State as being composed of many different factions. Even though men may differ in religious ideas they each may be loyal to the State. Jesus taught His disciples to render unto Caesar the things that are Caesar's and to God the things that are God's.

Christianity Not a Culture

Christianity does not create a culture but transcends all cultures. It is to influence all cultures. The church of our Lord is content to add its voice to whatever culture it finds itself in. The churches, made up of believers, were to be the salt of the earth. They were to have an influence on their society or culture. The Roman Government never understood this so when Christians added a religious voice, the State persecuted them.

Constantine

When Constantine wedded the State and Church the same concept of a State-Religious society resulted. All men and women within the State were to have the same religion. When true churches added their voice in religion they were persecuted. Roman Catholicism believed in State Religious Culture - one culture for all. The whole story of the persecution of the Donatists, Paulicians and the rest of our ancestors is the result of two different concepts of the nature of the church.

The Reformation

When Luther came on the scene with his Reformation, the battle between the two concepts of the true nature of a church had been going on for centuries. As we stated in the last chapter, the Anabaptists were, at first, drawn toward Luther and the Reformers. They thought, at first, religious freedom is coming.

The Same Problem

Before the Reformation was very far under way, the Reformers accepted the offered arm of the civil rulers. The Reformers drifted toward a new form of the old Constantinianism. On a smaller scale was developing exactly what existed under Roman Catholicism. They brought about the withdrawal of the Anabaptists from the Reformers. In turn, this brought on persecution of the Anabaptists by the Reformers.

The Anabaptists believed in the independence of the church and also that "honor" was due to the Emperor or State. They felt that a true church could not exist where the churches and the secular rule were blended into one. The Reformers said the opposite was true.

Verduin gives an interesting quote on this subject from John C. Wenger: "In 1519 Martin Luther began to write against the frightful abominations of the Babylonian Harlot and to disclose all her wickedness..., yes, as with thunder claps to bring it all down.... But as soon as he joined himself to the secular rule, seeking protection there against the cross... then it went with him as with a man who in mending the old kettle only makes the hole bigger, and raised up a people altogether callous in sin."[1]

Luther, Calvin and the other Reformers jumped but not far enough. They actually created little Roman Catholic Churches. Now there became several Catholic Churches and all of them opposed to the Anabaptists.

Religious Force

The Anabaptists believed that religion and all it includes (baptism, church membership, etc.), was to be a voluntary thing. People were not to be forced by the steel sword in matters of religion. State Religion is opposed to this. It believes coercion is to be used.

Augustine had argued, many years before the Reformation, that the Catholic Church had a divine right to force men into its confines. Let us look at a footnote given by Verduin:

"The length at which Augustine went in his effort to find New Testament warrant for coercionism is almost unbelievable. In his letter to Vincentius he wrote: 'have you not read how Paul ... was compelled by great violence ... to embrace the truth? For the light of men's eyes, more precious than money or gold, was suddenly taken away from him.... He did not get it back until he became a member of the Holy Church. You think no coercion should be used to deliver a man from his error, and yet you see ... that God does this very thing.' In a sermon on Luke 14:16 Augustine puts these words into the mouth of Christ: "Whom thou shalt find, wait not until they choose to come, compel them to come in. I have prepared a great supper.... I cannot suffer any place to remain vacant in it. The Gentiles come from the streets and lanes; let the heretics come from the hedges.... For those who make hedges have as their object to make divisions. Let these be drawn away from the hedges, plucked up from among the thorns. They have stuck fast in the hedges, unwilling to be compelled. 'Let us,' say they, 'come in of our own violation'; but this is not the Lord's directive. He says, 'Compel them to come in.' In his De Correctione Donatistorum Augustine comes back once more to this passage in Luke: 'Wherefore if the power, which the Church has received by divine appointment in its due season through the religious character and faith of kings, be instrumental in compelling those who are found in the highways and hedges - that is, in heresies and schisms - then let these not find fault for being thus compelled.'"[2]

At his instigation, thousands of Donatists (Baptists) lost their lives because they believed in freedom of religion. Remember, they also believed in rendering unto Caesar his due. They were the best citizens Rome had.

Luther's Choice

The word "heretic" means "to exercise option in the presence of alternatives." The Anabaptists, who believed religion to be a matter of choice, were called Heretics for that reason by those who believed in choiceless Christianity.

What would or what could Luther, Calvin and the Reformers do? If they went along with voluntary Christianity they would lose the support of the princes. How could they, without government help, oppose the Roman Catholic Church? Their other choice (rather than go it alone) was to make a deal with the local rulers. Thus was the choice the Reformers made. The Anabaptists could not embrace such a choice and as a result, were considered as enemies by the Reformers.

Church Requirements

The true churches have always believed in a pure church. They were called the Cathari (i.e. Puritans) by their enemies in previous ages. They believed in being separate from the world.

They preached that the churches were in the world but not of the world. Their members were to walk differently from the world.

If the Reformer's view that the church includes everyone in a given area be true then the Anabaptists' idea of a church could not be true. If the church consists of all in the world then how could it be distinct from the world? The "walk" of the Christian and the "walk" of the world would be identical according to the Reformer's definition.

The Reformers were forced to fight the Anabaptists because of this. They accused the Anabaptists of all sorts of heretical views. The Reformers must discredit the Anabaptists. This they did by calling them "dualists." The Reformers charged them with Perfectionism. The Anabaptists were charged with believing no one was going to heaven but them. These charges, of course, were false. They were the same charges with which the Papal Church had charged the ancestors of the Anabaptists.

Justin Menius, a close friend of Luther wrote: "Like the Donatists of long ago, they (The Anabaptists) seek to rend the Church because we allow evil men in the church. They seek to assemble a pure church and wherever that is undertaken the public order is sure to be overthrown, for a pure church is not possible, as Christ cautioned enough - we must put up with them."[3]

The Anabaptists believed in a converted church while the Reformers believed in a church of both believers and unbelievers - an unconverted church! This is but one more reason why the Anabaptists were not a part of the Reformation. They could not follow the Reformers as a matter of practice as well as doctrine.

Salvation by Faith Alone

Heathen religion had always laid emphasis upon rites and ceremonies. When Catholicism embraced heathenism she embraced this idea using the word "sacraments" (a name of grace). She taught (as the heathen religions did) that God was placed in you by the Lord's Supper and that you were placed in God by baptism.

All of the Anabaptists ancestors emphasized preaching and believing the preached Word. They taught that one was saved simply by believing the gospel. Baptism and the Lord's Supper were nothing in the matter of salvation itself. They were only symbolic of salvation.

When Luther first began to speak out against the papacy, he said the body of our Lord was not actually present in the Lord's Supper. He was speaking against the Catholic doctrine of transubstantiation. He and other Reformers, at first, said lay people as much as priests are able to administer the ordinances as well as those ordained by a bishop. The Anabaptists like this for this was their doctrine. They were, then, at first drawn toward Luther.

Then, when Luther attempted to combine "salvation by faith" with the administration of "sacraments", the Anabaptists recognized him as not of the true faith and left his "reformation." Luther's consubstantiation and the Reformers' "usual and specific presence," the Anabaptists saw as the old Roman doctrine in another dress.

When Luther gave up the idea of a church composed of believers only (he never really believed this but toyed with the idea) he ran the gauntlet of Roman error. The Anabaptists, like their ancestors and the Baptists of today, wanted nothing to do with the sacerdotalism (a salvation by sacraments). They were soon disillusioned with the Reformation. Here is one more reason they were not Reformers or "Protestants." It was also a reason why they were hated and persecuted by the Reformers.

Non-Public Worship

Jesus gathered His disciples together for worship without asking permission or license to meet. Early churches met in non-public places, such as private homes, to worship. Only those who had been admitted into the church's society participated. Others were permitted to come as "hearers" but the meeting was the property of the church. Only members partook of the Supper and voted, etc.

This non-public worship brought persecution from the Roman Empire. They were accused by the Empire of every imaginable evil going on in their "private" meetings. These Christians were up to evil and such meetings must be stopped.

When Constantine wedded Church to State, the same idea prevailed in the mind of the State-Church. Those who met privately must be up to no good or treason. They must by rooted out and stopped. Thus the Catholics sought to stop all such meetings. Persecution and death of these non-conformists resulted.

The Reformers, Calvin especially, felt the Anabaptists and their non-public worship were an obstacle to a creation of a Protestant Church in opposition to the Catholic Church. He wanted them to be a public cult like Lutherans and Presbyterians. Their idea of the nature of a true church prevented this, thus bringing the displeasure of the Reformers against them. There was no just way the Anabaptists and Protestants could live in the same house.

In concluding this last observation, I feel it appropriate to insert here another quote from Leonard Verduin: "The First Amendment is not so much the fruitage of the French Revolution as it is the legacy of Restitution (His term for the Anabaptist doctrine). All religious gatherings in these United States are Winckle (non-public) gatherings; they are all of them held off the streets and in non-public locales. Even the Catholic gatherings are Winckle gatherings. We say "even the Catholic gatherings" because the Catholic Church has never officially made its peace with the American version of things; wherever it is able to do so it demands for its services the status of public cult; it continues to be less than satisfied with the idea of a composite society."[4]

NOTES ON CHAPTER 25

1 *The Reformers and Their Stepchildren, page 37.*
2 *The Reformers and Their Stepchildren, page 68.*
3 *The Reformers and Their Stepchildren, page 104.*
4 *The Reformers and Their Stepchildren, page 187.*

Chapter 26

ANABAPTISTS AND THE REFORMATION CONCLUDED

From what we have seen in the two preceding chapters, it is difficult to understand why so many loudly proclaim the Baptists to have originated with the Reformation. Evidence abounds which separates the Baptists from the Reformers. Their whole doctrinal systems were different. Their views on the nature of the church were radically different. To identify the Baptists as a part of the Reformation is to ignore the plain facts of history.

In this chapter we will look at one more thing that forever separates the Anabaptists from the Reformers. That thing is the way that the Reformers persecuted the Anabaptists. Calvin never persecuted the followers of Luther nor Luther the followers of Calvin. So it was among the Reformers. Yet the Reformers were united in their persecution of the Anabaptists.

Peace Between Catholics and Reformers

Before we look at the persecution of the Anabaptists by the Reformers let us notice the Catholics and the Reformers. When Luther and others sought to reform the Catholic Church the Pope became angry. He led the Catholic Church to seek the suppression of the Reformers and even their lives. Since the Reformers had accepted the arm of the rulers in their respective countries, there became great danger of wars between the governments under Catholicism and the governments behind the Reformers.

The Peace of Augsburg 1555 A. D.

While there is much involved in the peace of Augsburg, simply stated, it was peace between the Lutherans and the Catholics. To avoid wars between the established religions, peace was made. This peace treaty kept the Lutherans from persecuting the Catholics and the Catholics from persecuting the Lutherans. In this peace treaty the Anabaptists were left out. They were fair game for both Catholics and Lutherans.

The Peace of Westphalia 1648 A. D.

There is also much involved in this peace treaty. Simply stated, it was peace between the Catholics, Lutherans and Presbyterians. To avoid confrontations between the established religions of the three, a peace treaty was signed. Again the Anabaptists were left out. They were left as fair game for Catholics, Lutherans and Presbyterians.

Lutheran Persecution

It is easy to see why the Lutherans persecuted the Anabaptists when you see how Luther, himself, felt about them. We are indebted to Baker Book House for re-printing Luther's unabridged Commentary on Galatians. In the preface of the book we may understand Luther's opinion of the Anabaptists. "For whoever heard (to pass over the abominations of the Pope) so many monsters to burst out at once into the world, as we see at this day in the Anabaptists alone? In whom Satan, breathing out, as it were, the last blast of his kingdom through horrible uproars, setteth them everywhere in such a rage, as though he would by them suddenly, not only destroy the whole world with seditions but also by innumerable sects swallow up and devour Christ wholly with his church."

"For at this day, the Papists and the Anabaptists conspire together against the church in this one point (though they dissemble in words), that the work of God dependeth upon the worthiness of the person. For thus do the Anabaptists teach, that baptism is nothing except the person do believe. Out of this principle must needs follow, that all the works of God be nothing if the man be nothing. But baptism is the work of God, and yet an evil man make it not to be the work of God. Moreover, hereof it must follow, that matrimony, authority, liberty, and are the works of God. Wicked men have the sun, the moon, the earth, the water, the air, and all other creatures which are subject unto man; but because they are wicked and not godly, therefore the sun is not the sun, the moon, the earth, the water, are not that which they are. The Anabaptists themselves had bodies and souls before they were re-baptized; but because they were not godly, therefore they had not true bodies and true souls. Also their parents were not lawfully married (as they grant themselves,) because they are not re-baptized; therefore the Anabaptists themselves are all _____s, and their parents were all adulterers, and whoremongers; and yet they do inherit their parents' lands and goods, although they grant themselves to be _____s, and unlawful heirs. Who seeth not here, in the Anabaptists, men not possessed with devils, but even devils themselves possessed with worse devils?"[1]

Thomas F. Curtis has the following quote about Luther and the Lutherans: "Luther says of false teachers, 'I am very averse to the shedding of blood. 'Tis sufficient that they should be banished' but he allows they may be 'corrected and forced at least to silence, put under restraint as madmen.' As to the Jews, he thought their synagogues should be leveled with the ground, their houses burned, and their books, even the Old Testament, taken from them.' Several of the Anabaptists were also put to death by the Lutherans 'for promoting their errors, contrary to the judgment of the Landgrave of Hesse-Cassel.'"[2]

Luther: A Persecutor

Luther may have started persecution slowly but he went the distance. Following is a paragraph from Thomas Armitage:

"Cardinal Hosius said truly that Luther did not intend to make all Christians as free as himself; thus, when they rejected his authority over their consciences, he treated them as the pope treated him; so Luther became a persecutor by slow degrees. He wrote to Spalatin, in 1522, concerning the Baptists: 'I would not have any who hold with us imprison them.' In 1528 he also said: 'I am very sorry they treat the Anabaptists so cruelly, seeing it is only on account of belief, and not because of the transgression of the laws. A man ought to be allowed to believe as he pleases. We must oppose them with the Scriptures. With fire little can be accomplished.' And still he sanctioned the decree of the Elector of Saxony, the same year forbidding any but the regular ministers to preach or baptize, under penalty of imprisonment. Charles V issued the terrible edict of Spire in 1529, commanding the whole empire to a crusade against the Baptists. He ordered that: 'All Anabaptists, male or female, of mature age, shall be put to death, by fire, or sword, or otherwise, according to the person, without preceding trial. They who recant may be pardoned, providing they do not leave the country. All who neglect infant baptism will be treated as Anabaptists.' This was worse than any thing in medieval persecution, for at least the form of a trial had been observed; but the Protestant princes who asserted to this edict left no way of escape, 'The design being,' as Keller says, 'to hunt the Baptists with no more feeling than would be shown to wild beasts.' The Peasants' war had only just closed when this ferocious edict was issued, yet it gives no hint that the Baptists were charged with sedition. The decree of 1529 was renewed in 1551, with this explanation: 'Although the obstinate Anabaptists are thrown into prison and treated with severity, nevertheless they persist in their damnable doctrine from which they cannot be turned by any amount of instruction.' If the remedy lay in 'severity' they ought to have been cured effectually, for everywhere they were treated much after the manner of serpents. A letter from a priest to his friend in Strasburg says: 'My gracious lord went hunting last Sunday, and in the forest near Epsig he caught twenty-five wild beasts. There were three hundred of them gathered together.'"[3]

Death Warrants

Luther signed death warrants for the Anabaptists. Erroll Hulse writes: "Luther hardened more in his attitude toward the left wing. By March 1530 he gave his consent to the death penalty for Anabaptists. This was further confirmed in 1536, when he signed a document clearly stating that the Anabaptists were to be put to death, not because their program entailed a complete re-orientation of church, state and society.

We can see the contrast of these later views with those held by Luther in 1520 when he wrote his Babylonish Captivity of the Church. In this work he considered the idea of reshaping the church as a body of believers only. We see then, in broad outline, why Luther moved further away from the Baptist concept of the church."[4]

John Calvin

We hear all too much praise for John Calvin now days. Yet few know of his persecution spirit. Much of what had been said of Luther may also be said of John Calvin and the Presbyterian Church of the Reformation he founded. His Reform had the government of Geneva behind it.

The burning of Michael Servetus illustrates Calvin's true spirit. Servetus held the Anabaptist principles somewhat. He opposed infant baptism and state-church government. Robert Robinson writes of this burning: "Calvin did not blush to say, 'I ordered it so that a party should be found to accuse him, not denying that the action was drawn up by my advice.' What a glorious reformation had been wrought at Geneva, when the proof of man's Christianity lay in his humble requesting the magistrates to burn a foreign gentlemen, over whom they had no jurisdiction, for the honour of God and his eminent servant Mr. Calvin."[5]

Listen also to the words of Leonard Verduin: "The burning of Servetus - let it be said with utmost clarity - was a deed for which Calvin must be held largely responsible. It was not done in spite of Calvin, as some over-ardent admirers of his are wont to say. He planned it beforehand and maneuvered it from start to finish. It occurred because of him and not in spite of him. After it had taken place Calvin defended it, with every possible and impossible argument. There is every reason to believe that if it had not been for the fact that public opinion was beginning to run against this kind of thing there would have been many more such burnings. The event was the direct result of the sacralism to which Calvin remained committed, a sacralism which he never discarded."[6]

Let us make a couple of observations here. Sacralism is the view that the church includes all individuals in a given location. This was always Calvin's view. His church was a State-Church and so opposed to a church only of believers. He planned Servetus' burning. This means he was a premeditated murderer. That is very bad but it is the testimony of history.

Again Verduin writes: "When the news was out that Servetus had died in the fire, a cry of outrage resounded over most of Europe. It is true that many of the leaders of the Reform applauded the burning (Melanchthon, for example wrote that the 'Church owes and always will owe a debt of gratitude to you for having put the heretic to death')."[7]

Of the burning of Servetus, Albert Henry Newman writes: "On October 27, 1553, having with rare courage refused to withdraw his objectionable teachings, he was burned at the stake along with his books. After writhing in the flames for half an hour, he cried aloud, 'Jesus, thou Son of the eternal God, have compassion upon me!' and gave up the ghost. The leading Reformers of Germany and Switzerland heartily commended Calvin and the Genevan Council for ridding the world of one who was regarded as an arch-enemy of the truth."[8]

The Reformers All Alike

We could take up pages with examples of the Reformers' persecution of the Anabaptists. Please read the Martyr's Mirror. I close the illustrations of persecution with the killing of Felix Manz - Anabaptist. This quote comes from Verduin but the incident is recorded by most of the church historians.

"Meanwhile the Radicals went about to organize a Church as they thought it should exist - by voluntary association. As one of their leader, 'Felix Manz, put it, their ambition was "to bring together those who were willing to accept Christ, obey the Word, and follow in His footsteps, to unite with those by baptism and to leave the rest in their present conviction." It will not escape the observant that here we have voluntarism secured (in the words "willing to accept") and coercionism precluded (by the phrase "leaving the rest in their present conviction").

This was certainly Restitutionism, without any ambiguity. For this ambition Manz was placed in a boat with his hands tied together at the wrists and passed over his knees, a heavy stick then thrust between his knees and his bent elbows. Thus bound, he was rowed to the far end of the Limmat and thrown overboard, so that he perished in the murky waters. This happened on January 5, 1527.[9]

Conclusion

Luther, Calvin, Zwingli, Melanchthon, Bullinger and all the rest of the Reformers hated or came to hate the :"believer's church" concept. This led them all to embrace the "State-Church" concept. This led them all to embrace "infant baptism." This led them to persecute the Anabaptists who rejected infant baptism, state-churches and all forced religion. To be sound on the nature of the church is an all important issue.

NOTES ON CHAPTER 26

1 A Commentary on Saint Paul's Epistle to the Galatians, pages XX-XXI.
2 The Progress of Baptists Principles, page 31.
3 The History of the Baptists, Volume 1, page 402.
4 An Introduction to the Baptists, page 7.
5 Ecclesiastical Researchers, page 339.
6 The Reformers and Their Stepchildren, page 51.
7 The Reformers and Their Stepchildren, page 52.
8 A Manual of Church History, Volume 2, page 195.
9 The Reformers and Their Stepchildren, page 74.

Chapter 27

THE ANABAPTISTS
OF MUNSTER

How many kinds of Baptists are there today? Are all Baptists in the true sense of the Word, who call themselves Baptists? Are there radical groups who call themselves Baptists? We all know that there are many gathered under the Baptist flag today who are not real Baptists and many who are quite radical. It is often the case that all Baptists are judged as being radical because some are.

Thus it was with the Anabaptists of the sixteenth century. There were many radicals among them who were not true Anabaptists. The actions of the radicals often stigmatized all the Anabaptists. Such was the case of the "Madmen of Munster." Madmen they were and not true Anabaptists at all.

W. A. Jarrel

W. A. Jarrel, in his most excellent book, quotes several historians as to the diversity among those called Anabaptists. It is necessary that we understand this if we are going to look at the Munster disorders. Following is a quote from Jarrel:

"There were several kinds of Anabaptists at the time of the Munster troubles. Says Hase: "These Anabaptists ... were ... a class of enthusiasts resembling each other, but very unlike each other in moral and religious character... Some of them were persons who renounced the world, and others were slaves of their own lusts; to some of them marriage was only an ideal religion communion of spirit; to others it resolved itself into a general community of wives; some did not differ from the reformers with respect to doctrine, but others rejected original sin and the natural bondage of the will, denied that we are to be justified by the merits of Christ alone, or that we can partake of his flesh and maintained that our Lord's body was from heaven, and not begotten of the virgin."

Mosheim: "It is difficult to determine, with certainty, the particular spot which gave birth to that seditious and pestilential sect of Anabaptists.... It is most probable that several persons of this odious class made their appearance at the same time in different countries.... The first Anabaptists doctors of any eminence were, almost all, heads and leaders of particular sects. For it must be carefully observed, that though all these projectors of a new, unspotted and perfect church were comprehended under the general name of Anabaptists, on account of their opposing the baptism of infants, and their rebaptizing such as had received the sacrament in childhood in other churches, yet they were, from their very origin, subdivided into various sects which differed from each other in points of no small moment. The most pernicious faction of all those that composed this motley multitude, was that which pretended that the founders of the new and perfect church, already mentioned, were under the direction of a divine impulse, and were armed against all opposition, by the power of the working miracles. It was this detestable faction which began its fanatical work in the year 1521, under the guidance of Munzer, Stubner, Storck and other leaders of the same furious complexion, and excited the most unhappy tumults and commotions in Saxony and other adjacent countries."

They were called Anabaptists, not because they were the same denomination, but solely because they rejected all baptisms not administered by themselves. Just as all immersionists of the United States are often, in books and newspapers, classed as Baptists, though radically different. Some who believed in infant baptism were classed as Anabaptists.

Says Dr. Ludwig Keller, the Munster archivist, a Lutheran, than whom there is no higher authority on this subject: "The name Anabaptist, which is used to designate alike all the South German societies, generally awakens the conception of a party of homogeneous and of like religious views. The conception, however, is an entirely erroneous one."[1]

The Munster Disorders

Now that we have seen that there were many different groups, even radicals, that were called Anabaptists, we are ready to see what the Munster disorders were.

Remember: All Anabaptists were charged as being of like-mind with those of Munster by the Catholics and many of the Reformers. The Anabaptists of Munster were of the very radical sort. A quote from John Henry Kurtz explains the "Munster Affair":

"Rottman had for some time embraced the Zwinglian doctrine of the Lord's Supper; his next step was to reject infant baptism. In a disputation with some theologians of Hesse, he was defeated. Nevertheless, he managed to remain in the city, and to strengthen his party by gathering in Anabaptist elements from other pages. On the festival of the Three Kings, 1534, the prophet John Mathys, a baker of Harlem, and his ardent apostle, John Bockelson, a tailor of Leyden, came to Munster. The populace, especially women, crowded to their preaching. Rottman, and a few other preachers, at once joined them. Their adherents soon multiplied in such an extent, that they thought they might bid defiance to the council. During an insurrection, the council was so weak and forbearing, that it made a treaty which secured to them legal recognition. Anabaptist fanatics then poured into Munster from all directions. After a few weeks they had the preponderance in the council. Mathys, the prophet, announced it as the will of God, that all unbelievers should be driven from the city. This was done, Feb. 27, 1534. Seven deacons divided the effects they left behind, among the believers. In May, the bishop laid siege to the city. By this means the disorder was at least confined to Munster. After having destroyed all the images, organs, and books (only saving the Bible,) the fanatics introduced a community of goods. Mathys, who imagined himself called to slay the besieging foe, fell during a sally by their sword. Bockelson took the prophet's place. In accordance with his revelations the council was deposed, and a theocratic government of twelve elders, who let themselves be inspired by the prophet, was established. That he might marry the beautiful widow of Mathys, Bockelson introduced polygamy. The still surviving moral sense of the citizens in vain resisted this enormity. Those who were dissatisfied rallied around Mollenhok, a blacksmith, were defeated, and all condemned to death. Rockelson, proclaimed king of the whole earth by one of his co-prophets, set up a splendid court, and introduced the most heinous abominations. He claimed authority to inaugurate the Millenium, sent out twenty-eight apostles to spread his kingdom, and appointed twelve dukes, to govern the earth as his vicegerents. Meanwhile the besieging army failed in an attempt to storm the city (Aug. 1534); had not help arrived from Hesse, Treves, Cleve, Mayence, and Cologne, they would have been compelled to raise the siege. All they could do was starve out the city, and this plan was succeeding well. But on St. John's eve, 1535, a deserter led the soldiers to scale the walls. After a stubborn struggle, the Anabaptists were over powered. Rottman plunged into the thickest part of the fight, and perished. King John, with his governor, Knipperdolling, and the chancellor, Krechting, were captured, pinched to death with red-hot tongs, and then hung up at the tower of St. Lambert's church in iron cages. Catholicism, in an absolutely exclusive form, was restored."[2]

Common Sense

Common sense should dictate that those described in Kurtz's History were not Anabaptists of the ordinary sort. If ever a person was adverse to war and murder it was the Anabaptists. They were also the people of high morals. It cannot be found where Anabaptists advocated polygamy. This part of their madness, these madmen of Munster probably got from Luther. Ten years before this time Luther had written: "'The husband must be certified in his own conscience and by the word of God that polygamy is permitted to him. As for me, I avow that I cannot set myself in opposition to men marrying several wives, or assert that such a course is repugnant to the Holy Scriptures.' About the same time he preached his famous sermon on 'Marriage,' which chastity may well pass in silence, beyond this one expression: 'Provided one has faith, adultery is no sin.'"[3] These "Madmen of Munster" were not true Anabaptists.

Anabaptists Denial

The Anabaptists of those days opposed the Munsterites. Menno Simons opposed them. Harold S. Bender writes the biography of Simons in The Complete Writings of Menno Simons translated from the Dutch by Leonard Verduin. In that biography Bender writes: "But finally a far more serious 'break' into his parish occurred when certain ones of the 'sect of Munster' reached Witmarsum and 'deceived many pious hearts in our village.' This occurred sometime in the year 1534, for the revolutionary kingdom of Munster was not set up until February of that year. The grievous error of the 'perverted sect of Munster,' as Menno repeatedly called them, was a very serious matter to Menno; the fight against this fanatical movement with every weapon at his command was Menno's chief concern in the years 1534 and 1535..."[4]

Some of Menno's own words about the men of Munster were: "My soul was much troubled, for I perceived that though they were zealous they erred in doctrine.... I did what I could to oppose them by preaching and exhortations, as much as in me was. I conferred twice with one of their leaders, once in private, and once in public, but my admonitions did not help.... I also faithfully warned everyone against the abominations of Munster, condemning king, polygamy, kingdom, sword, etc."[5]

Martyr's Testimony

Again and again, the martyrs in Martyr's Mirror disowned the "Madmen of Munster." Let me here give the words of J. M. Cramp. Some of what he says is taken from Martyr's Mirror.

"It is observable, also, that the Baptist martyrs of this period frequently and indignantly rebutted the calumny cast upon them, and maintained that they were not answerable for the disgraceful doings at Munster and other places."

"They also asked him (Brother Dryzinger, A. D. 1538), if it were true, that if we should become numerous, we would rise up against them and strangle them, if they would not join us? He told them, 'If we did so, we should be no Christians, but only such name.'"

Speaking of the word of God, Hans, of Overdam (martyred A.D. 1550), said, "That is our sword; it is sharp and two-edged. But we are daily belied by those who say that we would defend our faith with the sword, as they of Munster did. The Almighty God defend us from such abominations!"

"Were they not your people," said the lad, of the governor of Friesland, to Jaques Dosie, "that disgracefully and shamefully took up the sword against the magistrates at Amsterdam and Munster?" "Oh, no, madam," Jaques replied; "those persons greatly erred. But we consider it a devilish doctrine to resist the magistrates by the outward sword and violence. We would much rather suffer persecution and death at their hands, and whatever is appointed us to suffer."

I will only remark, in conclusion, that the history of these transactions has been written by enemies. We live in an age of impartial historical criticism. It is not improbable, therefore, that discoveries will yet be made which will enable future historians to tell the tale of the so-called Anabaptists of Munster much more clearly and fully than their predecessors.

"At any rate, this is certain, that the atrocities and impurities perpetrated at Munster were not more justly traceable to Baptist sentiments than the massacres of the Waldenses and the enormities of the Inquisition would be to Paedobaptism."[6]

Hardly a doubt exists that the true Anabaptists denounced and opposed the 'madness' of the men of Munster. All of their own writings and testimonies give voice to their opposition to the disorders at Munster.

Non-Baptist Vindication

It is not just the Baptist historians who disavow true Anabaptist connection to the "Madmen of Munster." Many non-Baptist historians clear the true Anabaptists of the whole incident. Following are a few quotes from them.

"The fanatical Anabaptists were universally taken as typical, and to this day when Anabaptism is mentioned it is supposed to be the equivalent of absurd interpretation of Scripture, blasphemous assumption, and riotous indecency. Munster, was, however, only the culminating point of fanaticism engendered by persecution, and Anabaptism in itself, strictly interpreted, is not responsible for it."[7]

Vedder lists some non-Baptists writings upon this subject. "Cornelius, the able and judicial historians of the Munster uproar, says justly, 'All these excesses were condemned and opposed wherever a large assembly of the brethren afforded an opportunity to give expression to the religious consciousness of the Anabaptist membership.' Fusslin, a conscientious and impartial German investigator, says: 'There was a great difference between Anabaptists and Anabaptists. There were those amongst them who held strange doctrines, but this cannot be said of the whole sect. If we should attribute to every sect whatever senseless doctrine two or three fanciful fellows have taught, there is no one in the world to whom we could not ascribe the most abominable errors.'"[8]

Much has been made of Munster; to this day, especially with men with a sacralist hangover, it affords an easy dismissal of all that the Stepchildren lived, and died, to achieve. But Munster was far from being typical of Anabaptism as such. As that great historian Tonybee has said, "Munster was 'a caricature of the movement.' Or to quote Professor Gooch once more, 'the tragedy of Munster drew attention to a phase of the movement that was far from typical of its real nature? Munster must be dealt with as the lunatic fringe of anabaptism.'"[9]

Conclusion

A whole movement should never be judged by one or two fanatics. A whole family should not be judged by one black sheep. The Anabaptist movement should not be judged by the Madmen of Munster. Actually, they were not true Anabaptists at all. I would like to refer my readers to the article on Anabaptists in William Cathcart's Baptist Encyclopedia. It is a long article and cannot be given here. He gives information aplenty on the whole Munster affair.

NOTES ON CHAPTER 27

1 *Baptist Church Perpetuity or History, pages 216-217.*
2 *Church History, Volume 2, pages 80-81.*
3 *Baptist Church Perpetuity or History, page 228.*
4 *The Complete Writings of Menno Simons, page 9.*
5 *The Complete Writings of Menno Simons, pages 669-671.*
6 *Baptist History, pages 256-257.*
7 *The New Schaff-Herzog Religious Encyclopedia, Volume 1, page 163.*
8 *A Short History of the Baptists, page 180.*
9 *The Reformers and Their Stepchildren, page 237.*

Chapter 28

THE WELSH BAPTISTS

The study and story of the Welsh Baptists is an interesting one. Wales is a part of Great Britain. It is located on the west of England about in the middle. To the west of Wales, across the Irish Sea lies Ireland. Wales is about 136 miles long from north to south and 96 miles wide at its broadest part. It is entirely flanked on the east by England. Scotland joins England to the north and the English Channel is on the south of England. Wales reaches neither Scotland nor the English Channel. This land is the center of British folklore and legend. It is the land of King Arthur and his Round Table, Lancelot and Camelot.

It also has a beautiful place in the history of the people called Baptists. How wonderfully God had His hand upon this little land! Our own American Baptist heritage has a close connection with Wales. Many of the earliest Baptists to come to America came here from Wales. Many of the early churches in America came from Wales or from people who were Baptists in Wales.

The Gospel in Wales

The Gospel was preached very early in Britain (in Wales). Tradition has it that Joseph of Armithea was the first one to preach the Gospel in Britain, at a place called Glastenbury. George Park Fisher tells of this legend: "The origin and development of the early Baptist Church are involved in obscurity. But although history is silent here, the credulity of later generations has never wanted for legends to supply its place. Some of these relate the story of missionary labors of Peter and Paul; others tell of Joseph of Armithea, of the church he founded at Glastenbury, and of his sanctity, which was so great that a hawthorn bush budded every Christmas day in his honor."[1]

Concerning Paul

Of Paul maybe preaching in Britain, here J. Davis: "That the apostle Paul also preached the gospel to the ancient Britons, is very probable from the testimony of Theodoret and Jerome; but that he was the first that introduced the gospel to this island cannot be admitted; for he was a prisoner in Rome at the time the good news of salvation through the blood of Christ reached this region. That the Apostle Paul had great encouragement to visit this country afterwards will not be denied."[2]

For one interested in various other ideas and opinions about how and when and by whom the gospel came into Britain, please read Thomas Crosby. There are 58 pages in this Preface which are interesting reading. Who first introduced the gospel into Wales is not really important. That is was introduced is. However, I will give my opinion. It is the same as that of most of the historians. The evidence seems pretty clear.

Claudia

Joseph Belcher writes: "It is believed that the Gospel of Jesus Christ was introduced into Britain about the year 63, by Claudia, a Welsh princess, converted under the ministry of the apostle Paul, at Rome. Her exertions to extend the reign of Christ were constant and successful. Bishop Burgess tells us, that the early British churches bore a striking resemblance to the model Institution at Jerusalem; and Mosheim tells us that 'No persons were admitted to baptism, but such as had been previously instructed in the principle points of Christianity, and had also given satisfactory proofs of pious dispositions and upright intentions.'"[3]

Of this Claudia, Thomas Crosby writes: "Now amongst the converts of the natives of this island, in the first age to Christianity, Claudia surnamed Ruffina, is refuted a principle; she was the wife to Pudence, a Roman senator; and that this is the Claudia, a Briton born, mentioned by St. Paul, then living at the exceptions of Parsons the Jesuit, by answering his objections to the contrary; and then says, 'The issue of all this is this: Claudia's story, as a British Christian stands unremoved, for any force of these objections; though one need not be much engaged herein.'"[4]

Again, let us read the words of Davis: "About fifty years before the birth of our Savior, the Romans invaded the British Isle, in the reign of the Welsh king, Cassibellan; but having failed, in consequence of other and more important wars, to conquer the Welsh nation, made peace with them and dwelt among them many years. During that period many of the Welsh soldiers joined the Roman army, and many families from Wales visited Rome; among whom there was a certain woman of the name of Claudia, who was married to a man named Pudence. At the same time, Paul was sent a prisoner to Rome, and preached there in his own hired house, for the space of two years, about the year of our Lord 63 (Acts 28:30). Pudence and Claudia his wife, who belonged to Caesar's household, under the blessing of God on Paul's preaching, were brought to the knowledge of the truth as it is in Jesus, and made a profession of the Christian religion (II Timothy 4:21). These, together with other Welshmen, among the Roman soldiers, who has tasted that the Lord was gracious, exerted themselves on the behalf of their countrymen in Wales, who were at that time vile idolaters."[5]

The comments of John Gill and Matthew Henry on II Timothy 4:21, seem to think Claudia was a Briton. Whatever, the gospel entered Britain very early. Since the early churches were Baptists, the early Christians in Wales were Baptists.

Baptists Alone

The first six centuries saw Britain mostly without the evils of Popery. I have a copy of a rare book called Saint Patrick and the Western

Apostolic Churches: or The Religion of the Ancient Britains and Irish, not Roman Catholic: and the Antiquity, Tenents and Sufferings of the Albigenses and Waldenses. My copy was published in 1857. This is a very interesting book with many source materials quoted. I would like to give a section of it showing that the early centuries of Christianity in Wales (Britain) were separate from the Roman error.

"This holy religion was introduced at an early period of the Christian era into Britain and Ireland. We have ample material to illustrate this, but shall not stop here to exhibit them." (He gives, in a footnote his source material).

"There is perhaps no point in ancient church history more clearly established than this, that the primitive, apostolic religion of Christ flourished in Britain and Ireland for the First Six Centuries, uninterrupted by any successful irruption of Popery."

"The following is a sketch of the proof of this important fact. Bishop Burgess has shown that there are seven remarkable epochs in the first seven centuries, relating to the ancient British Churches."

"Under the first epoch, Stillingfleet and Burgess have collected the ancient documents extant, to prove that 'St. Paul advanced into Spain,' and 'into the utmost bounds of the West,' and 'conferred advantages upon the islands which lie in the sea.' And Henry Spelman quotes a passage out of Fortunatus, bishop of Poictiers, stating that "St. Paul passed over the ocean, even to the British Isles."

"In the second epoch, in the second century, king Lucius publicly protected Christianity. In the ancient document called the British Triads, it is related that 'Lleirwig (in Latin, Lucius) called Lleuver the Great, gave the privilege of the country and the tribe, with civil and ecclesiastical rights, to those who professed faith in Christ.' The venerable Bede says: 'After the days of Lucius, the Britons preserved the faith which they had received, whole and inviolate, in a quiet and peaceable manner, until the reign of Diocletian.'"

"In the third epoch, and during the frightful persecutions which raged from the year 304, for many years; Bede says, 'The British Churches enjoyed the highest glory in its devoted confession of God.'"

"In the fourth epoch we find the British Churches sending eminent doctors to the Council of Arles, convoked, not by the Pope, who had no such power then, but by the emperor, Constantine the Great, in A.D. 314; also to the Council of Nice, in 325; and to the Council of Sardica, in 347. And these bishops were very unlike modern bishops. These ancient holy pastors, who preached every Sabbath, were so poor that 'the three delegates were constrained, through their poverty, to accept the public allowance in lodging and food, provided by the emperor.'"

"The fifth epoch is rendered famous for the unanimous condemnation of Pelagianism, by the British pastors and churches.

"In the sixth epoch, these faithful clergy and churches, in full council condemned Pelaganism for the third time.

"The seventh epoch is rendered painfully remarkable by the arrival of the emissaries of the Roman pontiff, to propagate Popery and idolatry. The first melancholy occasion was the marriage of 'a Papist,' namely, queen Bertha, by the king Ethelbert. This paved the way for St. Austin and his monks, who came into Britain in A.D. 600, and began their fatal operations shortly after."[6]

These above statements, written by Protestant writers, gives evidence that Britain (of which Wales is a part) was free from most of the Roman errors for 600 years after Christ.

Were Ancient World Christians Baptists?

We have already stated that there was only one kind of church back then and that kind was Baptistic. What did they believe and practice concerning baptism? Benjamine Evans writes: "It is not as to the mode of baptism. That is unquestioned. No man would risk his claim to accurate acquaintance even with English history, by denying that the ancient mode of baptism was immersion. Wales knew nothing else."[7]

Evans, though he doesn't seem sure of what American Baptists have said, writes of them: "Were the ancient British Christians Baptists? This question meets us on the threshold, and asks our attention for a time. Writers on both sides of the Atlantic, claim for Wales the honour of retaining primitive ordinances and church polity beyond any other nation in Europe. Removed from the influence of Rome, the authority of the ambitions and worldly-minded Pontiffs who ruled in that city was not acknowledged in Wales till about A. D. 600, and the growing corruptions of the Western church had not penetrated the fastness of that country. Some of our American brethren speak of the churches there as corresponding, up to the time of Austin's invasion, with our present polity. National Christianity was unknown, and everywhere the churches were based on Congregational principles, and union with them was the result of individual conviction, and was professed and secured by the immersion of the body in water. In other words, in a true and important sense they were Baptist churches."[8]

David Benedict

Benedict's History, probably the best History of Baptists to have if you have only one, has the following: "The Rev. Josiah Taylor, of England, in his Memoirs of the English Baptists, published many years since in the E. B. Magazine, gives the following account of the early history of these primitive British Baptists.

"About sixty years after the ascension of our Lord, Christianity was planted in Britain, and a number of royal blood, and many of inferior birth, were called to be saints. Here the gospel flourished much in early times, and here, also, its followers endured many afflictions and calamities from pagan persecutors. The British Christians experienced various changes of prosperity and adversity, until about the year 600. A little previous to this period, Austin, the monk, with about forty others, were sent here by Pope Gregory the great, to convert the pagans to popery, and to subject all the British Christians to the dominion of Rome. The enterprise succeeded, and conversion (or rather perversion) work was performed on a large scale. King Ethelbert, and his court, and a considerable part of his kingdom were won over by the successful monk, who consecrated the river Swale, near York, in which he caused to be baptized ten thousand of his converts in a day.

"Having met with so much success in England, he resolved to try what he could do in Wales. There were many British Christians who had fled hither in former times to avoid the brutal ravages of the outrageous Saxons. The monk held a synod in that neighborhood, and sent to their pastors to request them to receive the pope's commandment; but they utterly refused to listen to either the monk or the pope, or to adopt any of their maxims. Austin, meeting with this prompt refusal, endeavored to compromise matters with these strenuous Welshman, and requested that they would give Christendom, that is, baptism to their children; but with none of his propositions would they comply. 'Sins, therefore,' said he, 'ye wol not receive peace of your brethren, ye of others shall have warre and wretche,' and accordingly he brought the Saxons upon them to shed their innocent blood, and many of them lost their lives for the name of Jesus."

The Baptist historians in England contend that the first British Christians were Baptists, and that they maintained Baptist principles until the coming of Austin. "We have no mention," says the author of the memoirs, of the christening or baptizing children in England before the coming of Austin in 597; and to us, it is evident he brought it not from heaven, but from Rome. But though the subjects of baptism began now to be altered, the mode of it continued in the national church a thousand years longer, and baptism was administered by dipping, & c. From the coming of Austin, the church in this island was divided into two parts, an old and the new. The old, or Baptist church maintained their original principles. But the new church adopted infant baptism, and the rest of the multiplying superstitions of Rome."[9]

Conclusion

That there were Baptists in all centuries in Wales is evident. In some of our earlier chapters we saw the Paulicians, Waldenses and others entering Britain. We studied about the Lollards in England. At all times there was a Baptist witness there. All of the historians point this out. It is highly recommended that the student purchase Crosby's History of the English Baptists, published first in the 1700's and History of the Welsh Baptists.

NOTES ON CHAPTER 28

1 History of the Christian Church, page 89.
2 History of the Welsh Baptists, page 6.
3 Religious Denominations, page 125.
4 History of the English Baptists, Volume 1, second preface, page iv.
5 History of the Welsh Baptists, pages 6-7.
6 St. Patrick and the Western Apostolic Churches, pages 58-61.
7 Early English Baptists, Volume 1, page 3.
8 Early English Baptists, Volume 1, pages 2-3.
9 The History of the Baptists, page 343.

WALDENSIAN CONFESSIONS OF FAITH

WALDENSES CONFESSION OF 1120

1. We believe and firmly maintain all that is contained in the twelve articles of the symbol, commonly called the apostles' creed, and we regard as heretical whatever is inconsistent with the said twelve articles.

2. We believe that there is one God - the Father, Son, and Holy Spirit.

3. We acknowledge for sacred canonical scriptures the books of the Holy Bible. (Here follows the title of each, exactly conformable to our received canon, but which it is deemed, on that account, quite unnecessary to particularize.)

4. The books above-mentioned teach us: That there is one GOD, almighty, unbounded in wisdom, and infinite in goodness, and who, in His goodness, has made all things. For He created Adam after His own image and likeness. But through the enmity of the Devil, and his own disobedience, Adam fell, sin entered into the world, and we became transgressors in and by Adam.

5. That Christ had been promised to the fathers who received the law, to the end that, knowing their sin by the law, and their unrighteousness and insufficiency, they might desire the coming of Christ to make satisfaction for their sins, and to accomplish the law by Himself.

6. That at the time appointed of the Father, Christ was born - a time when iniquity everywhere abounded, to make it manifest that it was not for the sake of any good in ourselves, for all were sinners, but that He, who is true, might display His grace and mercy towards us.

7. That Christ is our life, and truth, and peace, and righteousness - our shepherd and advocate, our sacrifice and priest, who died for the salvation of all who should believe, and rose again for their justification.

8. And we also firmly believe, that there is no other mediator, or advocate with God the Father, but Jesus Christ. And as to the Virgin Mary, she was holy, humble, and full of grace; and this we also believe concerning all other saints, namely, that they are waiting in heaven for the resurrection of their bodies at the day of judgment.

9. We also believe, that, after this life, there are but two places - one for those who are saved, the other for the damned, which [two] we call paradise and hell, wholly denying that imaginary purgatory of Antichrist, invented in opposition to the truth.

10. Moreover, we have ever regarded all the inventions of men [in the affairs or religion] as an unspeakable abomination before God; such as the festival days and vigils of saints, and what is called holy-water, the abstaining from flesh on certain days, and such like things, but above all, the masses.

11. We hold in abhorrence all human inventions, as proceeding from Antichrist, which produce distress (Alluding probably to the voluntary penances and mortification imposed by the Catholics on themselves), and are prejudicial to the liberty of the mind.

12. We consider the Sacraments as signs of holy things, or as the visible emblems of invisible blessings. We regard it as proper and even necessary that believers use these symbols or visible forms when it can be done. Notwithstanding which, we maintain

that believers may be saved without these signs, when they have neither place nor opportunity of observing them.

13. We acknowledge no sacraments [as of divine appointment] but baptism and the Lord's supper.

14. We honour the secular powers, with subjection, obedience, promptitude, and payment.

BIBLIOGRAPHY

Armitage, Thomas. History of the Baptists, 2 volumes, 1877; Reprinted by James & Klock Christian Publishing Co., Minneapolis, Minnesota, 1977.

Asplund, John. Annual Register of the Baptist Denomination in North America, 1791; Reprinted by Church History Research & Archives, TN.

Backus, Isaac. History of New England With Particular Reference to the Denomination of Christians Called Baptists, 2 volumes, Newton, Mass. 1871.

Benedict, David. A General History of the Baptist Denomination, 2 volumes, Lewis Colby & Co., New York, 1848; Reprinted by the Baptist Historical Society, Aberdeen, MS.

Benedict, David. History of the Donatists, Nickerson, Silbey & Co. Pawtucket, RI, 1875.

Bright Lights In Dark Times, Bible Truth Publishers, Oak Park, Illinois, n.d. No author listed.

Brownlee, Dr. and King, Alexander. Saint Patrick and the Western Apostolic Churches: or the Religion of the Ancient Britains and Irish not Roman Catholic and The Antiquity, Tenets and Sufferings of the Albigenses and Waldenses - American & Foreign, Christian Union, New York, 1857.

Cathcart, William. Baptist Patriots and the American Revolution, 1876; Reprinted 1976 by Guardian Press, Grand Rapids, Michigan.

Carroll, J. M. The Trail of Blood, Ashland Avenue Baptist Church; 123 N. Ashland Ave. Lexington, KY.

Christian, John T. A History of the Baptists, 2 volumes, Baptist Sunday School Committee Texarkana, Ark.-Texas, 1922.

Christian, John T. Baptist History Vindicated, Baptist Book Concern; Louisville, KY, 1899.

Cook, Richard B. The Story of the Baptists, 1844; Reprinted by Attic Press, Inc. Greenwood, SC.

Cramp, J. M. Baptist History, American Baptist Publication Society, n.d.

Crosby, Thomas The History of the English Baptists, 4 volumes in 2, CHR&A, 1978.

Curtis, Thomas F. The Progress of Baptist Principles, Gould & Lincoln, Boston, 1856.

D'Aubigne, J.H. Merle. The Reformation in England, 2 volumes; Banner of Truth Trust, 1962, (First Published 1853).

Davis, A. A. Sermons on the Trail of Blood, First Baptist Church Nowata, OK. 1952.

Davis, J. History of the Welsh Baptists, 1835; Reprinted by the Baptist, Aberdeen, MS.

Dowling, John. The History of Romanism Edward Walker, New York, 1846.

Duncan, R. S. A History of the Baptist in Missouri, CHR&A.

Edwards, Morgan. Materials Toward a History of the Baptists, 2 volumes, 1770-1795; Reprinted by CHR&A.

Evans, Benjamin. The Early English Baptists, 2 volumes, 1862, Reprinted Attic Press, Inc., 1977.

Fisher, G. Park. History of the Christian Church, Charles Scribner's Sons, 1899.

Ford, S. H. The Origin of the Baptists, Baptist Sunday School Committee, 1950.

Gieseler, John. A Compendium of Ecclesiastical History, 5 volumes. T & T Clark, Edinburgh, 1846.

Gillette, A. M. Minutes of Philadelphia Baptist Association from A.D. 1707-1807, American Baptist Publication Society, 1851; Reprinted by Baptist Book Trust, Otisville, MI., 1976.

Goodby, J. J. Bye-Paths in Baptist History; Reprinted by CHR&A.

Graves, J. R. The First Baptist Church in America, 1887; Reprinted by Baptist Sunday School Committee, 1939.

Hagenback, K. R. A Text Book of the History of Doctrines, 2 volumes, Sheldon & Co., New York, 1862.

Harrison, E. F., Editor. Baker's Dictionary of Theology, Baker Book House, 1960.

Hassell, C. B. History of the Church of God, 1886; Reprinted by Turner Lassetter, 1948.

Jarrel, W. A. Baptist Church Perpetuity, 1894; Reprinted by the Baptist Examiner, Ashland, KY.

Jones, William. The History of the Christian Church, 2 volumes in 1, Ephraim A. Smith, Louisville, Ky. 1831.

Kurtz, J. H. Text Book of Church History, 2 volumes in 1, Nelson S. Quiney, Philadelphia, 1881.

Lorimer, Geo. C. The Baptists in History, Silver, Burdett & Co., Boston, 1893.

Madaule, Jacques. The Albigensian Crusade, Fordham University Press, 1967.

Masters, Lois W. The Gospel Traits in Ky. Baptists, State Board of Missions, n.d.

Mattoon, C. H. Baptist Annals of Oregon, 2 volumes, 1905; Reprinted by Elder Norman Wells, Central Point, Oregon.

Milner, Joseph. The History of the Church of Christ, 2 volumes, Hagan & Thompson, Philadelphia, 1835.

Milner, Vincent. Religious Denominations of the World, William Sarretson & Co., Philadelphia, 1871.

Mitchell, A. W., M. D. The Waldenses: Sketches of the Evangelical Christians of the Valleys of Piedmont, Philadelphia, Presbyterian Board of Publication, 1853.

Moreland, Samuel. The History of the Evangelical Churches of the Piedmont, 1658; Reprinted by Baptist Sunday School Committee; also CHR&A.

Mosheim, John L. Ecclesiastical History, Applegate, Poundsford Co., Cincinnati, 1874.

Neander, Augustus. History of the Christian Religion and Church, 5 volumes, Crocker & Brewster, Boston, 9th Edition.

Neander, Augustus. History of the Planting and Training of the Christian Church by the Apostles, 2 volumes, Henry G. Bohn, London, 1851.

Neander, Augustus. Lectures on the History of Christian Dogmas, 2 volumes, Henry G. Bohn, London, 1843.

Nevins, Wm. M. Alien Baptism and the Baptists, Economy Press, Ashland, KY, 1962.

Newman, Alfred H. A Manual of Church History, 2 volumes, American Baptist Publication Society, 1904.

Nowlin, Wm. D. Kentucky Baptist History, 1770-1922, Baptist Book Concern, 1922.

Orchard, G. H. A Concise History of Baptists, Ashland Avenue Baptist Church, Lexington, KY, 1956.

Overbey, Edward. A Brief History of the Baptists, The Challenge Press, Little Rock, Arkansas, 1962.

Ray, D. B. Baptist Succession, 1873; Reprinted by CHR&A.

Robinson, Robert. Ecclesiastical Researches, 1792; Reprinted by CHR&A 1984.

Robinson, Robert. The History of Baptism, Lincoln & Edmands, Boston, 1817.

Schaff-Herzog. Encyclopedia of Religious Knowledge.

Semple, Robt. B. History of the Baptists in Virginia 1810; Reprinted by CHR&A, 1976.

Simons, Menno. The Complete Writings of Menno Simons, Herald Press, Scottdale, PA, 1974.

Smiles, Samuel. The Hugenots, Harper & Brothers Publishers, New York, 1874.

Spencer, J. H. A History of Kentucky Baptists, 2 volumes, 1886; Reprinted by CHR&A.

Stovall, Chas. B. Baptist History and Succession, 1945; Reprinted by Bryan Station Baptist Church, Lexington, KY.

Taylor, John. A History of Ten Baptist Churches, 1823; Reprinted by Art Guild; Reprints Inc., Cincinnati, Ohio, 1968.

Thomas, Joshua. The American Baptist Heritage in Wales, 1663-1770, Reprinted by CHR&A.

Torbert, Robert G. A History of the Baptists, Judson Press, 1950.

Van Braght, T. J. The Bloody Theater or Martyrs Mirror, 1660; Published by Herald Press.

Vedder, Henry C. A Short History of Baptists, American Baptist Publication Society, 1907.

Verduin, Leonard. The Reformers and Their Stepchildren, Baker Book House.

Wall, William. The History of Infant Baptism - Together With Mr. Gales Reflections and Dr. Wall's Defence, 4 volumes, University Press, Oxford, 1844.

Wells, Norman H. The Church That Jesus Loved, The Challenge Press, 1973.

Wharey, James. Sketches of Church History, Philadelphia, Presbyterian Board of Publication, 1840.

Williams, Wm. R. Lectures on Baptist History, American Baptist Publication Society, 1877.

Zenos, Andrew C. Compendium of Church History, And Sabbath School Work, Presbyterian Board of Publication, 1920.

NOTES:

NOTES:

Baptist History Notebook and other Christian education resources are available for order online at:

www.baptisttrainingcenter.org

BAPTIST TRAINING CENTER PUBLICATIONS
WINTER HAVEN, FLORIDA

Also available from
Amazon.com and other retail outlets.

58979688R00163

Made in the USA
Columbia, SC
02 June 2019